Russian Literature and the Classics

STUDIES IN RUSSIAN AND EUROPEAN LITERATURE

A series edited by

Peter I. Barta
University of Surrey
and
David Shepherd
University of Sheffield

Volume 1

Russian Literature and the Classics
Edited by Peter I. Barta, David H. J. Larmour, and Paul Allen Miller

Forthcoming titles

The Contexts of Bakhtin, Edited by David Shepherd

Iurii Dombrovskii: Freedom Under Totalitarianism, Peter Doyle

Carnavalizing Difference: Bakhtin and the Other
Edited by Peter I. Barta, Paul Allen Miller, Chuck Platter, and David Shepherd

Discourse and Ideology in Nabokov's Prose, Edited by David H. J. Larmour

Polish Literature in the European Context, Edited by Patricia Pollock Brodsky

Russian Literature in the 1980s, Edited by Arnold McMillin

Gender and Sexuality in Russian Civilization, Edited by Peter I. Barta

This book is part of a series. The publisher will accept continuation orders which may be cancelled at any time and which provide for automatic billing and shipping of each title in the series upon publication. Please write for details.

Russian Literature and the Classics

EDITED BY

PETER I. BARTA
UNIVERSITY OF SURREY

AND

DAVID H. J. LARMOUR
PAUL ALLEN MILLER

TEXAS TECH UNIVERSITY, LUBBOCK

harwood academic publishers

Australia • Canada • China •
France • Germany • India • Japan •
Luxembourg • Malaysia • The Netherlands •
Russia • Singapore • Switzerland •
Thailand • United Kingdom

Emmaplein 5
1075 AW Amsterdam
The Netherlands

100324115⁷

British Library Cataloguing in Publication Data

Russian literature and the classics. - (Studies in Russian
  and European literature ; v. 1)
  1.Russian literature - History and criticism
  I.Barta, Peter I. II.Larmour, David H. J. III.Miller, Paul
  Allen
  891.7'09

  ISBN   3-7186-0605-4   (hardcover)
         3-7186-0606-2   (softcover)

CONTENTS

INTRODUCTION TO THE SERIES

Change and difference have become the cliched watchwords of Slavic studies in recent years. There is surely no need for further cataloguing — whether celebratory or cautionary — of the transformations in the practices and potential of our discipline wrought by the political, social, and economic turmoil of the former Soviet Union and the Eastern Bloc, not to mention the sweeping changes in interpretive practices within the study of the humanities in Western countries.

A series such as *Studies in Russian and European Literature* must in large degree be a response to those transformations; it cannot, however, be reduced to their mere product or reflection, and does not set out to impress by superficial novelty. In seeking to promote a comparative approach, with particular emphasis on the ties between Russian and other European literatures, and on the relationship between Western and Eastern European cultures, the series will extend long-established paths of inquiry. There will also be continuity in the embrace it offers theory, to which Russia and Eastern Europe are no strangers.

At the same time, such a venture must recognize that much of what passes for change and difference is all too often nothing more than an exchange of negative for positive which leaves old categorizations and oppositions in place, their valencies inverted by a mechanical operation of a kind characteristic of a world and a system which are supposed to have been discredited. The demise of one conceptual framework and the concomitant vindication of another might well hold out the prospect of rapid and dispiriting ossification. *Studies in Russian and European Literature* will resist this possibility. Like its global counterpart, literary history has not yet come to an end.

Peter I. Barta
David Shepherd

INTRODUCTION

Peter I. Barta, University of Surrey
David H. J. Larmour, Texas Tech University
Paul Allen Miller, Texas Tech University

Cum subit illius tristissima noctis imago,
Quae mihi supremum tempus in urbe fuit,
Cum repeto noctem, qua tot mihi cara reliquit,
Labitur ex oculis nunc quoque gutta meis.

Yes, the old world is "not of this world,"
yet it is more alive than it ever was

(Mandel'shtam 1979, 112)[1]

No monograph-length study has appeared to date which would undertake a more or less systematic study of the impact of the Classics on Russian literature and culture. Our volume is an attempt to remedy the situation. Of course, we do not aim at providing a complete survey of the subject. Rather, the articles published here examine aspects of the influence of antiquity on Russian literature at some particularly significant junctures: the beginning of the nineteenth century, the age of the great Russian realist novel, the "Silver Age," Stalin's terror, the "Thaw" after 1956 and the period just before the collapse of Soviet society. The articles in the volume study the firm foundations of westernized Russian literature in its European context.

In a real sense the Classical tradition has always been with the West. It is what defines both the continuities and the disjunctions of European culture. Our literature, our philosophy, our political systems all begin in Greece and

1

Rome. The Classical tradition cannot even be abandoned without being invoked, and abandonment, if it has occurred at all, is a very recent phenomenon. Thus, while we may routinely talk about the Renaissance and renascences, what we really mean is a series of changing points of view on the Classical tradition, rather than an actual loss or rediscovery.

From the fall of Rome in the fifth century to the dawn of Renaissance humanism in fourteenth-century Italy and the papal court in Avignon, three major sources kept the culture of the ancient Mediterranean alive: the Latin language and the literature that was associated with its teaching; the culture of the early Church fathers as it was passed on through the ecclesiastical tradition; and the Benedictine tradition of regular monastic reading and study. All these sources are inseparable from the institution of the Roman Catholic Church. It may seem odd that the Church becomes the primary conduit for transmitting the pagan culture it replaces, and to which at times it was unremittingly hostile, as in the case of the burning of the library of Alexandria and the stoning of its chief librarian, Hypatia, by a mob of rampaging monks. Nonetheless, after the fall of Rome the common written language in the West was Latin and the only way the institution of the Church could survive was through the teaching of it to future generations. The early Christian fathers, while at times profoundly exercised about the dangerous seductions of pagan literature, could never create an alternative pedagogy that was able to do without the school texts of antiquity. Therefore wherever education and learning survived after the barbarian invasions, Vergil, Horace, Ovid, Cicero, and Livy continued to be read.

Likewise, the early Church fathers themselves, Saints Augustine, Ambrose, and Jerome, as well as Tertullian, Boethius and others, were all the products of the best education late antiquity could offer. Well versed in the various philosophical schools and trained in the principles of rhetoric, their writings preserved much of the antique culture that first transformed Christianity from an odd Semitic cult, which was at most a curiosity to the cultured elite, into a legitimate philosophical and doctrinal adversary. This intellectual heritage, in turn, was passed on to succeeding generations in the form of the documents that laid the theological foundations for the Church itself. Thus, when Petrarch and others speak of Plato, they are frequently referring to the elements of Platonic and neo-platonic philosophy preserved in these patristic writings and not to the texts of the authors themselves. This is especially true in the case of Greek writers, since throughout the Middle Ages the Greek language was largely unknown in the West.

The entire process of transmission, both in the works of the patristic writers and in the texts of antiquity, however, was ultimately dependent upon something very mundane: the actual, physical existence of the books themselves. Apart from papyri buried in the dry sands of Egypt, virtually no manuscripts survive from the ancient world. The sheer corrosive power of mould and mildew could in the space of a couple of hundred years devour even the highest quality parchment antiquity was able to produce. Thus, the Latin and Greek books we read today are almost all printed from manuscripts copied over and over again by scribes. The Benedictine rule required that monks spend a certain amount of time each day in reading and study. Such a rule also required that there should be something to read. Consequently, every monastery was equipped both with a library and a facility for copying and preserving its collection, called a *scriptorium*. It is thanks to these institutions that we possess the vast majority of the Classical texts in existence today.

The Medieval world and the Roman Catholic Church in Western and Central Europe that dominated its intellectual horizons, then, did not so much replace Classical culture as appropriate it. As the eminent scholar Thomas Greene and others have recognized, what constitutes the crucial difference between the Middle Ages and that beginning of the modern world which we call the Renaissance is the recognition that this ecclesiastical appropriation of pagan culture also involved a large measure of historical naivete and repression, a failure to recognize the differences that separated the Medieval from the ancient world by what retrospectively seemed an unbridgeable gap (1982, 8–9, 12, 81–126). While in the culture of the Middle Ages it seemed perfectly reasonable to allegorize Ovid's lascivious *Remedia Amoris* as a form of praise for the Blessed Virgin (Nolhac 1965, 178), or for the pagan Vergil to lead Dante to the brink of heaven itself, this sense of immediate continuity between present and past was lost in the Renaissance. The ancient world ceased to be continuous with the present and became instead something lost that had to be recovered. The Renaissance, then, did not discover Classical culture (which was never really lost or the texts would not have been there to be rediscovered in the first place): it discovered history. By learning to recognize that Classical culture was fundamentally different from that of their Medieval predecessors, the Renaissance humanists also learned to separate themselves from those who had immediately preceded them. The civilization of the Classical world became the means whereby a new cultural formation was able to construct itself in opposition to its understanding of the Medieval culture that had gone before. What the Renaissance discovered was difference. Thus for the literature of Western Europe between the fourteenth and the sixteenth centuries, as for most of the works discussed in this volume, the study of the ancient world was in reality an exercise in self-fashioning (Greenblatt 1980).

The price paid for this discovery of historical difference and for the great cultural energies released in the new search for an authentic antiquity was an increased level of disenchantment within the word. When the texts of antiquity could no longer be so easily allegorized as the word of God, when the contingent and material signifier could not be firmly anchored in the transcendental signified, the status of language itself had fundamentally changed (Waswo 1987, 59–60). The word had fallen irredeemably into history and could no longer be redeemed by a hermeneutic that viewed everything *sub specie aeternitatis*. The anxieties which this fall into the contingent provoked can be seen most clearly in the work of Petrarch. His status is crucial since he is both the founding figure of Renaissance humanism and a man whose religious and philosophical views still bear the stamp of Medieval piety. The *Canzoniere* and the *Secretum* echo repeatedly with his fears that he has condemned himself to everlasting damnation through his pursuit of earthly fame and poetic glory, two phenomena which were in turn inseparable from his knowledge, and imitation, of ancient literature. Yet these same texts also demonstrate his refusal to bow to those fears. The result is not only two great works of art, but also the inaugural moments in a tradition of increasingly secular literature that came to define modernity itself.

In all cases, the Renaissance "rediscovery" of antiquity involved the adaptation of a stance towards the present and the immediate past every bit as much as an understanding of antiquity. Thus, in Joachim Du Bellay's landmark *La deffense et illustration de la langue Française*, the call to imitate the ancients is couched primarily in terms of establishing the criteria whereby the generation of poets represented by the Pléiade could distinguish themselves from the preceding group known at the "Grands rhétoriqueurs." At stake here was not just poetic prestige, and the attempt to create a vernacular literature which could rival not only that of contemporary neo-Latin writers, but that of the ancients themselves: what was also at stake was the patronage of the mighty. The poets of the Pléiade by claiming to speak a transhistorical poetic language that transcended the parochial concerns of the previous generation's vulgate courtly literature were able to trace their poetic genealogy to the primal sources of Greece and Rome and to present themselves to their potential patrons as having access to a type of discursive power unavailable to their rivals. At the same time, this very transhistorical language — embodied in a poetry that traced its power to its ancient lineage — empowered the poets to speak to and for their social superiors in ways which would have been inconceivable in daily life, given their generally middling social situations. Thus the study of the ancients, in a real sense, can be said to have provided the raw materials for the construction of a new subject position that allowed the speaker to give voice to ideas and sentiments that might well have seemed presumptuous or completely inappropriate if spoken from the position of the poet's social status as a private individual (Greene 1982, 195; Ferguson 1983, 34–52; McGowan 1985, 6). The imitation of antiquity became a way both to sanction and to counter feudal power.

Indeed at times the literature of the ancients provided the writers of the Renaissance a kind of Aesopian language that allowed them to articulate concerns that were otherwise literally unspeakable, whether because of external political pressures or because of internal censorship and psychic contradictions. In this respect, the literature of the ancients at times served for the writers of the Renaissance the same sort of function as it did later for the writers of Tsarist Russia and, in particular, the Soviet Union; it became a code that allowed the unspeakable to be spoken. Thus, in the case of a Protestant writer such as Sidney, who vigorously defended the morally edifying power of literature in his *Defence of Poesie*, his use of Ovidian imitation in the sonnet sequence *Astrophil and Stella* revealed the presence of an erotic imagination quite at variance with the poet's stated theoretical goals (Miller 1991). Likewise Shakespeare's *Julius Caesar* allowed the poet to investigate such sensitive questions as when it is legitimate to assassinate a reigning monarch, and what the appropriate relations between the competing ideals of aristocratic freedom and subjection to an absolute monarch are, issues that might well have been difficult to dramatize if set in a time and place more closely approximating Elizabethan England.

This liberating potential of the Classical languages and literatures, as manifested in both the construction of new subject positions and the ability to discuss issues which might otherwise be relegated to the realm of the unspeakable, was drastically curtailed with the dawning of seventeenth- and eighteenth-century Classicism. It is probably no coincidence that the emergence of French Classicism coincides with the growing consolidation of absolutism in Western European politics. With the latter, the freewheeling and often experimental nature of the early humanists' explorations of antiquity becomes codified in an ever more rigid set of rules. The result was often an art of an astounding purity and power as in Racine's *Phèdre*, Corneille's *Le Cid*, or Molière's *L'école des femmes*. Yet the strong sense of a need to circumscribe all potential forms of change and disorder, be they social, political, or aesthetic is strongly in evidence both in Boileau's *Art poétique* and in those satires where he associates Molière's more farcical comedies with the motley and dangerous Parisian mob. Likewise La Bruyère's *Les caractères* represents an attempt to define a series of human essences which should be unchanging and to which it is necessary to adapt rather than to try to change them. It is perhaps no accident that this same work also contains the passage cited by Bakhtin in *Rabelais and His World* to demonstrate the loss of that sense of open exuberance that accompanied the early Renaissance and its essays at self-construction (1968, 107–08). The creation of a closed set of aesthetic rules that corresponded to the imposition of an ever more closed political and social order in Western Europe in general and in France in particular also resulted in the creation of an ever more rigidly codified view of Greek and Roman culture. Ideals of unity and decorum came more and more to stand metonymically for the sanction of the ancients, and so replaced the much more open-ended and potentially destabilizing study of the Classics themselves. In the new European Classicism there was no more room for the decentered scatology of an Aristophanes and a Catullus, or for the homosexual desire of a Sappho (DeJean 1989, 43–197) or Tibullus, than there was for the ribald humor of traditional Gallic wit or the epic messiness of Shakespeare.

It is at this point that the Classical heritage in Russia becomes closely associated with the western Classical tradition just described. For, in spite of its close links with Byzantium, the first Russian state inherited only a small part of the legacy of Classical civilization. Kievan Russia and its successor states received their literacy and their orthodox religion, not to mention the foundations of their statehood, from the last remnant of the antique world, in its final stage of development before it fell to the expanding Ottoman Turks. Because of the monopoly of Christianity, the cultural package that arrived in Kiev from Byzantium failed to include the anthropomorphic heritage of ancient Greece and Rome. For well-known historical reasons, Russia did not experience the rediscovery of the Classical world during the centuries when Renaissance humanism was reshaping Western Europe. It was not until Peter I's irreversible efforts to westernize his country in the eighteenth century that a real interest in the heritage of Classical antiquity appeared. No poet expresses this new literary sensitivity with greater verve than Gavrila Romanovich Derzhavin.

The first article in our collection, Charles Byrd's "Thunder Imagery and the Turn Against Horace in Derzhavin's 'Evgeniyu. Zhizn' Zvanskaya' (1807)" studies the poet's famous autobiographical poem. By establishing the context of "Evgeniyu" in the tradition of the European "country-house" poem, and by drawing upon the theoretical support of Harold Bloom's *The Anxiety of Influence*, Byrd analyzes Derzhavin's "filial" treatment of Horace's "Second Epode." He sees the "subversion" of patriarchal authority in Derzhavin's extensive use of thunder imagery. The article traces not only Derzhavin's complex relationship with his predecessors but also looks upon the poet as a predecessor of his own successors.

In many ways, Russia's greatest twentieth-century literary theorist, Mikhail Bakhtin, was emblematic of the pervasive influence of Classical culture and literature on Russian writers of the nineteenth and twentieth centuries. Of all the critics and theorists, he was perhaps the most deeply read in the literature of Greece and Rome. Having studied philology under Zelinksy at the University of Saint Petersburg, his understanding of the byways as well as of the broad avenues of Classical literature is virtually unparalleled among modern theorists. He knew not only Homer and the tragedians, but also Boethius, Macrobius, and the writers of the second sophistic. He produced substantial readings of Greek romance, ancient epic, and the narrative and biographical elements in authors as diverse as Plato, Plutarch, Petronius and Apuleius. By the same token, his understanding of Menippean satire, of carnival's ancient ancestor, the Roman Saturnalia, and of the dynamics of dialogue as manifested in Socratic dialect and Lucianic parody formed the crucial intellectual background against which he constructed both his general theory of the novel and his famed readings of Dostoevsky and Rabelais (Bakhtin 1981, 1–40, 51–68, 84–146; 1984, 106–37; 1968, passim; Clark and Holquist 1984, 30–34).

In "Mediating the Distance: Prophecy and Alterity in Greek Tragedy in Dostoevsky's *Crime and Punishment*," Naomi Rood examines the role of prophecy in Athenian tragedy and in Dostoevsky's novels. Her primary focus is on *Crime and Punishment*, where she studies the concept of the divine within the text's intelligence. Rood relies on Bakhtin's conceptions of "monologue" and "dialogue" to develop her argument. Whereas antique tragedy "monologically" accepts the divine word, Dostoevsky's novels fail to re-confirm the validity of prophecy: this adds dialogic momentum to his discourse. Dostoevsky, Rood argues, gives a new significance to prophecy. The question of how genetic features of tragedy inform Dostoevsky's novels provided the basis of a debate between two famous Russian classicists in the beginning of the twentieth century, Vyacheslav Ivanov and Lev Pumpyansky. After the author analyzes the arguments of this debate, she proceeds to examine *Crime and Punishment*: the novel's hero, Raskolnikov, searches for a prophetic word, which, by its very nature, is monologic. His attempt to find the "new man" prompts him to ignore the past. The text, however, does not allow Raskolnikov to unlearn the past and the result is a combination of the new and the old. In conclusion, Rood establishes that whereas antique tragedy emphasizes the proximity of the hero to the divine, the Dostoevskian novel highlights the distance of the two from one another.

It appears that the twentieth century in Russia marks a particular increase of interest in matters Classical. At the fin-de-siècle, Russian symbolist poets responded enthusiastically to Nietzsche's reinterpretation of Classical trag-

edy whose moving force was seen in the figure of Dionysus. The beginning
of the century also witnessed the dynamic activity of the famous Classical
scholar, Faddei Zelinsky. Like Vyacheslav Ivanov, Zelinsky advocated the
view that a rebirth of Slavic culture could only be accomplished by finding
its Greek origins.

The city of Petersburg, with its neo-classical architecture, caryatids and
statues depicting figures of ancient mythology, has always expressed the
attempt by some Russians to bridge the gap between Russian civilization and
the Classical foundations of European culture. The first three decades of the
twentieth century produced literature which can justifiably be considered as
a culmination of the "Petersburg Text," generated by the myth of the city.

Mary Jo White's article, "The Source of Andrei Bely's Literary *Mifotvorchestvo*: The Case of the Ableukhovs," offers a key to the complex ring of
interconnected imagery upon which the novel *Petersburg* draws. White's
study is informed by an awareness of the synchronizing urge in Russian
symbolism. Ancient Greek mythology, religion and philosophy are projected
as a united force. For the writing of *Petersburg*, Bely assimilated Nietzsche's
interpretation of Classical mythology with Vyacheslav Ivanov's and Mikhail
Solovyov's visions. The article offers a *prolegomenon* to the Classical symbolism of the novel *Petersburg*.

St. Petersburg physically embodies the desire to overcome that sense of
"cultural inferiority" which Brodsky talks about in his essay, "The Child of
Civilization" (Brodsky 1986, 130). Many a Russian intellectual also felt an
acute concern for the survival of civilization in the face of a barbaric and
oppressive political monolith. Turning to Classical subjects not only afforded
an Aesopian language of sorts for challenging the powers of the Soviet state,
but also made it possible to emphasize Russia's cultural links with the
intellectual heritage to the rest of Europe. Vyacheslav Ivanov as Classicist
and poet is the subject of Pamela Davidson's article, "Hellenism, Culture and
Christianity: The Case of Vyacheslav Ivanov and his 'Palinode' of 1927."
The attempt to integrate Classics and poetry in a Christian world-view played
a vital part in Vyacheslav Ivanov's career. The links between Classical
antiquity and Christianity in Russia at the beginning of the twentieth century
are the focus of Davidson's attention. The poem "Palinodiya" was written in
1927, and it offers a retrospective view of the history of Vyacheslav Ivanov's
relationship with Classical culture. The article presents a detailed analysis of
the biographical context, textual history and meaning of "Palinodiya."
Davidson's reading of the poem is supported by her study of the Russian and
Italian versions of the text in each other's light. The author offers a close
reading of the last section of the poem which develops an aspect of Pushkin's

"Prorok" ("The Prophet"). Davidson then discusses the theme of spiritual purification in Ivanov in the light of Pushkin's poems.

While some émigré writers, like Vyacheslav Ivanov, were well-known in the West, this was certainly not the case with many authors inside the Soviet Union who were equally ignored at home and abroad. Vasilii Grossman was "discovered" only in the 1980s. Frank Ellis argues in his article, "Soviet Russia Through the Lens of Classical Antiquity: An Analysis of Greco-Roman Allusions and Thought in the Oeuvre of Vasilii Grossman," that in his perceptive analysis of the Soviet system, Grossman is on a par with such writers as Pasternak, Bulgakov, and Solzhenitsyn. Ellis examines Grossman's handling of Classical allusions to Greek and Roman writers and philosophers against the background of official Soviet views on the same ancient figures.

The final two articles in the volume consider the role of Classical culture in Russian poetry of recent times. David Wells's article, "Classical Motifs in Aleksandr Kushner," looks at how the poet draws upon the world of antiquity for the artistic expression of both himself and his country. In Kushner's poems, the ancient world is part of a unity which incorporates contemporary Russia. Kushner became a poet during the "Thaw" after 1956 and looked to Russian Modernism for inspiration, but his interest in the "Silver Age" tends to be connected with Classical culture. Wells surveys and interprets the thematic units into which Kushner's Classical motifs fall. The other contemporary Russian poet who most frequently alludes to the mythology, art and history of Greece and Rome is Joseph Brodsky. Like Kushner, Brodsky alludes to Roman history to make more or less overt political references to the decline of Soviet society. "The Wandering Greek: Images of Antiquity in Joseph Brodsky" by Dan Ungurianu studies the poet's use of several Classical motifs. Ungurianu's article devotes almost as much attention to Mandel'shtam as to Brodsky: Mandel'shtam's "Hellenicism" formulated Brodsky's understanding and appreciation of Classical culture. Unlike the late "Roman" poems, Brodsky's "Greek" poems exhibit mainly mythological imagery, lacking in a directly political content. Ungurianu relies on the poems in Russian and the numerous essays Brodsky wrote in English to support his observations. He emphasizes that Brodsky is not limited to *littérature engagée*; rather than being a political poet, his view of the world — which includes, but is not limited to, Russia — is broadly historical.

We standardized the forms of submissions but we have respected as much as possible the authors' decisions in matters of style, spelling and punctuation in so far as these conform to American or British standard usage. The editors would like to express their gratitude to the members of the editorial board and many other colleagues who provided invaluable help in refereeing submissions. We would also like to thank Elizabeth Bilbro for her excellent technical assistance.

NOTE

1. The quotation is from Mandel'shtam's essay, "The Word and Culture." Mandel'shtam cites the Latin verse from Ovid's *Tristia*, I.3.

WORKS CITED

Bakhtin, M.M. 1968. *Rabelais and His World*. Trans. Hélène Iswolsky. Cambridge: MIT Press.

_____. 1981. *The Dialogic Imagination: Four Essays by M.M. Bakhtin*. Trans. Caryl Emerson and Michael Holquist. Ed. Michael Holquist. Austin: University of Texas Press.

_____. 1984. *Problems of Dostoeveky's Poetics*. Ed. and Trans. Caryl Emerson. Theory and History of Literature, Vol. 8. Minneapolis: University of Minnesota Press.

Brodsky, Joseph. 1986. *Less than One: Selected Essays*. New York: Farrar, Straus, Giroux.

DeJean, Joan. 1989. *Fictions of Sappho: 1546–1937*. Chicago: University of Chicago Press.

Ferguson, Margaret. 1983. *Trials of Desire: Renaissance Defences of Poetry*. New Haven: Yale University Press.

Greenblatt, Stephen. 1980. *Renaissance Self-Fashioning: From Moore to Shakespeare*. Chicago: University of Chicago Press.

Greene, Thomas. 1982. *The Light in Troy: Imitation and Discovery in Renaissance Poetics*. New Haven: Yale University Press.

Holquist, Michael and Katerina Clark. 1984. *Mikhail Bakhtin*. Cambridge: Harvard University Press.

Mandel'shtam, Osip. *The Complete Prose and Letters*. Ed. and Trans. Jane Gray Harris. Ann Arbor: Ardis.

McGowan, Margaret M. 1985. *Ideal Forms in the Age of Ronsard*. Berkeley: University of California Press.

Miller, Paul Allen. 1991. "Sidney, Petrarch, and Ovid, or Imitation as Subversion," *ELH* 1991: 499–522.

Nolhac, Pierre. 1965. *Pétrarque et l'humanisme.* Vol. 1. Paris: Champion, first printed in 1907.

Waswo, Richard. 1987. *Language and Meaning in the Renaissance.* Princeton: Princeton University Press.

THUNDER IMAGERY AND THE TURN AGAINST HORACE IN DERZHAVIN'S "EVGENIYU. ZHIZN' ZVANSKAYA" (1807)

Charles Byrd, Washington University

Readers interested in psychological and intertextual approaches to the poetry of Gavrila Romanovich Derzhavin (1743–1816) are likely to find his last major work in verse, "Evgeniyu. Zhizn' Zvanskaya" [To Evgenii. Life at Zvanka], a particularly inviting subject.[1] As the title suggests, this odic, long country-house poem was written as an epistle to Derzhavin's friend and regular guest, Evgenii Bolkhovitinov, an Orthodox priest. By addressing the work to an actual historical personage, Derzhavin encourages his readership, even today, to consider the biographical contexts he created around the poem as much as the enduring artistry of the words themselves. Rich in the quotidian details of Derzhavin's stylish retirement — his choice of tea, his preferred card-games — the work also resounds with references to the poet's earlier achievements as a writer, concluding, for example, with direct allusion to "Felitsa," his famous ode to Catherine the Great. "Evgeniyu. Zhizn' Zvanskaya" may thus readily be taken as Derzhavin's greatest poetical celebration of self, his most bluntly autobiographical work in verse.[2] At the same time, the long Russian country-house poem is preoccupied with a wide range of ancient and modern literary precedent in mythic, odic, and pastoral genres. Derzhavin's spectrum of reference extends from the works of Hesiod, Pindar and Theocritus to those of Mikhail Vasilevich Lomonosov (1711–66) and the contemporary Vasilii Andreevich Zhukovsky (1783–1852).

13

Derzhavin's commemoration of life on an independent, rural estate mirrors autobiographically his delineation of independent poetic space both within and against the boundaries of literary tradition. Derzhavin gained access to the property through his second wife, who, after the marriage, purchased it from her mother; but the private ownership of landed estates in Russian and Western culture is, more generally, inseparable from the basic system of patrimonial inheritance. One might then wonder whether the literature celebrating that ownership also depends in some way on systematic patriarchal laws of affiliation. These latter, poetic codes of influence have been analyzed in engaging, universalist terms by Harold Bloom in his work on the English Romantics (1966). According to Bloom, "strong" poets engage in any number of a series of revisionary ratios with regard to parent poems, competing with them much as a son, from a psychoanalytic viewpoint, tends to compete with the father.[3] In "Evgeniyu," Horace's Second Epode may be regarded as the primary object of filial interest; Derzhavin extensively quotes and revises passages from it.[4] Moreover, in its unusually sustained and playful deployment of thunder imagery, "Evgeniyu. Zhizn' Zvanskaya" engages and challenges the urbane irony of Horace's complex pastoral vision. The motif of thunder is particularly powerful for Derzhavin because it allows him to achieve partial identification with poetic fathers who seem even stronger (Hesiod, Pindar, Theocritus) and more immediate (Lomonosov) than the great Roman predecessor.

Horace's Second Epode had been widely translated and imitated throughout Europe by the end of the eighteenth century. Along with the concluding passage of Virgil's second book of *Georgics* and the description of the "fortunate woodlands" of Elysium in Virgil's *Aeneid*, Horace's Second Epode has been a basic source for later European poems in praise of country life. The speaker in Horace's epode, an urban money-lender, catalogues at length the virtues of such rural pursuits as viniculture, caring for livestock, and hunting wildfowl. He also praises the simple pleasures of home-grown foods and notes the joyful fidelity of a typical country wife. A number of long country-house poems, including Ben Jonson's "To Penshurst" (the most notable English example), are derived in part from Horace's model. Although it is highly unlikely that Derzhavin knew Jonson's work, he was clearly familiar with the basic premise of generic poems in praise of country life through his extensive readings of Horace's epodes and James Thompson's nature poetry in German translation. Another important source of nature poetry for "Evgeniyu" was the work of Vasilii Zhukovsky, whose long poem "Vecher" [Evening] (1806), as Zapadov has shown, provided the exact verse form which Derzhavin later chose to use in his own long work. Important philosophical justifications of nature and country-house poetry had been provided much earlier by Aleksandr Petrovich Sumarokov (1717–77), who catalogued rural virtues in his 1759 "Pis'mo o krasote pirody" [Letter on the Beauty of Nature]. As Baehr has shown, Sumarokov in turn had been influenced by the tradition in European rhetoric which came to be known as the "locus amoenus" [description of a pleasant place] (1991, 68–71).

The stylized behavioral context which Derzhavin created around "Evgeniyu" clearly establishes, however, the poet's primary concern with Horace. Having begun work on "Evgeniyu" in May of 1807, Derzhavin wrote four lines of verse, dated July 22 of that very summer, on the back of a watercolor, specially commissioned for Evgenii Bolkhovitinov, to whom Derzhavin eventually addressed the final version of his long poem:

> На память твоего, Евгений, посещения
> Усадьбы маленькой изображен здесь вид.
> Гораций как бывал Меценом в восхищении,
> Так был обрадован тобой мурза-поэт. (Derzhavin 1869, 2:411)

> In memory of your visit, Eugene,
> A view of the little estate is here portrayed.
> Horace used to be as enthused by Maecenas
> As the poet-mirza was by you. (trans. Hart 1978, 137)

This gift must have been intimately connected in the poet's mind to the long poem, which in initial drafts had been punningly titled "Zhizn' moya na zvanke, il eshchyo inache Kartina zhizni zvanksoi" (Derzhavin 1869, 2:412) [My Life at Zvanka, or Still Another Picture of Zvankan Life]. The wording plays on the notion of pictorial representation, both in the strictest, most literal sense, and as a metaphor for verbal description. Derzhavin's title is, in fact, a subtle twist on one of Horace's most famous formulas, "Ut pictura poesis" [As in painting, so in poetry] from the *Ars Poetica*, which like "Evgeniyu" was written as an epistle. Derzhavin's original title subtly reverses the temporal scheme implied by the Latin topos. While Horace suggests the priority of painting, simply by listing it first, Derzhavin had begun his long poem before commissioning the watercolor, which thus seems secondary to the impetus for verbal creation. Maecenas, a wealthy Roman aristocrat, was friend and patron to Horace for some 30 years (c. 38–8 B.C.E.), and even donated the tract of land in the Sabine Hills about thirty miles northeast of Rome on which Horace's country estate was later built. The term "poet-mirza" alludes to the oriental persona Derzhavin himself adopted for his much earlier cycle of poems written to Catherine the Great. A mirza (usually transliterated "murza") was a Tatar prince. Derzhavin had used this persona — which he abandons in the writing of "Evgeniyu" — earlier in his career as an exotic mask for the purpose of genially satirizing Catherine's courtiers.

Derzhavin's identification with Horace, as in the simile on the back of the painting, is evident from the very beginning of the final version of "Evgeniyu," which paraphrases, as Grot has indicated in his notes, the opening of Horace's Second Epode. Compare:

> Блажен, кто менее зависит от людей,
> Свободен от долгов и от хлопот приказных,
> Не ищет при дворе ни злата, ни честей,
> И чужд сует разнобразных![5]

> Happy, he who depends as little as possible on people,
> Free from debts and from the hassles of being ordered around,
> Not looking at court for either gold or honours
> And a stranger to a wide variety of cares.

> Happy the man who, far from business and affairs
> Like mortals of the early times,
> May work his father's fields with oxen of his own …
> Avoiding busy forums and the haughty doors
> Of influential citizens. (Horace 1983, 99)

Derzhavin's initial near-quotation attunes the reader to a number of later echoes, including references to the netting of wild birds, the processing of honey, and the joys of freedom from marital discord. Later use of "Flakk," from the full tripartite Latin name Quintus Horatius Flaccus, places the echoes of the Second Epode within a larger, hypothetical context of friendship. The selection of "Flakk," to designate Horace, is familiar, if not affectionate; the formal Russian version of Horace's name is "Goratsii," based, as is its English equivalent, on the highly respectable and aristocratic Roman family name (*nomen*) Horatius. This was Derzhavin's choice in the occasional verse on the back of his gift to Evgenii. "Flakk," on the other hand, is based on the Latin "Flaccus," meaning "flap-ear," and is a kind of playfully derisive nickname (Campbell 1924, 85). "Flaccus" was an unflattering "extra" name (*cognomen*) typical for servants; as such, it is reminiscent of Horace's family history, for his father was a slave. The move from "Goratsii" to "Flakk" in designation of the Roman predecessor hints at the genial spirit of competition characteristic of Derzhavin's long poem as a whole.

Although significant differences in rhetoric and tone are noticeable, Derzhavin, like the speaker in Horace's epode, goes to great lengths to express his preference for home-grown, as opposed to exotic, food:

> I would not ask for oysters from the Lucrine Lake
> Or turbot any more, or scar,
> Which winter, the roaring in an eastern sea, drives west
> With waves until they reach these parts;
> No Afric bird into my stomach would descend,
> Nor heathfowl from Ionia,
> More tasty than the plumpest olives gathered from
> The branches of my orchard trees. (Horace 1983, 100)

> Я озреваю стол, — и вижу разных блюд
> Цветник, поставленный узором:
> Багряна ветчина, зелены щи с желтком,
> Румяно-желт пирог, сырь белый, раки красны,
> Что смоль, янтарь-икра, и с голубым пером
> Там щука пестрая — прекрасны!
> Прекрасны потому, что взор манит мой вкус,
> Но не обилием иль чуждых стран приправой,
> а что опрятно все и представляет Русь:
> Припас домашний, свежий, зравый. (406–07)

> I gaze at the table — and see a flowerbed
> Of many dishes, laid out in colorful pattern:
> Scarlet ham, green cabbage soup with egg yolk,
> The blushing rose and yellow of a pie, white cheese, red crayfish,
> Black-amber caviar, and garnished with a sky-blue feather
> A brilliantly colorful pike — all beautiful!
> Beautiful because they summon my glance, my palate,
> With no excess of exotic, foreign spice,
> But purely because everything is representative of Russia:
> A home-grown pantry, everything fresh and healthful.

Horace's rhetoric is full of negation, and ironically reveals the speaker's familiarity with a wide variety of exotic culinary imports. The ironic tone is consistent with the surprise ending to the epode, in which we learn that the major part of the poem in praise of country life had been merely the wishful daydream of a city-dweller. The phrasing of Derzhavin's praise for native Russian sustenance, on the other hand, minimizes the Horatian pattern of negation and its suggestions of irony. While Horace had used the negative particle (*non*) three times, always in an emphatic position at the beginning of lines,[6] Derzhavin negates only once, and weakens even this use by moving it to the second syllable of a line. Derzhavin does not use the description of a country feast to boast of a well-travelled palate; cabbage soup and pike, quintessentially Russian dishes, are sincerely and lavishly praised.

The removal of irony from Horace's model is most obvious in the complete excision of the epode's ending, which introduced a distinction between author and speaker alien to Derzhavin's seemingly genuine, autobiographical voice. The urban money-lender Alfius, we learn in Horace's final stanza, decides not to abandon the city for the joys of the country he has just enumerated:

> With these words the money-lender Alfius,
> Soon, soon to be a country squire,
> Revoked all mid-month loans at interest, —
> But plans relending on the first. (1983, 100-101)

Thus, Horace retrospectively locates his entire epode in the city. The irony of the *volte-face* ending is achieved through, among other devices, the duplication "soon, soon" (*iam, iam*), since repetition can serve to figure doubt. The reader is prone to feel that Alfius may never move to the country. The greater part of the entire epode now must be reconceived as a "skit on fashionable Arcadianism" (Bailey 1982, 6). Derzhavin, by contrast, purges the model of its ironic conclusion, and unambiguously locates all of "Evgeniyu" in the country. The poet explicitly mentions the "northern capital" in his last stanza only to verify that his speaker is *not* actually situated within the city.

It has been shown that Horace's eighteenth-century European translators and imitators often deliberately omitted the ironic, urbane conclusion of the Second Epode (Wilkinson 1969, 297). The same point has been made specifically with regard to many of the German and Russian translations which Derzhavin would have read (Baehr 1991, 69). But the decision to erase all trace of Horace's ending must have been, in Derzhavin's case, a highly conscious one, for in an earlier imitation of the Second Epode, "Pokhlvala sel'skoi zhizni" [In Praise of Country Life], Derzhavin concludes with a direct paraphrase of Horace's final five lines:

> Так откупщик вчера судил,
> Сбираясь быть поселянином;
> Но правежем долги лишь сбрил,
> Остался паки мещанином,
> А ныне деньги отдал в рост. (1869, 2:104)

This was how the merchant judged yesterday,
Planning to become a rural settler;
But by force he's managed only to shave off his debts,
And he's remained hitherto only a petty city-dweller,
Though he's invested his money.

The close relation of the final passage of this early work to the epode makes the many swerves away from Horace in "Evgeniyu. Zhizn' Zvanskaya" all the more noticeable.

The revision of Horace in the latter poem returns it to the myth of a golden pastoral age such as those found in the writings of Theocritus or Hesiod, the poetic predecessors on whose poems Horace's irony depends. A hint of a time when gods and men lived as equals in the same idyllic paradise appears when Derzhavin describes himself feasting with deities. In locating his work squarely in a rural paradise, Derzhavin gently subverts Horace's authority by making him seem merely the modern child of a grander, more ancient vision: "gods and men have come from the same starting point"; "The race of men ... was of gold ... they lived like gods, with carefree heart, remote from toil and misery" (Hesiod 1988, 40). In what has come to be called the "Panegyric of Ptolemy," Idyll XVII, Theocritus describes a time when Ptolemy, a man, enjoyed "equal honor with the Blessed; a golden mansion is builded him in the house of Zeus" (1928, 211). Such a pastoral, idyllic vision carries with it certain conventions of meteorological imagery. Later in Theocritus' work, the sky-god Zeus is treated exclusively as nurturer. He brings gentle rain to ten-thousand lands; the thunder one might associate with such activity would have to be, according to the archaic logic of pastoral, harmless.

The paradoxical notion of "sweet thunder" — to use a Shakespearean formulation (1987, 101) — remains more implicit than explicit in ancient pastoral. Yet for Derzhavin in "Evgeniyu" the metaphor of "gentle thunder" becomes a particularly fruitful and unifying motif. Not only does this oxymoron figure prominently in the long poem's conclusion; the motif appears throughout the work. Moreover, the sustained thunder imagery of "Evgeniyu" itself may be taken as the culminating achievement of many years of poetic experiment. "Grom," associated with "thunderous Pindar" and the hyperbolic style required for solemn and triumphant Pindaric odes, became a veritable cliche in Russian neoclassicism, often assuming the meaning of any deafening or loud noise. Derzhavin inherited this generalized usage, but he spent much of his poetic career further expanding the number of semantic fields associable with the term. Yet at other times he returns the word to its archaic meteorological contexts. So pervasive and idiosyncratic is Derzhavin's use of the image that Lev Pumpyansky, an important Russian scholar of the early twentieth century, was forced to use the distinctive formulation "gromopodobnaya poeziya" [thunderlike poetry; 1928, 47], to describe it.

The nearly automatic association of thunder with Pindar in Russian neo-classicism allows Derzhavin to achieve at least partial identification with this most important of Horace's chosen rivals. In *Odes* 4.2, the Roman poet compares his own style to Pindar's in an ultimately deflating catalogue of praise, typified by the ironic use of exaggerative epic similes:

> Like a river headlong from mountains pouring
> Forth to drown its banks with the glut of rainfalls,
> Pindar's language, seething with boundless power,
> Bursts like a torrent. (Horace 1983, 311)

In an exemplary illustration of poetic father–son conflict, Horace compares Pindar's verse not to the power of thunderstorms, but to their unpleasant residue. Derzhavin, on the other hand, is more interested in thunder proper, which, in seeming identification with Pindar, he restores and reconstitutes throughout his career. The use of thunder imagery thus undermines Horace's authority by returning to the mythic poetic systems of a still more ancient, and hence stronger, odic poetic father.

The many references to thunder, only a few of which can be considered here, in Derzhavin's military ode "Na vzyatie Ismaila" [On the Taking of Izmail] (1957, 156–66) typify the widespread neoclassical fascination with thunderous bombast. "Furious thunder" roars and shakes the axis of the universe. An epic simile compares soldiers hesitating before fire to lions "chasing the thunder of tigers." And thunder announces eventual military victory, as in the famous line from another of Derzhavin's poems which was set to music and popularized by O.A. Kozlovsky: "Grom pobedy razdavai-sya!" [Thunder of victory, resound!] (1868, 1:268). In all these examples, thunder functions as a periphrastic, ornate way of referring to a simple historical referent: the actual sound of cannon or gunfire. Thus, when Der-zhavin, in his poem on the discovery of the Crimea, writes that "thunderbolts are hung on the wall" we clearly understand, by aural metonymy, that he means weapons are being put aside; no wonder Mars is annoyed.

But not all of Derzhavin's thundering is so obviously linked to the tradition of the military ode as it was established in Russia by Vasilii Kirillovich Trediakovsky (1703–69) and Mikhail Vasilievich Lomonosov (1711–65). In Derzhavin's Anacreontic poetry not only drums, but also pianos, Sappho's harp, and even a balalaika thunder, the last, strangely, in a lyric entitled "Tishina" [Silence] (1868, 2:76). In still another lyric, Derzhavin, looking into a glass of wine, dismisses the thunder of oceanic storms, humorously expressing in this way his preference for domestic, as opposed to epic, styles of drowning. Following the precedent of Mikhail Dmitrievich Chulkov (1743–92), who codified and embellished Russian folklore for literary purposes, Derzhavin invents a mythopoeic "Knyaz' Grom" [Prince Thunder] in a playful poem entitled "Luch" [The Sunbeam].[7] Chulkov, in his *Kratky mifologichesky leksikon* [Short Mythological Lexicon] (1767), itemized a pantheon of Slavic deities to complement the well-known ancient Greek model. The ludic tone of Derzhavin's later lyric is equally reminiscent of Chulkov's collection of stories, *Peresmeshnik, ili slavenskie skazki* [The Mocker, or Slavic Tales] (1768) in which the author invented Slavic deities clearly unheard of in his sources. It has been shown that Chulkov's inventions often simply russify Greek models, as in the use of "Zimtserla" for Aurora (Garrard 1970, 49). Given this pattern, Derzhavin's "Prince Thunder" might clearly be understood as a lesser relation of Zeus, the sky-god associated with thunder in ancient Greek mythology.[8]

Thunder is also prominent in Derzhavin's experiments with the short nature poems characteristic of pre-Romanticism and Romanticism. In a particularly memorable work, "Solovei" [The Nightingale], a bird's singing reminds the poet of thunder in a peculiar apostrophe:

Твой глас отрывный, перекаты
От грома к нежности, от нег
Ко плескам, трескам и перунам,
Средь поздних, ранних красных зарь,
Раздавшись неба по лазурам,
В безмолвие приводят тварь. (1957, 230–31)

Your fragile voice, the bursts
From thunder to tender caress, from contentment
To handclaps, cracks, thunderbolts,
Amidst the red twilights of evening and morn,
Which, having spread out against the light blue hues of the sky
Bring Creation into silence.

The syntax is particularly arresting; it suggests that the nightingale's range begins and ends with thunder: "Ot groma ... perunam." Elsewhere in this lyric, the bird is said to "capture thunder" (lovit grom). Having inserted thunder into the mellifluous songs of a nightingale, Derzhavin is nevertheless able to bury thunder in the alliterative line of his memorial tribute to Suvorov: "Severnye gromy v grobe lezhat" [The northern thunderbolts are lying in the grave] (1986, 125). Here thunder serves as a figure for the body of the great Russian general himself. The onomatopoeia of lines such as these has previously been noted by Helmut Koelle in his treatment of what is perhaps Derzhavin's most striking use of the device: "Grokhochet ekho po goram / Kak grom gremyaschy po gromam" [An echo rumbles through the mountains / Like thunder thundering from thunderclap to thunderclap] (qtd. from Koelle 1966, 33).

Despite its sonorous guttural presence, "grom" does not remain a strictly auditory concept for Derzhavin; by association with lightning, thunder blazes in his "Vodopad" [The Waterfall] (1957, 178–90). Able to move in and out of clearly distinct semantic environments, taking on a wide range of meanings, "grom" for Derzhavin is a "migratory word" (perelyotnoe slovo). This term is taken from one of Aleksandr Blok's well-known lyrics, "Net kontsa lesnym tropinkam" [There is no end to wooded paths]. It has been further defined for criticism by David Sloane as a word accumulating the implications of the texts which contain it, remembering its previous habitats as part of its aesthetic potential (1988, 136–93). Despite its many wanderings, "grom" does not lose its most basic substantive meteorological sense for Derzhavin. In a devotional ode written only one year before "Evgeniyu," and actually entitled "Grom," the word is returned to the context of a powerful hail- and rainstorm. In brief, this spiritual, almost pantheistic poem argues at length for a position of intellectual humility in the face of the Creator, whose immortal power, beyond human comprehension, is exemplified for Derzhavin by the natural forces of thunder and lightning.

One might suggest that a larger aesthetic of the Baroque determines Derzhavin's exaggerated use of "grom." Such an aesthetic prescribes for all verse forms the high-flown conceits and complex periphrases through which Derzhavin's thunder often reverberates. Indeed, Pumpyansky has related what he identifies as Derzhavin's more than one hundred thunderous lines to the "acousticism" of the German Baroque and, specifically, to the influence of Barthold Heinrich Brockes (1680–1747).[9] And yet, as Pumpyansky admits, Derzhavin's preoccupation with thunder is highly unusual: "In general, there is perhaps no other phenomenon in Russian poetry more distinctively characteristic of Derzhavin than the play of thunder, its sudden bursts, echoes, and sustained reverberations" (1928, 47).

Derzhavin's fascination with the various acoustic potentials of thunder imagery seemingly allows him to usurp on the level of poetic fantasy some of the patriarchal authority traditionally belonging to Zeus, Jove, and Perun, the ancient Slavic thunder god. More specifically, in "Evgeniyu" the rhetorical mastery of thunder permits Derzhavin to compete aesthetically with Horace as the chosen poetic father, while, at the same time, appearing to claim momentary identification with such other poets as Hesiod, Pindar,

Theocritus, and Lomonosov. In his revisions of the Horatian model, Derzhavin thus defeats the "anxiety of influence" (Bloom, 1966) to achieve his own, independent, poetic definition of self. One might object that neoclassical poets were little concerned with matters of originality, but it has been suggested that Derzhavin was familiar with Edward Young's *Conjectures on Original Composition*, published in German during the 1770s (Brown 1980, 406), a work which theorizes that originality is a determinant of overall poetic worth.

After invoking the aesthetic of a peaceful, quiet garden, Derzhavin's "Evgeniyu. Zhizn' Zvanskaya" soon thunders gently against itself and its Horatian model, a total of ten times. Thunder first intrudes upon the restful quiet of Zvanka in the hammering of woodpeckers, in what Derzhavin emphasizes with spondaic assonance as "grom zhyoln" [the thunder of woodpeckers] (128). The bird described is the black woodpecker (*Drycopus martius*), by far the largest and the loudest of Russian woodpeckers (Flint 1984, 184). Its hammering is clearly associated with the spring mating season (Menzbir 1895, 347). Derzhavin's thunderous metaphor for the hammering reconstitutes the mythology of the ancient Romans, who knew the red-crested species as "the incendiary bird" (*avis incendiaria*), which was thought to carry heavenly flames, readily associable with lightning (Afanas'ev 1970, 1: 492). It was held sacred to Mars by the Sabines, who believed the bird had led them on their way to Italy (Thompson 1966, 249). More generally, the woodpecker has been regarded as the European representative of the "thunder-bird," a recurring character in mythology from Ancient Greece to Native American culture.[10] In Aristophanes's *The Birds*, Euelpides jokingly remarks: "Zeus won't easily yield the sceptre to the woodpecker." One might wonder if the humor here depends precisely on the incommensurability of god and bird. Yet the joke is not without a certain mythic logic, and, according to an early twentieth-century interpretation, has been regarded as evidence for the existence in prehistoric times of ritual oak-kings, who were believed, when they died, to assume the form of the woodpeckers which attack oak trees. Whatever the mythological resonance of Derzhavin's woodpeckers, their vernal exuberance contrasts vividly with Horace's "queruntur in silvis aves" [birds which murmur in the woods], autumnal harbingers of the "wintry season" and of "thundering Jove" who "brings on the falls of rain and snow" (1983, 100). The changes in weather lead to an extensive fantasy in the epode about the types of wild game available late in the year, but the *queruntur* of Horace's *aves* connotes a certain ambivalence in narrative tone. Related etymologically to "querel" (Old French) and "quarrel" (English), the word suggests "whining" or "complaint." One may wonder if Horace's diction and the references to rain and snow are meant subtly to anticipate and cohere with Alfius's ultimate decision to avoid the country, seemingly based only on financial worries. In any case, the harmless noise of Derzhavin's much louder birds is substituted in "Evgeniyu" for any explicit mention of adverse weather. Elsewhere in the work, the Russian poet, no less than Horace, celebrates the pleasures of hunting and of wild game, but unlike Horace, Derzhavin is able to do so in a mythical world of endless spring and summer.

The boisterous woodpeckers belong to a larger system of avian imagery related to thunder in Derzhavin's poem. The doves mentioned a few lines prior to the woodpeckers may be taken to allude to their ancient Greek precedent: doves brought the young thunderbolt-thrower Zeus his ambrosia. In Slavic cultures, it was thought that if a household offered food to doves, it was protected from fire (Afanas'ev 1970, 1: 540–41). Later in Derzhavin's work, the most obvious avian emblem of thunder in Western culture, the eagle, also appears: "The gaze of the young leaders blooms with victories, but the glory of the gray-haired eagle is hidden" (132). It has been noted by I.O. Ionin that the bird represents the military prowess of Count M.F. Kamensky (1738–1809), retired as commander in chief because of illness (Derzhavin 1986, 458). Yet the presence of specific political allegory here, as elsewhere in Derzhavin's highly topical and biographical poem, need not deafen ears to occasional mythic overtones. In Homer, the eagle is "an omen sent from Zeus," in Pindar, "the bird of Zeus." Aristophanes refers to "Zeus, with an eagle on his head" (Pollard 1977, 15, 123, 143). In modern Anatolia, dead eagles were impaled against the doors of houses in the belief that they could ward off lightning (Pollard 1977, 142), a practice, however far from Russia, which suggests that the tendency to associate eagles with destructive thunderstorms was hardly limited to the ancient Greek world.

Human inhabitants of Zvanka enjoy their table and drink "with thunder" to the tsar and his family (s gromom p'yom; 407). It is well known that such toasts were regularly accompanied by a cannon salute (Khodasevich 1931, 259), to which the "grom" in Derzhavin's image periphrastically refers. Yet should this relation of the image to its actual primary historical referent provide an end to interpretation? If so, reading the poem as a whole may begin to seem little more than an exercise in historical or biographical decoding. One might alternatively ask whether the cannon fire accompanying toasts participates in a larger, stylized behavioral system worthy of analysis. The use of the cannon in domestic ritual would seem to have certain psychological, unconscious advantages to the participants. War is temporarily turned into something highly organized and regular; the tools of military aggression are made to seem harmless, clock-like. In the context of Derzhavin's extended pastoral, the domestication of cannon figures a larger domestication, or taming, of thunder, which broadly characterizes the aesthetic of the poem. Here linked with woodpecker-hammering and celebratory toasts, thunder is made to seem innocent. It is dissociated from fearful memories of the destruction wrought by lightning and floods.

The metaphoric linking of thunder with firearms continues in a description of hunting: "dich'gromim svintsom" [We slay the game with lead](130). The very sound of the verb "gromit" contributes phonetically to the development of the aural motif of thunder in the poem as a whole. Although in this context, the word means primarily "to slay" or "rout," the word has long been used in connection with thunder (Dal' 1978, 1:397). Derzhavin returns to the sound of thunder to invoke the image of festive shooting among his peasants at holiday time:

> Из жерл чугунных гром по праздником ревет;
> Под звездной молнией, под светлыми древами
> Толпа крестьян, их жен вино и пиво пьет,
> Поет и плащет под гудками. (408)

> From iron gun-barrels thunder roars for all the holidays;
> Under starry lightning, under the well-lit trees,
> A crowd of peasants and their wives drink wine and beer,
> Sings and dances to the music of the *gudki*.[11]

Reconstituting meteorological associations, Derzhavin links the thunderous, celebratory shots to lightning. Aristocrats both in Russia and Europe frequently organized courtly feasts including illuminations and gun salutes, and it is known that Derzhavin celebrated his birthday and name day in such a fashion. But in this description, the poet and his family are absent, enjoying more refined activities indoors. Since Derzhavin later refers to a "volkhva" [sorcerer], the boisterous mood of the drinking peasants here is subtly suggestive of pagan ritual. In particular, the metaphoric reference to thunder evokes the presence of Perun, the ancient Slavic god of thunder, whose name is hidden several stanzas later in a standard eighteenth-century figure for weaponry ("peruny"). Although it is doubtful that many archaic rituals of pre-Christian Russian peasantry persisted into the late eighteenth century, the pagan Eastern Slavs once celebrated a series of "thunder holidays" (gromovye prazdniki) in July and early August to honor Perun (Brokgauz 1990, 9:761). Earlier reference to oak trees on the estate at Zvanka is consistent with the hint of such festivity in the name of the thunder-god. Oak trees are comparatively tall, and thus prone to attract lightning-bolts. For this reason, the oak has been sacred to thunder-deities in a number of European cultures, and it is believed that the oak had an important function in pre-Christian Slavic Perun-worship.

From ballistics and festive contexts, Derzhavin's thunder migrates into psychological and musical environments:

> Там с арфы звучныя порывный в души гром,
> Здесь тихогрома с струн смягченны, плавны тоны
> Бегут, — и в естестве согласия во всем
> Дают нам чувствовать законы. (409)

> There from the harp, here from the strings of the pianoforte
> The struck and ringing, soft tones
> Run into the thunder of the soul, and in their natural harmony with all
> They let us feel their laws.

Thunder appears, in a typical example of Derzhavin's highly experimental, convoluted word-order, to enter the soul from a harp. Continued development of the motif in a psychological context occurs when, in a subsequent stanza, Derzhavin muses on the "burei shum" [noise of storms] (409), which the poet imagines in a state of near-sleep rather than hearing directly. The poet's drowsiness extends the archaic pastoral argument of thunder's harmlessness, here but a function of mind.

Back in the previously cited harp stanza, thunder is inserted into what Yakob Grot notes is a literal translation of "pianoforte," "tikhogrom" (Derzhavin 1868, 2:414). The usual translation, used by Derzhavin in an earlier lyric, is "fortep'yano" (1986, 51). The invention of a new term invites interpretation. The use of Slavic morphemes in "tikhogrom" is perfectly consistent with the desire of Admiral Shishkov and his followers to oppose the linguistic Westernization espoused by the Karamzinians; yet I have found no evidence to suggest that anyone other than Derzhavin created or used the word. The only other use of it I am familiar with occurs in a long poem, "Tselenie Saula" [The Wrath of Saul], which Derzhavin wrote in 1809, two years after "Evgeniyu": "O, kol' sei diven tikhogrom / I l'yot garmoniyu takuyu" [Oh, how wondrous is the pianoforte / And it pours forth such harmony] (1868, 3:12). It is perhaps not accidental that the setting here is explicitly celestial, for the earlier poem evokes the mood of an earthly heaven in the long European tradition of Edenic gardens.[12] "Tikhogrom" suggests gentle noise; the neologism contributes to the domestication of gods and cannon basic to the aesthetic strategies of behavior and creation at Zvanka.

Thunder also figures in the elegiac, concluding part of the poem, where it is used in an elaborate figure to describe the creaking sounds of rusted metal gates and a bronze harness (133). Finally, the climax of the poem includes thunder in what initially seems a paradoxical simile: Evgenii, having heard the poet's songs, commemorates him: "Shepnesh' v slukh stranniku, v dali kak tikhy grom / Zdes' Boga zhil pevets, 'Felitsy'" "[You will whisper to a wanderer, in the distance like quiet thunder, / Here lived the singer of God, of 'Felitsa'"] (410). Derzhavin's word order is again experimental, and the cluster of metaphors complex, for it contains two challenging, but essential comparisons. Memory is first likened to a whisper. Then the whisper is compared to the sound "quiet thunder," (tikhy grom). How are we to interpret this oxymoron? On the most literal level, the thunder merely sounds quiet because of its distance. Yet the unusual formulation cannot fail to excite memories of Derzhavin's earlier periphrasis for "piano," and suggests a musical context for the entire poem.

The highly unusual phrasing of the previously cited passage gives any reader pause, but the syntax is not without a purpose. The name "Felitsa" refers to Catherine the Great in Derzhavin's most famous eponymous ode and is clearly associated with court politics, harmonizing here with religion. Yet the fact that "Bog" and "Felitsa" are paralleled in the genitive case invites additional interpretation. Both terms designate not only cosmic and imperial beings, but also eponymous literary works and the types of poetics they represent. The allusion to Derzhavin's own poem entitled "Bog" [God] is particularly significant, for the poetic taming of thunder achieved in "Evgeniyu" illustrates the boasting of the speaker in this earlier, religious ode: "Umom gromam povelevayu" — "With reason I rule the thunderbolts" (1957, 116). Mikhel'son glosses this line as a periphrastic reference to the discovery of the lightning rod, known in eighteenth-century Russian as "thunder rod" [gromootvod] (1912, 1044). Although "lightning rod" [molnieotvod] is the term now considered more scientifically correct, "gromootvod" continues to be the more popular word. It is well known that Lomonosov, a continual subject of Derzhavin's ambivalent poetic admiration and competition, contributed to the invention in Russia of the lightning rod. Lomonosov had followed Benjamin Franklin's experiments and worked on the invention of a lightning-rod with Richmann in St. Petersburg (Menshutkin 1947, 101–05). The power of this discovery has been suggested by Ernst Benz in his use of the phrase "theology of electricity," which designates what he treats as the most important scientific paradigm of the seventeenth and eighteenth centuries (1989). It was known that Lomonosov made one of the first "thunder rods" in Russia for his official residence and that this instrument, improperly used, had the power to kill. It had indeed caused the death of one of Lomonosov's fellow experimenters. Lomonosov gave several public lectures in St. Petersburg on the scientific study of atmospheric electricity.

In his poetic taming of thunder, Derzhavin identifies with Lomonosov's technological and scientific mastery at the same time as he competes with Horace's ironic treatment of the pastoral. In effect, "Evgeniyu" may be read as a rhetorical lightning-rod. Thus Derzhavin resolves what George Orwell, in an entirely different context, calls "the jealousy of the modern literary gent who hates science because science has stolen literature's thunder" (1958, 22). Orwell uses a common English idiom, "to steal someone's thunder," with no exact counterpart in Russian. The idiom is nevertheless indicative of the Enlightenment's characteristic fascination with technological mastery. The phrase is attributed to John Dennis, a stage manager, who invented a new technique for producing theatrical thunder for an ill-fated show, *Appius and Virginia*. The play flopped. In 1733, watching a performance of *Macbeth*, Dennis exclaimed: "Damn them!... They will not let my play run, but they steal my thunder!" (OED 1989, 18:36). An unconscious wish that thunder might become an object of possession and control by human beings may account for the enduring popularity of the idiom. It is tempting to dismiss the basic presuppositions of the idiom — which can only be hypothesized — as peculiar to English speakers, but the present analysis of the strength and originality of Derzhavin's thunder imagery would suggest that the fantasy of manipulating thunder cuts across European cultural boundaries.

Surrounded by associations of Lomonosov with the technology of thunder-taming, Derzhavin relates his influential predecessor poetically to thunder in lines composed to his portrait:

> Се Пиндар, Цицерон, Виргилий — слава Россов.
> Неподражаемый бессмертный Ломоносов.
> В восторгах он своих где лишь черкнул пером,
> От пламенных картин поныне слышен гром. (1868, 3:259)

> Pindar, Cicero, Virgil — the glory of Russians,
> The inimitable Lomonosov.
> In flights of rapture wherever he made his mark in pen
> Today is heard the thunder from fiery pictures.

Note the onomatopoeic alliteration: "ar ... ro ... ir ... ro / ... ra ... er / ... or ... er ... ro / ... ar ... ro." The rhyme of "pen" and "thunder," also used as the penultimate rhyme of "Evgeniyu," suggests a larger metaphoric association of writing and meteorological mastery. Such an association may be unconsciously reinforced by the partial echo of the thunder-god's name in the very word for "pen": "Perun" — "pero." The immortality consistent with the mastery of the thunder — here ascribed to Lomonosov — provides a context for the parallel immortality Derzhavin gives himself at the end of "Evgeniyu." One might object that Derzhavin does not mention Lomonosov explicitly in this later poem. And yet Lomonosov's presence may be subtly felt in Derzhavin's citing of Pindar's name, which suggests a common contemporary epithet designating Lomonosov "the Russian Pindar." Given the rivalry between Horace and Pindar mentioned privately in Horace's *Odes* 4.2, Derzhavin's identification with Lomonosov thus directly works to subvert Horace's authority. Irina Reyfman has shown that inaccurate, "mythological" images of Lomonosov as the founding "father" of Russian poetry — at Trediakovsky's expense — achieved wide circulation by the end of the eighteenth century (1990, 95). Her analysis explains why Lomonosov is generally a privileged object of Derzhavin's interest, for poetic creation by definition occurs in strife with poetic fathers.

Within the larger patriarchal laws of poetic influence, Bloom identifies and discusses six particular "revisionary ratios," one of which most aptly characterizes the success of Derzhavin's poem in the face of Horace's poetic authority. The specific type of intertextual thunder-stealing illustrated by Derzhavin is identified as "apophrades" (1966, 139–55). The term is borrowed from the Ancient Greek calendar; *apophrades* were days on which the dead were thought to return to their former houses. According to Bloom's reformulation for poetics of the apophradic relation, a strong poet subverts the authority of a poetic father through identification with that father's father. In other words, a successful poet engaged in this particular revisionary ratio seems to assume the voice not of his poetic father, but of a poetic grandfather. In imitating directly the idyllic visions of Hesiod and Theocritus, as well as the odic flamboyance of Pindar, Derzhavin achieves an illusory imaginative priority over Horace; he seems to become Horace's father. Like ghosts, Hesiod and Theocritus return to inhabit the magnificent country house of pastoral poetry Derzhavin has occupied, lending the powerful voice of their authority to his creation. In genial competition with Horace, Derzhavin illustrates a Theocritean principle of composition, that of the country singing match. Theocritus' competing shepherds issue friendly summonses such as the following: "Ho friend! hither and lend us your ears awhile. / We two have a match toward, to see who's the better man at a country-song" (1928, 69).

In conclusion, Derzhavin's multiple symbolic hushings of thunder gently subvert the patriarchal authority which the ability to manipulate meteorological electricity represents. Ultimately, Derzhavin is able to claim that authority as his own. The complete structural interpretation which "Evgeniyu. Zhizn' Zvanskaya" deserves has not been offered here; rather the poem has been used to isolate a term of particular significance for psychological and intertextual understanding of the poet. I have suggested that Derzhavin poetically steals the thunder of new technology and of one of the greatest poets in his tradition, Horace. The analysis might be extended to include other names of patriarchal authority at both ends of the biographical spectrum: the biological father, and the tsar, with whom, late in life, Derzhavin came into considerable conflict. But the primary goal pursued here has been more modest: to account for the striking impressions of originality arising from a single long poem.

So unparalleled, in fact, does the work of Derzhavin appear to posterity that he has won for himself the name of "father" in his own right. Pumpyansky aptly calls Derzhavin the "father of colorful styles" in reference both to his place in Russian literature as a whole and to the complex kinship of Fyodor Tyutchev (1803–73) with the prior poet in particular (1928, 39). The metaphor of Derzhavin's "fatherhood" is particularly irresistible in consideration of Tyutchev's thunderous conceits. Perhaps the most extravagant example of Tyutchev's thunder imagery appears, not surprisingly, in a poem entitled "Vesennyaya groza" [A Spring Thunderstorm]:

> Ты скажешь: ветреная Геба,
> Кормя Зевесова орла,
> Громокипящий кубок с неба,
> Смеясь, на землю пролила. (1965, 2: 12)

> You will say fickle Hebe,[13]
> Was feeding Zeus's eagle, and
> Laughing, emptied a cup of boiling thunder[14]
> From heaven down on the earth.

The entire preceding discussion would suggest, at the very least, that Tyutchev's striking neologism "gromokipyashchy" [thunder-boiling] is not simply an isolated verbal curiosity, but rather, a term loaded with a number of complex intertextual affiliations. Who is the mysterious "ty" [you] addressed and playfully mocked by the extravagant lines? Tyutchev's memorable stanza seems not merely to engage the memory of Derzhavin's manipulations of thunder, but to recycle the apophradic relations of the prior poet with authoritative representatives of Antiquity. One might wonder whether Tyutchev, by returning to the mythical figures of ancient Greece, momentarily even beats Derzhavin at his own game. The stanza carries with it the convincing illusion of a folkloric, mythic world seemingly as old or even older than Theocritus, the pastoral tradition, or formal literary creation itself.

NOTES

1. I would like to thank Nina Perlina and Vadim Liapunov of Indiana University, and Anna Lisa Crone of the University of Chicago, for their suggestions. Except when otherwise noted, all English renditions of Russian titles, poetry and scholarship are my own. In translating Derzhavin's poetry, I have striven for literal accuracy rather than overall aesthetic effect. Derzhavin's verses often strike the modern Russian reader as awkward not only because of their use of eighteenth-century idiom, but also because of their highly unusual word order and syntax. It is hardly surprising, then, that English versions which try to match the peculiarities of the original also seem cumbersome.

2. This long work has been previously appreciated and commented upon. Brown calls "To Evgenii. Life at Zvanka" "the most complete example" of the poet's "delight in the beauties of life and his consummate ability to enshrine them in vivid word pictures" (1980, 402). Hart comments on "To Evgenii" in his monograph, arguing that the final fifteen stanzas, in their highly conventional themes, all but spoil the otherwise masterful work (1978, 129–31). Zapadov has treated at length the unusual stanzaic structure of Derzhavin's poem (1958, 150–54). Despite the abundance of reference and opinion, the imagery in the poem has not yet been subjected to systematic analysis.

3. One cannot help wondering whether Bloom's theory applies only to male poets, or at least only to poets who can be said to operate within, rather than challenge, the basic assumptions of patriarchal literary tradition.

4. Discussion of Derzhavin's relation to Horace has a considerable scholarly history. Bush provides useful information about the history of Horace's reception in Russia and discusses Derzhavin's role as a translator (1964). Pinchuk itemizes Derzhavin's many borrowings from his Roman predecessor (1955).

5. All quotations from the poem are taken from pp. 401–11, vol. 2 of the 1868–78 *Sochineniya Derzhavina*, edited and annotated by Yakob Grot. Henceforth only page numbers are given.

6. While all translations of Horace are by Charles Passage (see Works Cited for Horace), occasional reference to the wording of the original is based on the Latin text of the epode given with a parallel English translation in Horace, *Odes and Epodes*, Cambridge: Harvard UP, 1988, pp. 364–68.

7. Chulkov's books are rarities, and the discussion here is based on summaries provided in Garrard (1970). Additional information on Chulkhov may be obtained in Blaigoi, D.D., *Istoriya russkoi literatury XVIII veka*, Moscow: Gosudarstvennoe uchebno-pedagogicheskoe izdatel'stvo, 1951: 459–81.

8. A definitive, two-volume study of Zeus in ancient Greek mythology was written by Arthur Bernard Cook: *Zeus: A Study in Ancient Religion*, New York: Biblo and Tannen, 1965. Part one of the trilogy's second volume, *Zeus, God of the Dark Sky (Thunder and Lightning)*, is of particular interest here.

9. Pumpyansky's argument has been commented upon critically by Zapadov (1958).

10. Here I follow a summary provided by Thompson (1966, 175) of arguments propounded earlier by E.A. Armstrong and J. Rendel Harris. Later parts of this paragraph are also indebted to Thompson's work.

11. "Gudki" are three-stringed folk music instruments played with bows.

12. The history of gardens and their "poetics" has been treated extensively by Likhachyov (1982).

13. Hebe, an ancient Greek goddess of eternal youth and wine-server on Mount Olympus, was often depicted in the graphic arts giving Zeus's eagle a cup of nectar.

14. Not surprisingly, a number of translations for "gromokipyashchy kubok" have been suggested: "thunder-boiling goblet" (Jessie Zeldin, trans., *Poems and Political Letters of F.I. Tyutchev*, Knoxville: Tennessee University Press, 1973, 29); "seething cup of thunderstorms" (Eugene M. Kayden, trans., *Poems of Night and Day*, Boulder: University of Colorado Press, 1974, 6) and "thunder-bubbling goblet" (Richard Gregg, entry for "Tyutchev," in Victor Terras, Ed., *Handbook of Russian Literature*, New Haven: Yale University Press, 1985, 492).

WORKS CITED

Afanas'ev, A.N. 1970. *Poetischekie vozzreniya slavyan na prirodu.* 2 vols. The Hague: Mouton.

Baehr, Stephen Lessing. 1991. *The Paradise Myth in Eighteenth-Century Russia: Utopian Patterns in Early Secular Russian Literature and Culture.* Stanford: Stanford University Press.

Benz, Ernst. 1989. *The Theology of Electricity.* Trans. Wolfgang Taraba. Allison Park, PA: Pickwick.

Bloom, Harold. 1966. *The Anxiety of Influence: A Theory of Poetry.* New York: Oxford University Press.

Brokgauz, F.A., and I. A. Efron, Eds. 1990. *Entsiklopedichesky slovar'.* Yaroslavl': Terra.

Brown, William Edward. 1980. *A History of 18th Century Russian Literature.* Ann Arbor: Ardis.

Bush, Wolfgang. 1964. *Horaz in Russland.* Munich: Eidos.

Campbell, Archibald Y. 1924. *Horace: A New Interpretation.* London: Methuen.

Dal', Vladimir. 1978. *Tolkovy slovar' zhivogo velikorusskogo yazyka.* 4 vols. Moscow: Russky yazyk.

Derzhavin, G.R. 1868–78. *Sochineniya. S primechaniyami Ya. Grota.* 7 vols. St. Petersburg: Akademiya nauk.

_____. 1957. *Stikhotvoreniya.* Leningrad: Sovetsky pisatel'.

_____. 1986. *Anakreonticheskie pesni.* Ed. G.P. Makogonenko, G.N. Ionin and E.N. Petrova. Moscow: Nauka.

Flint, V.E., et. al. 1984. *A Field Guide to Birds of the U.S.S.R., Including Eastern and Central Asia.* Trans. Natalia Bourso-Leland. Princeton: Princeton University Press.

Garrard, J.G. 1970. *Mixail Chulkov: An Introduction to His Prose and Verse.* The Hague: Mouton.

Hart, Pierre R. 1978. *G.R. Derzhavin: A Poet's Progress.* Columbus: Slavica.

Hesiod. 1988. *Theogony and Works and Days.* Trans. M.L. West. New York: Oxford University Press.

Horace (Quintus Horatius Flaccus). 1983. *The Complete Works of Horace.* Trans. Charles E. Passage. New York: Ungar.

Khodasevich, V. F. 1931. *Derzhavin.* Paris: Soveremennye Zapiski.

Koelle, Helmut. 1966. *Farbe, Licht und Klang in der malende Poesie Derzhavins.* Munich: Fink Verlag.

Likhachyov, S. 1982. *Poeziya sadov: k semantike sadovo-parkovykh stilei.* Leningrad: Nauka.

Menshutkin, B.N. 1947. *M.V. Lomonosov.* Moscow: Izdatel'stvo Akademii Nauk USSR.

Mikhel'son, M.I. 1912. *Russkaya mysl' i rech'. Svoyo i chuzhoe: opyt russkoi frazeologii. Sbornik obraznykh slov i inoskazanii.* St. Petersburg.

Menzbir, M.A. 1895. *Ptitsy Rossii.* 2 vols. Moscow: Kushnerev.

Orwell, George. 1958. *The Road to Wigan Pier.* New York: Harcourt.

The Oxford English Dictionary. 1989. 20 vols. Ed. J.A. Simpson and E.S.C. Weiner, Oxford: Clarendon.

Pinchuk, A.L. 1955. "Goratsii v tvorchestve G.R. Derzhavina." *Uchyonye zapiski Tomskogo gos. universiteta im. V.V. Kuybysheva* 24: 71–86.

Pollard, John. 1977. *Birds in Greek Myth and Life.* Plymouth: Thames and Hudson.

Pumpyansky, L.V. 1928. "Poeziya F.I. Tyutcheva." *Uraniya: Tyutchevsky al'manakh.* Leningrad: Priboi, 9–57.

Reyfman, Irina. 1990. *Vasilii Trediakovsky: The Fool of the New Russian Literature.* Stanford: Stanford University Press.

Shackleton Bailey, D.R. 1982. *Profile of Horace.* London: Duckworth.

Shakespeare, William. 1987. *A Midsummer Night's Dream.* New York: Signet.

Sloane, David. 1988. *Aleksandr Blok and the Dynamics of the Lyric Circle.* Columbus: Slavica.

Theocritus. 1928. "The Poems of Theocritus." Trans. J.M. Edmonds. In *The Greek Bucolic Poets*. Ed. T.E. Page, E. Capps and W.H.D. Rouse. New York: Heinemann (Loeb Classical Library), 5-362.

Thompson, D'Arcy W. 1966. *A Glossary of Greek Birds*. Hildesheim: Georg Olms Verlagsbuchhandlung.

Tyutchev, Fyodor I. 1965. *Lirika*. Ed. K.V. Pigarev. 2 vols. Moscow: Nauka.

Wilkinson, L.P. 1969. *The Georgics of Virgil: A Critical Survey*. Cambridge: Cambridge University Press.

Zapadov, A.V. 1958. *Masterstvo Derzhavina*. Moscow: Sovetsky pisatel'.

MEDIATING THE DISTANCE: PROPHECY AND ALTERITY IN GREEK TRAGEDY AND DOSTOEVSKY'S CRIME AND PUNISHMENT

Naomi Rood, Princeton University

We have corrected Thy work and have founded it upon *miracle, mystery* and *authority*.

The Grand Inquisitor in *The Brothers Karamazov*
(Dostoevsky 1976, 237)

All literary art presupposes conventions, and Athenian tragedy is surely one of the most conventionalized genres. Some conventions arise out of the demand upon a fictional work to provide motivations for the events of its plot; as Aristotle deemed, the best kind of plot is that in which things happen by probability or necessity.[1]

One way of supplying causation to a plot, of course, is simply to involve or to invoke the divine. If the phrase, "and the will of Zeus was accomplished," as in *Iliad* I.5, prefaces all the actions to come, no further explanation of motive is needed.[2] Furthermore, when the divine becomes expressed in language, the resulting divine word takes on the supplementary authority of a performative utterance, i.e. speech identical with action.[3] Divine speech which is not differentiated from its actualization encloses necessity within itself. For an author, then, it can provide necessary and sufficient causation.

As Oedipus acknowledges at the beginning of *Oedipus Tyrannus* (278–86), however, the gods do not necessarily speak just at those times when we might wish them to. In the second best case, mortals can learn their will and words from prophecy, the speech of the oracle who speaks forth for another (*prophemi*).[4] For the majority of mortals, that is, for those not continually graced with divine epiphanies, prophecy supplies the primary vehicle of the divine word. This article considers the use of prophecy within two different but associated genres, Athenian tragedy and the novels of Dostoevsky.

I.

The questions behind this comparison concern the attitude of these two genres to the use of prophecy: under what conditions is prophecy the awesome expression of the divine word to humanity which contains causality within it? And when might this capacity of divine speech to create causality be exploited for literary demands, thus utilizing prophecy as a convention? I have chosen to focus on prophecy for the wider view to which I believe it provides access: to the text's conception of the divine, and subsequently, to the ways in which language signifies. For it seems that when prophecy in a text is of the monologic, "singularly-signifying" sort, it is thus determined by a close proximity to the divine. But when prophecy becomes wider, not quite dialogic, but with some room for choice, it is caused by a more distant relation to the divine. For dialogue presupposes the presence of a complete other:[5] in tragedy, the word of the divine cannot yet be dialogic because the divine is not yet sufficiently other. In tragedy, the gods often speak and act on stage, or second best, become heard through oracles. As another and supreme actor and interlocutor, their speech-acts are effected directly. In the world of Dostoevsky's novels, by contrast, the divine word has grown more distant both in space and time. The imagined (and singular) epiphany of Christ in the Grand Inquisitor, for example, in which Christ remains perfectly silent, affords only an opportunity to remind him that having spoken, he can add nothing to what he has spoken of old. But this completion of the divine speech itself comprises the freedom of humans: as the alterity of the divine other becomes more complete, the possibility for dialogue increases. The following discussion of prophecy, then, ultimately refers to the particular relationship to the divine expressed in these two versions of the genres of tragedy and novel. I will seek to show that, while both tragedy and the Dostoevskian novel centrally include prophecy in their plots, tragedy reaffirms the inevitable dynamic of the divine word, whereas, in the construction of his novels, Dostoevsky rejects this kind of divine causality. Prophecy in tragedy provides, at least in part, a genuine motivation for the events of the plot; this type of prophecy is laid bare in Dostoevsky as a conventionalized device for *falsely* creating necessity. In other words, to invoke the familiar Bakhtinian categories, tragedy operates according to the monologic word, whereas Dostoevsky's rejection of prophecy constitutes one aspect of his dialogic word. But in the end, as I hope to demonstrate (*contra* Bakhtin), Dostoevsky is still not free from the dynamics of prophecy. Instead, he only slightly complicates the matter when he gives humans more of an initial choice; after this point things grow generally more inevitable. Thus, while Dostoevsky does not absolutely import Greek antiquity's conception of prophecy into his novels, he nevertheless underscores its continuing importance as he raises it to a new and more complex level of significance.

The debate over the "tragic" reading of Dostoevsky began with two of his earliest and most influential posthumous critics, both of them Classicists. These were the Symbolist poet and philosopher Vyacheslav Ivanov (1866–1949), and the quasi-Formalist/Symbolist member of the Bakhtin circle, Lev Pumpyansky (1894–1940). Ivanov, following the cues of Dmitry Merezhkovsky, promoted the notion of Dostoevsky's works as tragedy. Starting in 1917, he published in *Russkaya mysl'* [*Russian Thought*] a series of revisions of earlier lectures which interpreted Dostoevsky's major works as "novel-tragedies." Ivanov's view of Dostoevsky's writings as tragedies forms one part of a larger concept of tradition as cultural agglutination which was common to the Symbolists. Part of their philosophy included the incorporation of past texts into a mystical synthesis which would culminate in their own writings. Such a philosophy of history and literature, in its eagerness to detect syntheses, often led to an exaggerated perception of likenesses between literary works and genres. In this instance, Ivanov claimed to perceive both the form and content of Classical tragedy in Dostoevsky's prose.

Formally, Ivanov understands all the episodes in Dostoevsky's plots as mini-tragedies, each leading to an inevitable catastrophe. He explains that the tragic episodes are interrupted by digressions characteristic of the storytelling of his times, as seen in Balzac or Dickens. Yet every particular action participates in the unity of the successive episodes.

These episodes, in turn, are worked into the shape of acts, so to speak, in a continually unfolding drama; and these acts, finally, represent in their sequence the iron links of a chain of logic — on which, like a planetary body,

hangs the main event which was from the beginning the theme and purpose
of the whole work, with all the weight of its contentual and solemn significance. (Ivanov 1952, 10–11)

Such a catastrophic end hung on the fatal decision of the hero: whether to be
with God or without God. Once such a choice has been made, all else
inevitably follows. Ivanov frequently refers to Dmitry Karamazov's famous
statement that life is a struggle between God and the Devil and the battlefield
is the heart of man.[6] Thus, like a drama which demands the expression of
every spiritual development portrayed in action, the one who chooses against
God becomes the transgressor of the cosmic and social orders. Crime then
becomes the center of Dostoevsky's tragic world, much like the content of
ancient tragedies. Ivanov discusses at length Dostoevsky's exposition of
solitude, which always threatens to collapse into solipsism. The sole relief
from such solitude comes through *proniknovenie*, the penetration into the
Other as another subject. This kind of penetration, more suggestive and
powerful than the "I–Thou" relationship, approaches another I and happens
only through God. Essentially, then, Ivanov's argument is this: Dostoevsky's
writings consider man's position in relation to the divine, just as tragedy
continuously explores man's tense connection with the gods.[7]

Soon after Ivanov's syncretic reading of Dostoevsky's novels had cap-
tured the imagination of the Russian public, a voice arose in objection. In
1922, Lev Pumpyansky published his argument against Ivanov in an article
entitled "Dostoevsky and Antiquity." Pumpyansky had been a close friend
and "partner in dialogue" of Bakhtin since their undergraduate years in the
Department of Classics at Petersburg University under the direction of the
evangelical and charismatic scholar, Faddei Zelinsky. Unlike Ivanov, who
received a traditional Classical training under Mommsen in Germany, Pumpyansky studied Classics in Russia during the frenetic pre-revolutionary
years, when antiquity was enjoying an oddly active revival. Perhaps in
connection with the idealization of the war of independence in Greece,
Hellenism became a movement espousing the eventual resurrection of an
ancient model of society in Russia, a projection they referred to as the "Third
Renaissance." The circle which formed around Bakhtin — who was somewhat reminiscent of Zelinsky — valued independence of thought, unconven-
tionality, and eccentricity.[8] Thus Pumpyansky approached Dostoevsky with
the aim of debunking any dogmatic approach to literary canons and texts, and
so sought in him the new and the different. In response to Ivanov's invocation
of ancient genres, Pumpyansky remarked almost sarcastically:

дошло ли эстетически непоколебимым трагическое искусство за столь долгое странствие от Афин до Петербурга? осталось ли тем же дионисическое божество на всем протяжении страстного путешествия?[9]

Like most members of the Bakhtin circle, Pumpyansky insisted on the effects of historical time. He concluded that the changes of the Renaissance had necessarily transformed the genre of tragedy in an essential way. In a nonconformist spirit, he wrested Dostoevsky's writings out of the grasp of their Classical, and even Russian genre associations, and wedged them into a typology alongside other more modern — although not modernist — European works, such as Shakespeare's *Hamlet* and Hugo's *Les Miserables*. What was Pumpyansky's thesis against Ivanov? In brief, he objected to the understanding of Dostoevsky as tragic on the grounds that neo-Classicism and Romanticism in Europe had corrupted the idea of the "truly Classical." In consequence, Russia received a somewhat damaged Muse, already self-conscious and anxiety-ridden. While Classical poetry could be marked by a definite distinction between author and hero, the modern hero rebels against the author and eventually assumes the authorial function and position. Thus Pumpyansky conceived of the shift from antiquity to modernity as the change from the author's dream about the hero, to the hero dreaming his own dream, or nightmare, about himself. This has its parallel in Bakhtin's view of the Dostoevskian hero, published in 1929, whose dominant feature will be self consciousness. Because the hero is without an external author, he wanders through life, hallucinating his own reality. Ultimately, dream space becomes the hero's — and specifically Raskolnikov's — "aesthetic homeland, that is, his Classicism." For herein the hero assumes authorship of himself as an "envisioned hero." Finally, Pumpyansky conclusively dismantles Dostoevsky as tragic poet through the orientation of the dream. In Dostoevsky, the coincidental dreaming of the poet and hero is always prophetic, a "son prorochesky [prophetic dream]." This evaluation of the dream informs Dostoevsky's whole perspective, and his difference from tragedy: "Трагедия есть всегда *память* о событии никогда *пророчество* о нем" [Tragedy is always a *memory* about an event, never a *prophecy* about it] (italics in original). Tragedy, Pumpyansky elaborates, is the last wave of an event already fictive and no longer real; the poetry of Dostoevsky, on the other hand, is the wave of an event still to be. In other words, tragedy moves out of reality into fiction, while Dostoevsky's poetry moves from fiction into reality. From this it follows, Pumpyansky concludes, that Dostoevsky is not a tragic poet: "ego slovo ni vspominaet, a predvaryaet [his word does not remember, but anticipates]" (Pumpyansky 1922, 8–25). Pumpyansky's commitment to Dostoevsky's "anticipatory word" reminds us of Bakhtin's famous gloss on the Dostoevskian opposition to Aristotelian catharsis:

> Certain scholars (Vyacheslav Ivanov, Komarovich) apply to Dostoevsky's works the ancient (Aristotelian) term "catharsis" (purification). If this term is understood in a very broad sense, then one can agree with it (without catharsis in the broad sense there is no art at all). But tragic catharsis (in the Aristotelian sense) is not applicable to Dostoevsky. The catharsis that finalizes Dostoevsky's novels might be — of course inadequately and somewhat rationalistically — expressed in this way: *nothing conclusive has yet taken place in the world, the ultimate word of the world and about the world has not yet been spoken, the world is open and free, everything is still in the future and will always be in the future.* (italics in original) (Bakhtin 1984, 165–66)

Thus, we can see that both Ivanov and Pumpyansky discern the central role of fate in Dostoevsky's novels, although they define this role differently. For Ivanov, fate consists in the direction of events once man has chosen for or against God. Prophecy, we can thus deduce, would occur at the moment of this human choice, with God or Devil marking the events to come. Pumpyansky, on the other hand, calls the *totality* of a Dostoevskian novel prophecy. Tragedy portrays events already completed in the past; Dostoevsky describes events yet to occur. In either case, both Ivanov and Pumpyansky foreground the human construction of the prophetic word, with its relation to the divine being perceived as secondary; rather than the divine word coming through the oracle to man, prophecy appears as the human word which aims at approximating to a more distant relationship to the divine. Prophecy has thus lost its intrinsic causality. It will be the task of the second half of this essay to demonstrate that Raskolnikov in *Crime and Punishment* suffers from this transformation of prophetic speech.

In antiquity, as we have noted, prophecy comprised the most traditional means of divine communication to man. If man communicated to the gods through hymn and sacrifice, the gods communicated to man, equally obliquely, but equally reliably, through the riddling words of the oracle. The most obvious example of this in tragedy is the *Oedipus Tyrannus*. Prophecy, or prophecy configured as curse, functions to some degree in almost all the tragedies. The traditional hermeneutics of prophecy entails a kind of "bindingness" of word and deed; because the prophetic word originates in the divine will, speech and action contain their consequences within themselves. In such a divinely bound cosmos, there is no arbitrarily signifying word, even if that signification cannot be understood until later, the time of the tragically "too late." Prophecy then, traditionally, describes a single path of action, the effect of which makes necessary every step upon that path.

Prophecy denotes an ordered and meaningful universe, albeit inexplicably so. For example, Oedipus had to become upset by the offhand remark of the drunken guest that Polybus was not his true father, in order to set out to question the oracle. Eteocles had to arrange his men so that he would fight last, and thus against his brother. It makes little sense to keep asking ourselves: "Why didn't Ajax just stay in his tent?" In a universe which plays by the rules of prophetic speech, that is, speech which signifies its realization because of its divine referent, things simply *have* to happen. Yet the first dream in *Crime and Punishment* and Raskolnikov's response to it suggest the breakdown of these traditional assumptions. When Raskolnikov tries to read it like an ancient prophecy, the surrounding narrative opposes his misreading. Already in the *Oedipus Tyrannus* the materialized "path" of prophecy is depicted as treacherous: both Oedipus and his father left home to consult the oracle (868–70; 130–31), and both arrived at disaster. In this way, Sophocles suggests that the road to the oracle is a dangerous one, which can even lead to murder. As Creon says of Laius' death: "He went to consult an oracle, Apollo said, and he set out and never came home again" (130–31; Sophocles 1977, 165). Raskolnikov demonstrates this danger again, with greater insistence, in his own search for the prophetic.

For Raskolnikov, born into the post-Hamlet world of doubt and self-consciousness (Pumpyansky 1922, 13), necessity has grown elusive. There are no more prophecies, even for heroic men. There are no more assured definitions. As Ivan Karamazov envisioned in his story of the Grand Inquisitor, Christ chose not to enslave man with miracles, mystery and authority. Instead he gave the respectful, but difficult gift of freedom.[10] In a sense, Christ widened the possibilities of signification, removing the necessity of a single referent; by introducing choice into destiny, he thereby dismantled the dynamic of prophecy.

But Raskolnikov is not yet ready for this freedom. Rather than the great freedom of acting in a dialogically signifying world, Raskolnikov desires the lesser, monologic freedom from doubt. He wants the certainty of extreme definition and classification: Am I a Napoleon? Or am I a louse? With prophecy erased from the universe, Raskolnikov endeavors to reestablish such a constricted universe for the sake even of a constructed, illusory necessity.[11] So Raskolnikov explains his idea of the "ordinary" and the "extraordinary," which he published in an article:

> As for dividing people into ordinary and extraordinary, it's a bit arbitrary, I agree, but I don't insist on exact figures. I believe only in the basic conception. Merely that people *in general* are divided by a law of nature. The lower part, ordinary people I mean, just stuff, so to speak, good only to reproduce

their own kind. The other part consists of people in the true sense. I mean
those who are gifted, those who have the talent to shape a *new word* in the
context of their environment. The subdivisions, of course, are endless. Yet the
distinguishing features of both parts are clear enough. (italics in original)
(Dostoevsky 1968a, 258)

As the novel uncovers Raskolnikov's self-construction of divine speech,
we perceive the deceit inherent in his progression; we see Raskolnikov as
though we were witnessing one who, although he is in the process of carving
a false idol, tries to convince himself that he is engendering God in his own
creation. Raskolnikov searches for an authoritative and absolute prophetic
word vis-à-vis himself, not the universe. He wants God's voice, in response
to his problem of self-consciousness, to answer his question: who am I? But
this desperate search unravels only to reveal the impossibility of such a
singly referential word's existence in the world of the polyphonic novel. We
meet Raskolnikov as a seeker after the new, determinedly forgetful of the old
and the past. The problem with Raskolnikov's conception of prophecy is that
he has forgotten, along with much else, the ancient prowess of the prophet:
not just one who foretells, the prophet knows the things having been, the
things being, and the things yet to be.[12] The prophecy desired early on by
Raskolnikov is a naive and partial one, which looks only toward the future
and speaks solely in signs particular to the individual.

Raskolnikov's failure, and concomitantly the novel's success in exposing
it, is rooted in his obstinate desire for a regressive, obsolete prophetic word
which plots a singular monologic path. Raskolnikov's yearning for prophecy
becomes indistinguishable from his mission for the new: the new step, the
new word, the new man. Having embarked on this crusade for the new, the
forward, the authoritative-prophetic, Raskolnikov continuously "forgets" (as
Freud would have it) to see the old and past, yet without these the new
becomes meaningless. Raskolnikov clumsily stumbles "singularly" forward,
necessarily half-asleep or in delirium in order to ignore the other half of the
new, the old and past. The following reading seeks to show the way in which
the text, in a crosscurrent to Raskolnikov, consistently and explicitly presents
the new in combination with the old. In other words, the archaic type of
prophecy, as the singularity of forward-moving plot and action, is consistently coupled with its opposite — past and memory. The very presentation
of this duality or plurality of signification inherently defies the false conception of the traditionally prophetic word. Raskolnikov always has a choice
throughout the novel; the text again and again presents a plurality of options.
But as Raskolnikov repeatedly chooses from only one set of options, consciously refusing to acknowledge the other of the old and past, the blindness

of his vision becomes apparent. Not until the road of the new leads him right back to the old does he come to see his own self-deception. The final destination of Raskolnikov's story of murder reminds us of Ivan Karamazov's tale of the Grand Inquisitor; when Ivan has finished his narration, his brother Alyosha declares: "Your poem is in praise of Jesus, not in blame of Him — as you meant it to be" (Dostoevsky 1976, 241). So also the gradual dismantling of Raskolnikov's authoring of divine speech turns into praise of Christ; the deconstruction of Raskolnikov's false prophecy praises a universe ruled not by monologic miracle, mystery, and authority, but by the freedom of people to speak and act dialogically as *agents* in the world.

The rest of this article, then, will trace the definitive dismantling of the authoritative prophetic word primarily through a consideration of Raskolnikov's first dream, which he finds to be a major source of his prophecy. This analysis concentrates on two areas. First, it attempts to show how the dream, which blends past and future, remembering and forgetting, becomes "monologized" by Raskolnikov, who reduces it solely to a sign of the future and its correlative, forgetting. Secondly, in an effort to show the inadequacy of Raskolnikov's interpretation of the dream, it will also focus on the dream's commentary on Raskolnikov's relation to the divine. Raskolnikov's discomfort in the state of separation from the divine both explicates his yearning for the monologic word in the way he seeks to destroy the old woman, and further illustrates the more distant position of the divine in a dialogic universe. The discussion of the divine, then, reverts to the discussion of prophecy.

II.

The first description of Raskolnikov names his general condition in terms reminiscent of not-remembering: "He soon plunged into deep thought, or rather, into a kind of oblivion [zabyt'e]" (Dostoevsky 1968a,14).[13] Indeed, variations of "zabyvat' [to forget]" and "zabyvat'sya [to forget oneself, to doze off]" figure prominently in the narrative. The first dream, a sojourn into memory and densely surrounded by a haze of forgetting, thoroughly examines the coexisting relationships of these juxtaposed forces. Raskolnikov's second and third dreams are introduced simply yet significantly: "He lost consciousness [On zabylsya]" (Dostoevsky 1968a, 120, 272; 1989, 111, 261). Forgetting, and subsequently, remembering, intersect directly with dreaming. Thus the preface to Raskolnikov's first dream says:

> Such dreams, pathological dreams, make a powerful impression on man's disordered, already aroused organism, and are always remembered for a long time [vsegda dolgo pomnyatsya]. (Dostoevsky 1968a, 62; 1989, 54)

A vivid dream comprises that which is long remembered; a dream creates, or triggers memory. Raskolnikov's forgetting himself causes his dream visions, sites in which, as the first dream shows, memory returns.

A series of "forgettings," while Raskolnikov is walking across Vasilevsky Island, precedes the first dream. "When he raised his head again with a start, he immediately forgot [zabyval] what he had been thinking about and where he had gone" (Dostoevsky 1968a, 61; 1989, 54). After noting several summer houses and flower beds, he comes across carriages and riders on horseback: "He followed them with curious eyes and forgot [zabyval] about them even before they disappeared from sight" (Dostoevsky 1968a, 61; 1989, 54). Finally, he pauses to count his money, accounting for his recent expenditures, "but soon forgetting [zabyl] why he had taken his money out" (Dostoevsky 1968a, 61; 1989, 54). The series of things forgotten, which leads up to his dream, occurs not by coincidence but clearly shows Raskolnikov's need or desire — yet ultimately his inability — to forget. For while he almost succeeds in forgetting while conscious, he can no longer do so while dreaming.

Raskolnikov's dream takes him back to childhood. The time, the day, and the place are just as they are preserved in his memory, but they are even sharper in his dream: "The neighborhood was very much as he remembered it, though he did not remember it as clearly as he saw it in his dream" (Dostoevsky 1968a, 62). Thus, dream not only presents a memory, but a memory more vivid and accurately detailed than one held in mind and subject to conscious recall. Dream then goes back beyond memory, to something beyond recall, to something *forgotten*. What is it that dream recalls and memory has forgotten? It must be that, like Raskolnikov's sudden recollection that he is planning to commit murder, memory usually forgets the thing buried and unlawful. And so what does Raskolnikov's first dream recall?

First, the dream reveals Raskolnikov's innocence; he is a little child, afraid of the unruly crowd around the tavern, attached to his father, innately reverent towards the rites and symbols of the Church. When he sees the beating of the old mare, encouraged by the jeering crowd, he tears himself away from his father in passionate empathy. Indeed, Raskolnikov identifies with the poor innocent beast: upon waking up: "His whole body felt as if it had been beaten" (Dostoevsky 1968a, 67). But Dostoevsky's later extrapolations of this theme suggest that, in his universe, the very conception of innocence necessarily signifies a knowledge of guilt.[14] The dream, in fact, portrays the very conjunction of Raskolnikov's innocence and guilt; the moment he understands that he is, or was, innocent signifies the loss of innocence. Raskolnikov, because of his hyper-consciousness, perhaps more extremely than the rest, becomes part of the despicable crowd; his horror and his fascination draw him deeper and deeper into their midst. He, too — he especially — cannot stop looking. Thus, Raskolnikov dreams of the time when he was still innocent and yet already guilty; his dream presents to him the drama of his loss of innocence. Yet the beating of the mare does not recall the source of his guilt as much as the scenes with his father do.

Raskolnikov's father is absent from the novel. Having died many years earlier, he exists once in the closing words of his mother's letter and then again in this dream. The beginning of the dream recalls Raskolnikov's activity of walking with his father past the tavern, whose drunken and brawling crowd frightens him. He responds to his fear of encountering the terrifying crowd by drawing closer to his father: "He would pull himself close [tesno] to his father and tremble" (Dostoevsky 1968a, 62; 1989, 55). But by the end of the dream, the closeness to his father becomes a tightness in his chest: "He throws his arms around his father, but his chest feels very tight [tesnit, tesnit]" (Dostoevsky 1968a, 67; 1989, 59). What has occurred to create this subtle, yet significant, change?

Raskolnikov first responds to the beating of the mare with an appeal to his father: "'Daddy, Daddy,' he shouts to his father, 'Daddy, what are they doing!'" (Dostoevsky 1968a, 64). The father responds by urging Raskolnikov away from the horrible "sight": "You mustn't look, let's go!" (Dostoevsky 1968a, 64). And, though his father endeavors to lead him away, Raskolnikov "tears himself loose from his father's hands" (Dostoevsky 1968a, 64). The father returns only at the end of the dream after the mare has finally been beaten to death. Having long chased after Raskolnikov, he seizes him and carries him out of the crowd. Again he responds to Raskolnikov's imploring query with an imperative "let's go," adding the explanation, "it's not our business" (Dostoevsky 1968a, 67). Although less conspicuous, if perhaps more consequential than the beating of the mare, Raskolnikov witnesses in his dream the crime of betrayal by his father. Here Raskolnikov experiences the limitations of his father's moral and physical power. The father, omniscient and omnipotent in the world of the child, falls into the realm of the weak and merely human in his willingness *not* to see the suffering of the mare and of his son. In this dream the father betrays the son when he urges him to come away and not to look. And just as the father betrays the son, the son then betrays the father, tearing himself away from the father's hand. And in the same way that the conception of innocence simultaneously comes to exist and ceases to be through the acknowledgement of guilt, the moment of the betrayal of the father marks the recognition of the self through the not-self; or, in terms of that other Father, Raskolnikov learns here of God through himself as not-God. The road that leads to the Sacred, to the church with the green cupola, winds past the tavern, the temple of earthly sin and vice. Raskolnikov never reaches the destination of the Sacred in this dream; instead of the Sacred, he discovers, through the rebellion against the father, the not-Sacred, himself.

One could read this dream, then, as Raskolnikov reexperiencing his first conception of the other and of himself as separate from it. But more than the trauma of the experience of separation, the dream portrays the problem of the incompleteness of the division; the very connectedness between the self and the other becomes the source of Raskolnikov's mad sense of necessity to act. In this dream, Raskolnikov is too much like too many of its characters; both as Mikolka and the mare, both as innocent child and part of the guilty crowd, Raskolnikov stands in clear distinction only from his father. Only the act of breaking away from the father, only the uncoverable and unrecoverable distance from the tavern to the Church, seems an irremediable break. And yet, the very violence of this severing and the absence of overt signs characterizing the similarity (as with the mare and Mikolka) between f/Father and son, mark the extreme and unbearable character of this closeness and separation. Two possibilities arise from this position of bound separation: one may, emphasizing either the connection or the division, strive to bridge the distance and thereby to minimize it, or conversely, to complete the division and render it absolute. Raskolnikov chooses the second option, only to discover that the attempt to divide absolutely produces the opposite result; Raskolnikov identifies both with Mikolka and the mare. The attempt to separate by violence yields only to a deeper degree of non-separability. In the dream, Raskolnikov is both murderer and murdered, as he will be in his dream-filled life after the murder.

Appropriate to the motifs with which the dream is concerned, Raskolnikov's connection to the old pawnbroker is figured in terms of memory and forgetfulness. When Raskolnikov goes to the old woman's apartment for a trial run, he presses her doorbell which rings with a tinny and weak sound:

> In the cramped little apartments of such houses, there are always bells that sound like that. Its tone had slipped his mind [on uzhe zabyl]. Now this peculiar tone reminded [emu chto-to napomnil] him suddenly of something. (Dostoevsky 1968a, 16; 1989, 8)

Already on the doorstep of the old woman's apartment, Raskolnikov experiences a progression of forgetting and then recollecting (a process similar to that of a dream and the language associated with the dream, "predstavil"). What does imminent contact with the old woman call to mind?

When Raskolnikov first addresses the old woman, he bows slightly, "recalling [vspomniv] that he had to be more polite" (Dostoevsky 1968a, 17; 1989, 9). Her very proximity produces remembering. And Raskolnikov, introducing himself as having visited a month earlier, prompts the old woman's first speech: "Oh, I remember [pomnyu],[15] my good man, I remember quite well [ochen' khorosho pomnyu] that you were here" (Dostoevsky 1968a, 17; 1989, 9). The old woman, in contrast to Raskolnikov's continual forgetting, defines herself here by absolute memory. Clearly, the old woman presents in her remembering a difference from Raskolnikov. The otherness of the old woman stems from her association with memory; she represents the past, the old and faded in all the yellowness that surrounds her. Raskolnikov, on the other hand, is the new, striving towards a fearlessness of the "new step, an authentic new word" (Dostoevsky 1968a, 14). Their difference is encapsulated in their very appellations: "young man [molodoi chelovek]"/"old woman [starushka]." But also, as in the dream, the otherness never exists as a distinct separation, but signifies a connection. Thus, while Raskolnikov so drastically opposes the old woman, as new versus old, future versus past, their difference turns into likeness. When Raskolnikov stands on her threshold prepared for murder, he bends his ear to her door and hears her movements behind it:

> Someone was standing silently at the threshold, and exactly as he was doing on the outside, was lurking and listening within; also, it would seem, with an ear to the door. (Dostoevsky 1968a, 81)

Raskolnikov imagines the old woman as mirroring his every movement, enacting his actions simultaneously with him. Thus, while she stands opposite to him, she also becomes like him in this stance, reflecting him like a mirror. Just behind the very penetrable divider of a door, she performs the same actions as he does. Can there now be an answer to the question of what the old woman causes Raskolnikov so discomfortingly to recollect?

It was argued earlier that the dream presented the horror not simply of a brutal murder, but also of the recognition of guilt which comes from the rebellion of separating from the f/Father and the recognition of one's individuality. But while the act of separation constituted a division, it also revealed a connectedness, compromising the division into incompleteness. On the one hand, the lingering bond can be a source of continued nurture and sustenance; on the other hand, the attenuation of the previous whole can be unbearable. For Raskolnikov, the desire for completion then arose as a relief from the tension of being both bound and apart; he mistakenly believes that murder will overcome the division by fully severing the remaining bonds, yet the violent act only tightens the inextricability between murderer and victim, thus casting him as both Mikolka and the beaten mare.

Raskolnikov stands in just such a tense relation to the old woman. When we think about the role of prophecy as indicative of the position of the divine, his relationship to her takes on significance when she becomes an attainable substitute for God. A beacon of memory, she causes him to recognize her as different, but also to remember uneasily the significance of that difference. The otherness of the old woman recalls the initial pain of separation from the father when the wholeness becomes irremediably divided but still bound; she recalls the original conception of the self in view of the other, a self eternally divided. She reminds him of the separation from God on a journey that arrives not at the Church, but at the understanding of the self as not-God. Raskolnikov cannot "kill" God in his effort to obliterate the object from which he is separated, and thus relieve his pain. Instead, he can destroy a different other, the old woman; ironically, the "louse" becomes a stand-in for God. The distinction of the self demands the sacrifice of the whole; the knowledge of the self demands the distance of the other. Raskolnikov, "the split one," tries to forget the pain of the loss of the whole but cannot endure the tension of the distance. He murders the old woman in an effort to obliterate the other, to relieve the tension of the distance by destroying that from which one is separated. Raskolnikov's act is tragic because of the futility of his effort; the desire to obliterate the tension by completing the division through the destruction of the other unavoidably becomes the destruction of the self. I suggest that Raskolnikov here occupies the exact position of the tragic hero as described by Vernant, situated in the not-divided-enough division out of which tragedy arises:

> For there to be tragic action it is necessary that a concept of human nature with its own characteristics should have already emerged and that the human and divine spheres should have become sufficiently distinct from each other for them to stand in opposition; yet at the same time they must continue to appear as inseparable. (Vernant 1990b, 46)

There is too much likeness between the self and the other to destroy successfully the distanced object of desire, and therefore the source of pain, without also destroying the self. Thus Raskolnikov cries to Sonya: "Did I kill the old hag? No, not the old hag — I killed myself! I went there, and all at once I did away with myself forever!" (Dostoevsky 1968a, 407). And thus the road to the church also leads to the cemetery, where the grave of the little brother lies alongside the grave of the grandmother.

At this point, we can see how Raskolnikov interprets his dream as prophetic. Raskolnikov, the dreamer of the new word, the "forgettor" of the old and the past, reads his dream exclusively with an eye to the future. Upon awakening, he responds to his dream:

> "God!" he exclaimed. "Will I really? ... Will I really take the ax, will I really hit her on the head, split open her skull ... will I really slip in the sticky warm blood, break open the lock, steal, and shiver ... and hide, all bloody ... with the ax ... Good Lord, will I really?" (Doestoevsky 1968a, 67)

Raskolnikov reads his dream strictly "forwardly," as a prophetic warning dream. Although it recalls to him the past and the road to God, Raskolnikov forgets this fact again. He "forgets" the past when he sees the dream as a picture of the possible future, just as he "forgets" God when he kills the old woman.

Raskolnikov has already shown himself as a forward-looking reader in areas other than his reaction to his dream. Throughout the first part of the novel, Raskolnikov several times admits that he knows something is going to happen, that he has a presentiment. Early on, his response to the drunken man's ridicule of his hat introduces his general stance toward events: "'So I knew!' he muttered in confusion. 'I thought so!'" (Dostoevsky 1968a,15). Raskolnikov's first look at Marmeladov has special significance for him: "Later, Raskolnikov would recall that first impression and think of it as an omen [predchuvstviyu]" (Dostoevsky 1968a, 21; 1989, 13). Walking through the park the next day, the horrible thought comes into Raskolnikov's mind: "For he had known, he had *felt [predchuvstvoval]* that inevitably it would 'flash,' and he had been waiting for it" (italics in original) (Dostoevsky 1968a, 53; 1989, 46). This sensation of presentiment recurs to Raskolnikov when he later considers how he unnecessarily detoured through the Haymarket on the way home after his dream:

> Subsequently, when he recalled everything that happened to him in those days, moment by moment, point by point, bit by bit, he was always struck, almost superstitiously by that one circumstance, not in itself unusual, but which afterward constantly seemed to him a kind of predestined turning point of his fate.... Yet why, he always asked, why did such an important meeting, for him so decisive and yet so extraordinarily accidental, take place in the Haymarket (where he had no reason to be going) just then at just that hour at just that moment of his life when he happened to be in just the mood and under just those circumstances when that meeting alone could have exerted the most decisive and the most conclusive influence on his entire destiny? It was as though it had purposely been lying in wait for him! (Dostoevsky 1968a, 68)

Circumstances have grown fateful in Raskolnikov's mind; the very accidental nature of this encounter in the Haymarket engenders its contrary sense of
necessity. As a further explanation of Raskolnikov's developing feeling of
being "dragged along by a wheel in which his coat became entangled," he
provides a second anecdote similar to his learning the fateful piece of news
in the Haymarket. That other encounter involves overhearing a student tell a
soldier in the tavern Raskolnikov's exact thoughts about killing the old
pawnbroker. Intellectually, they debate the morality of killing the shrewish
old pawnbroker for the improvement of the general welfare: "For one life,
thousands of lives saved from ruin and collapse. One death and a hundred
lives — there's arithmetic for you!" (Dostoevsky 1968a, 73). The student
concludes that the only justice consists in murdering her oneself. Raskolnikov's reaction to this as a sign of his destiny is symptomatic of his general
tendency towards searching after oracles and omens:

> Recently, however, Raskolnikov had grown superstitious. Traces of supersti-
> tion remained in him for a long time afterward, too. And he was always
> inclined to see a certain strangeness, a mystery, in the whole affair; he as-
> sumed the working of special influences and coincidences. (Dostoevsky
> 1968a, 70)

Raskolnikov becomes superstitious; particular events assume special significance, as prophetic of the future or as logical steps in the progression of his
unfolding destiny. In his interest in the prophecy of a straight and single
forward path, Raskolnikov forgets the other, backward-looking half of the
dream.

For readers of the novel, more aware of what has been and then what will
be, the dream does not appear disconnected from the earlier events. Rather,
just as we sometimes anticipate "bad dreams" from watching a horror movie
late at night, themes and images from Raskolnikov's waking life cross over
into his dream. Thus, the imagery of Raskolnikov's dream finds correspon-
dences in where he has been and in what he has experienced prior to it. His
trip to the old woman with the "offering" of his father's watch recalls the visit
to his grandmother's grave accompanied by his father and the gift of the rice
dish. The drunken peasant who "rode past him on the street, in an enormous
cart drawn by an enormous dray horse" (Dostoevsky 1968a, 15), prefigures
Mikolka in his large cart (usually drawn by a large horse) tormenting the
mare. Raskolnikov's first visit to a tavern presumably marks taverns as
significant places, towards which he is drawn and wherein he encounters the
crowd. Marmeladov conveys himself to Raskolnikov as both the sacrificer
(of Sonya, his wife and her children) and also as the sacrifice in his bestial

form: "I am the shape [obraz] of a beast" (Dostoevsky 1968a, 24; 1989, 17), the victimized end of his wife's physical aggression, that is. The letter from home links his mother and sister with Sonya in the ranks of women who sacrifice themselves, and who, like the mare, live on with determination. The closing words of his mother's letter further remind Raskolnikov of his childhood and the time of happiness when his father was alive, that is, the time of the dream: "Remember, my dear, how when you were still a child, when your father was still alive, you used to babble your prayers on my knee and how happy we all were then!" (Dostoevsky 1968a, 47). Lastly, the maternal letter arouses his indignation at her willingness *not to see*, to accept the way things "seem," rather than are, particularly in Luzhin, the despicable fiancé (Dostoevsky 1968a, 49). The final event before the dream, the encounter in the park with the abused girl, cements the motif of the beaten women — Sonya, Dunya, his mother. In this last situation, Raskolnikov behaves both like the child and father in the dream. First he does intervene to help the suffering girl, but then he shifts to speak his father's words ("it's not our business"), but with even greater malice when he advises the policeman to stop his efforts at helping the girl: "'Stop! Why bother? Let it go! Let him have his fun.' He pointed to the dandy. 'What's it to you?'" (Dostoevsky 1968a, 57). Also the very last images on Vasilevsky Island play a role in his dream: the interrupted journey (to Razumikhin), the tavern again, the carriages and horses, and the general sensation of the countryside. Clearly, the events of the chapters preceding it become recast in the images and events of the dream.

The dream, then, provides a pre-telling and a retelling, yet Raskolnikov chooses to see only the former. The very irony of his prophetic reading, however, is that it reverses linearity — he has to read backwards, to remember, in order to see how the dream reads forwards. For the text explains Raskolnikov's consideration of his walk home via Haymarket as fatefully laden upon his *later* contemplation of events.

It is worth making several observations about the nature of dreaming itself as Dostoevsky understood it and aesthetically presented it. First, although dream must be told in narrative, one of its marvels is the way it functions in absolute disregard of the laws of narrative.[16] The dream, not subject to space and time, poses a challenge to the causality and linearity which narrative imposes. When Raskolnikov reads his dream as strictly prophetic, he loses sight of it as dream, and sees it only in narrative terms. He forgets that the law of causality intrinsic to narrative need not extend beyond it, into, for example, the non-narrative of dream.

Thus the contents of the first dream, and Raskolnikov's partial response to it, reveal the *complexity* of time and motivation. Raskolnikov endeavors to

draw a sharp line between past and future, turning exclusively towards the latter, in his murder of the old woman; yet any such violent division only binds the two sides together more tightly. Raskolnikov's "loss of memory" initiates his return to it: in his dream, in his attraction to the old woman, even in the murder. Raskolnikov acts from a deep immersion in memory and demonstrates in his action the inextricability of past and future, of memory and novelty. And when he ceases to dream in the second half of the novel, turning over his position of dreamer to Svidrigailov, it seems that he has seen what his dreams made visible: the past, the time of his childhood. Raskolnikov comes to see that there is no obliteration of the past in light of the future. Raskolnikov's act of murder reestablishes the totality of the dialogic word. His reading of the exclusively new implies, even if violently, another signification, that of the old. Thus the demon of Raskolnikov's monologic self-appointed prophecy is exposed.

III.

An application of this reading to Athenian tragedy seems more radical. Vernant's analysis, building upon Lesky's, of the shared, albeit tense, responsibility of both man and god in the enacting of destiny in ancient tragedy seems to me persuasive and satisfying. To make it work, we must to a certain extent approach the question of agency differently, without the modern requirements of the term; for tragedy occurred at the crossroads between old and new. On the one hand, tragic guilt arises from the ancient religious conception of an inherited familial or tribal defilement, an *ate* or madness sent by the gods; on the other hand, the rule of law has begun to define a person as an individual acting independently and unconstrainedly, and so deliberately committing crime. Thus, tragic man is always divided, between *aitios*, his character, and *daimon*, the urging of the gods. The earmark of tragedy consists in the tension between the two areas of decision and guilt: the categories remain open and inseparable (Vernant 1990a, 49–84). But what happens if we entertain for a moment the possibility of taking a less moderate viewpoint, and stand together with Peradotto and his "Sophist Other" to see tragedy from a very rational and scientific glance? For in a recent article, having nothing to do with Dostoevsky, Peradotto seeks a reconsideration of *Oedipus Tyrannus* without the concession to the convention of prophecy. Peradotto deplores what he sees as the degradation of the standards and goals of literary interpretation and in assigning blame for this, he has a bone to pick with Aristotle. Seeking the reinstatement of reason as the primary hermeneutic tool, which naturally discounts chance as a force of

causation, Peradotto wonders how Aristotle, the greatest scientist of antiquity, could esteem the *Oedipus Tyrannus*, "a play so riddled with chance, so
crippled by coincidences" (1992, 4), most highly. It is as though we have all
been coerced into reading like Raskolnikov, making inferences and connec-
tions where none necessarily exists. Despite the fact that Sophocles admit-
tedly wrote an "anti-Sophist" (1992, 1) play, Peradotto encourages us to free
ourselves from the shackles of authoritative ideology and reinstate our
disbelief, like full Sophists, not the "half-baked Sophist" Oedipus (1992, 13).
Then we will be free to rewrite Sophocles' play into one of "emancipation"
rather than "enslavement" (1992, 2). While Peradotto acknowledges at the
outset the "particular contemporary perspective" (1992, 1) of his reading, I
suggest that he would be a happier reader of Dostoevsky than of Sophocles.
In my opinion, Peradotto reads either anachronistically, aiming to reroute the
ancient text into a modern one, or non-poetically as a scientist, rather than a
literary critic. Peradotto raises the question of the moral and social implications of a literary work (1992, 6). He wonders why Aristotle's *Poetics* aligns
itself more closely with his *Rhetoric* than with the *Physics* or *Metaphysics*
(1992, 5–6). While Peradotto attributes this to some fault in Aristotle's
thinking, or to his falling to the degraded logic of the general public, it seems
important to keep in mind the consistency of Aristotle's categories and his
brilliance; Poetics *is* like Rhetoric and different from Physics, as Aristotle
clearly demonstrates. Literary narrative is not science: *chance in the "real"
world ceases to be chance once it is plotted*. While Peradotto understands this
capacity of language to turn the "merely *accidental* into the *necessary*"
(1992, 6), he rejects precisely this poetic and narrative function of language.
Peradotto longs for the dialogic, for the prophecy of Dostoevsky's novel. Yet
I fear that this is premature for a reading of the *Oedipus Tyrannus*, and I think
this may be seen based on Peradotto's own insights on the narrative and
performative nature of ancient prophecy:

> Prophecy is not conceivable apart from narrative. It *derives from* narrative,
> from the representation of causal continuity in time. It is, I believe, less
> accurate to say that a narrative represents a prophecy than to say that proph-
> ecy represents that narrative, and does so by *pre-presenting* it, the frame
> paradoxically embedded in what it frames. Prophecy derives from the narra-
> tor's foreknowledge (in reality, his afterknowledge) of his own products, from
> a process of retrogressive composition — from end to beginning (the end
> coming first and justifying the means), disguised in performance as a progres-
> sion from beginning to end. (italics in text) (1992, 10–11)

Peradotto here summarizes the workings of prophecy in ancient drama,
which he sees as the most suspicious genre; drama masks the author as the

source of discourse and does not allow for rereading, thereby creating an audience disabled from producing meaning (1992, 9). But herein lies the crux of Peradotto's insight and blindness: to reject the monologic prophecy of ancient drama is to reject ancient drama itself. For, essentially, there is no difference between prophecy and narrative performance. Prophecy was a verbal genre, and, like tragedy, a performative one. The delivery of a prophecy took place through an "oracular performance." I agree with Peradotto: "Prophecy is not conceivable apart from narrative" (1992, 10). And this is so because prophecy *is* narrative. Thus Vernant's categorization of the *Oedipus Tyrannus* as a riddle has been extended to liken the structure of the play to an oracle: "Since riddles and oracles are often indistinguishable, we may also say that the *Oedipus Tyrannus* is constructed like an oracle" (Maurizio 1993, 139). The play is essentially an oracular performance, whence its context and power. I think we could claim that monologic prophecy denotes the genre of tragic drama, and it is not until the change to the genre of the polyphonic novel, which blurs the distinction between author and hero and allows for rereading, that the construction of prophecy can be exposed and dethroned. Thus, unwittingly, Peradotto — in his desire in contrast to his material — has demonstrated for us the difference between the genres of ancient tragedy and the modern polyphonic novel. Had Peradotto sat amongst the 5th century sophists at a performance of the *Oedipus Tyrannus*, he alone would have been uncomfortable. It seems to me, that like Aristotle, the sophists recognized the difference between poetics and physics. And if the power of poetics to make the accidental necessary upsets one's civic order, ban it from your city, but let it remain itself, poetry, not science.

As suggested earlier, Dostoevsky in part escapes the interdependence of prophecy and narrative by displacing false prophecy into the non-narrative of dreams. But he does not escape it entirely. We recall that Pumpyansky called the whole of the Dostoevsky novel "prophecy." Why? Perhaps ironically, it is his rival, Vyacheslav Ivanov, who clarifies Pumpyansky's pronouncement. Dostoevsky portrays a universe significantly changed from that of antiquity. His perception of the Divine as unwilling to enslave with miracle and mystery opens up the word, allowing for true dialogicity. Raskolnikov's search for the prophetic led to the past: he no longer inhabits a universe permissive of simple prophetic speech which describes a single path of action. Rather, his is a universe of choice, of agency, of freedom and respect for man. Yet within this freedom, Dostoevsky's heroes face a choice, to be with or without God. Once the choice is made, there remain two directions with innumerable permutations of events within them. In the beginning, Raskolnikov chooses against God and in favor of the Grand Inquisitor when he tries to set up the idol of the prophetic speech of his own making. But once its false mechanics have become exposed, he chooses God, and moves along that other general path. In a sense we can conceive of this as another form of prophecy, but a kind which allows for two described paths rather than one. We may go as far as to say that Dostoevsky exposes one kind of prophecy almost as a foil in order to elevate another kind. Prophecy in the Dostoevskian novel becomes wider, more complete and inclusive. This greater prophecy offers the more complete vision of past, present and future which views the overall direction for humankind. This is not a one-to-one type of prophecy, either between signified and signifier or between divinity and individual. Rather it outlines a direction within which man as agent speaks and acts with a large margin of choice and reference. In a sense it is also a more enclosed prophecy as the universe itself has become teleological.

In conclusion, we can spatially reformulate some of the discussion above. If we conceive of both the *Oedipus Tyrannus* and *Crime and Punishment* as stories of self-discovery in relation to the divine, we could picture the moment of Oedipus' separation from his father on the road to Apollo's oracle as not unlike Raskolnikov's on the road to the Church. A difference, however, consists in the trajectory of those paths. Oedipus kills his father because the path does not allow for two to pass: this road to the word of God is straight and narrow. In *Crime and Punishment*, the road to the Church, "the word of God," bends around in a circle: this road never leads directly to the divine, yet makes room for both father and son. Both Oedipus and Raskolnikov stand in a tensely bound and discreetly separate relation to the divine. Yet there is a difference of emphasis: tragedy underscores the closeness, while the novel highlights the distance. From this we have our two kinds of prophecy, indicative, it seems, along with Pumpyansky, of two distinct genres separated by the great waves of literary evolution.

NOTES

1. *Poetics* (1752a). Unless otherwise indicated, all translations refer to the editions cited in the bibliography.
2. This is not to say that Homer wrote epics of fate: Achilles's wrath was his own and his *choice* to kill Hektor and thus himself be killed was completely commensurate with his own character, while simultaneously fulfilling the plan of Zeus. See Vernant 1990a, 49–84. Vernant shows tragic decision rooted in two types of reality: *ethos* and *daimon*, character and divine power (77). He summarizes: "The nature of tragic action appears to us to be defined by the simultaneous presence of a 'self' and something greater that is divine at work at the core

of the decision and creating a constant tension between the two opposed poles"
(75).

3. Two matched lines of Achilles and Athena in Book I of the *Iliad* demonstrate
    this capacity of divine speech, in contrast to human:

    all' ek toi ereo, to de kai teleesthai oio (204) (Achilles)
    ode gar exereo, to de kai tetelesmenon estai (212) (Athena)
    [Yet I will tell you this and I think it will be accomplished;
    For I will tell you this and it will be a thing accomplished.]

    The change of verbs at the end of the line summarizes the matter: while Achilles
    thinks that what he says will be accomplished, for Athena it *will be*. See Parry
    1981, 24. Vernant paraphrases this weakness of human speech: "What it lacked
    was the power of realization, the efficacy that was the exclusive privilege of the
    divine" (1990a, 83).

4. Nagy provides an etymology for *prophetes*: a *nomen agentis* of the verbal stem
    *pha- "to say," "to speak" and the prefix *pro-*, which means "forth," rather than
    "in advance," where the dependent object has no relation to the future. Thus the
    word means most often "one who proclaims publicly." *Prophetes* = declarer
    (1990, 162–64).

5. This model of dialogue comes, of course, from Bakhtin. Morson and Emerson
    summarize thus: "Bakhtin argued, without a finalizing other, 'I' cannot achieve
    an image of myself, just as I cannot be aware of how my mind works when I am
    unself-conscious, and cannot know how I really appear to the world by looking
    in a mirror. An integral self, a tentative self-definition, requires an *other*. To
    know oneself, to know one's image in the world, one needs another's finalizing
    outsideness" (italics in original) (1990, 91).

6. It is probably worth noting that the significance of Ivanov's aesthetics is based
    on Dmitry, the most iconic, revelation-oriented, and dramatic of the four broth-
    ers. Bakhtin summarizes Dmitry's binary character in his comments on the
    picture of false psychology portrayed in the scenes of his preliminary investiga-
    tion and trial. "The investigator, judges, prosecutor, defense attorney, and
    commission of experts are all equally incapable of approaching the unfinalized
    and undecided core of Dmitry's personality, for he is a man who stands, in
    essence throughout his entire life, on the threshold of great internal decisions
    and crises" (1984, 62). Such a threshold position characterizes Ivanov's concep-
    tion of the hero in Dostoevsky's universe.

7. See Vernant 1990b, 43–48. For the collected essays of Ivanov in English
    translation, see Ivanov 1952, esp. 3–47.

8. See Clark and Holquist 1984, 30–42. See also Emerson 1993, 125–26.

9. "Did aesthetically unshakable tragic art arrive, after such lengthy wandering,
    from Athens to Petersburg? Did the Dionysian divinity remain the same during
    the whole period of the passionate journey?" (Pumpyansky 1922, 9; my trans-
    lation).

10. Dostoevsky elaborates on the state of this new, prophecy-seeking world, in *The Brothers Karamazov*. In the chapter of the same name, The Grand Inquisitor makes clear to Christ that he can now add nothing to what he has said and done. He could have converted the people by miracle, but instead gave them freedom: "Thou [Christ] did not come down [from the cross], for again Thou wouldst not enslave man by a miracle, and didst crave faith given freely, not based on miracle" (1976, 236). Christ left man in a state of too much freedom, without miracles and mysteries, which were binding upon the world of prophecies. As Ivan Karamazov formulates, in his great respect for humankind, Christ refused to enslave man with miracles.

11. So the Grand Inquisitor understood: "Is the nature of men such, that they can reject miracle, and at the great moments of their life, the moments of their deepest, most agonizing spiritual difficulties, cling only to the free verdict of the heart?... But Thou didst not know that when man rejects miracle he rejects God too; for man seeks not so much God as the miraculous. *And as man cannot bear to be without the miraculous, he will create new miracles of his own for himself*" (my italics) (Dostoevsky 1976, 236).

12. For example, the following is said of Calchas in *Iliad* I.70: "os ede ta t' eonta ta t' essomena pro t' eonta [he knew the things being, the things yet to be, and the things having been]."

13. I am using Sidney Monas' translation of *Crime and Punishment*, with several slight alterations. I include words of special significance from the original in transliteration in brackets. The first citation refers to the English translation, the second to the Russian in Dostoevsky 1989.

14. Cf. *The Dream of a Ridiculous Man*: "When they [the inhabitants of the star] became wicked, they began talking of brotherhood and humanity and understood the meaning of those ideas. When they became guilty of crimes, they invented justice" (Dostoevsky 1968b, 734).

15. "Pomnyu" actually comprises her first word.

16. Cf. *The Dream of a Ridiculous Man*: "Dreams as we all know, are very curious things: certain incidents in them are presented with quite uncanny vividness, each detail executed with the finishing touch of a jeweller, while others you leap across as though entirely unaware of, for instance, space and time" (1968b, 724).

WORKS CITED

Bakhtin, Mikhail M. 1984. *Problems of Dostoevsky's Poetics*. Tr. Caryl Emerson. Minneapolis: University of Minnesota Press.

Clark, Katerina and Holquist, Michael. 1984. *Mikhail Bakhtin*. Cambridge: Harvard University Press.

Dostoevsky, Fyodor M. 1968a. *Crime and Punishment.* Tr. Sidney Monas. New York: Penguin Books.

_____. 1968b. "The Dream of a Ridiculous Man." Tr. David Magarshack. *Great Short Works of Fyodor Dostoevsky.* New York: Harper & Row, 715–38.

_____. 1976. *The Brothers Karamazov.* Tr. Constance Garnett. New York: W.W. Norton & Company, Inc.

_____. 1989. *Prestuplenie i nakazanie. Sobranie sochinenii v pyatnadtsati tomakh.* Tom 5. Leningrad: Nauka.

Emerson, Caryl. 1993. "Irreverent Bakhtin and the Imperturbable Classics." *Arethusa* 26: 123–40.

Ivanov, Vyacheslav. 1952. *Freedom and the Tragic Life.* Tr. Norman Cameron. New York: The Noonday Press.

Maurizio, Lisa. 1993. "Delphic Narratives: Recontextualizing the Pythia and Her Prophecies." Diss.: Princeton University.

Nagy, Gregory. 1990. *Pindar's Homer.* Baltimore: Johns Hopkins University Press.

Parry, Adam. 1981. *Logos and Ergon in Thucydides.* New York: Arno Press.

Peradotto, John. 1992. "Disauthorizing Prophecy: The Ideological Mapping of *Oedipus Tyrannus.*" *Transactions of the American Philological Association* 122: 1–15.

Pumpyansky, Lev V. 1922. *Dostoevskii i antichnost'.* Petrograd: n.p. (Pumpyansky first delivered the thesis as a paper on 2 October 1921.)

Sophocles. 1977. *Oedipus the King.* Tr. Robert Fagles. New York: Penguin Books, 158–251.

Vernant, Jean-Pierre. 1990a. "Intimations of the Will in Greek Tragedy." *Myth and Tragedy in Ancient Greece.* Tr. Janet Lloyd. New York: Zone Books, 49–84.

_____. 1990b. "Tensions and Ambiguities in Greek Drama." *Myth and Tragedy in Ancient Greece.* Tr. Janet Lloyd. New York: Zone Books, 29–48.

THE SOURCES OF ANDREI BELY'S LITERARY MIFOTVORCHESTVO: THE CASE OF THE ABLEUKHOVS

Mary Jo White, University of Washington

At a critical point in the murderous plot of Andrei Bely's *Petersburg*, Apollon Apollonovich Ableukhov is seized by a desire to spy on his son. Only an instant before, as he heard what he took to be the distant sound of galloping horses, Apollon Apollonovich had been thinking about this same son's violent beginnings. This spawn of terror, he remembers, was conceived in an act of rape. For his part, his son, Nikolai Apollonovich Ableukhov, had recently had a companion vision, or perhaps it was a memory, of a similarly violent act of creation. As he leapt from a carriage bearing the legend "1905" on its license, Nikolai Apollonovich had caught sight of a stone unicorn goring a stone knight, a sculpture of the family emblem emblazoned on the family home. Immediately Nikolai Apollonovich had experienced a kind of blurred or doubled vision and had understood that it was his father, and by extension he himself, who was being gored. For reasons he could not explain, he then pictured his father at his conjugal duties (Bely 1978, 150–51).

Now, drawn on to satisfy his desire to spy, Apollon Apollonovich enters his son's study where he finds things in disarray. His eye falls first on a red domino sprawled over a spotted leopard. It does not escape his notice that the domino is headless, nor does he miss the half-mask hanging on a spear above it. His eye travels next to a portrait of Nikolai Apollonovich painted the previous spring. Sword at his side, his son stands "suffering inside the frame"

(1978, 249). Finally, and most fatefully, his gaze is attracted to a photograph of a certain brunette on his son's desk. Without thinking, he picks up this image of beauty and loses himself in contemplation. When he emerges from his reverie, he finds himself holding what the reader knows to be a bomb — the sardine tin of terrible contents — rather than a picture of a woman. Entranced by the tin's mechanism but oblivious of its fiery content, Apollon Apollonovich carries it out of his son's room and into the drawing room where he deposits it on a Chinese tray. This is the same tray that had, at the start of the story, pointedly held an unread letter from his violated and faithless wife — the wife who has now returned to the city and who will soon join him in a carriage ride.

The Chinese tray and a few key letters, the carriage, the red domino, and the bomb have travelled the length of the novel together. They have circulated throughout it and now spiral toward its denouement in a whirlwind of images which gathers in horses, statues, emblems, masks, and paintings and photos as well. These and allied images fill the emotional landscape of *Petersburg* and construct the house of Ableukhov, the family whose story Bely might well have called "a religious tragedy of the suffering resurrection," in the language of his essay "The Phoenix" (1969b, 148). For the suffering Ableukhovs are not merely a family unhappy in its own way, but a noble family of ancient lineage whose unhappiness embodies the city's past and portends its future as if in a myth of Greek tragedy. And within the frame of the story, the Ableukhovs present a portrait of family life whose rich detail reveals not only the nature of the plot, but also some of Bely's more complex notions, worked out in his theory and criticism, about the unity of philosophy, history, poetry, myth-making and cultural renewal. Indeed, Bely's act of thinking in images, this act of creation that results in *Petersburg*, reflects the leading and intertwined concerns of religious symbolism and religious philosophy in the Silver Age and their common focus on popular religious myth and its roots in ancient Greece.

During the religious renascence of the Silver Age modern Russia came to know the authentic power and original purpose of ancient Greek myth-making for the first time. No longer viewed through the tales and images of Virgil and Ovid, no longer Roman in aspect, the gods and heroes whose names now stood for the religious thought of archaic Greece looked more familiar to Russian eyes, their struggles and triumphs more native. "Only a cloud separates us from the Greeks," Nietzsche was sometimes quoted as saying, by the religious-minded of the period. And what Nietzsche had proposed be done with German myth, Russian poets and thinkers now did with Russian myth, joining their belief in Russian *mifotvorchestvo* to their hopes for cultural renewal throughout Europe. Some went further and, like Nietzsche himself on the eve of his madness, tried to live their faith in the antique gods, in the regenerative spirit symbolized by the *agon* of dream and intoxication, the contest of statue and song, and the marriage of Apollo and Dionysus.[1] These were Nietzsche's images for the creative spirit that had made the Greeks — or so he said — the only people strong enough to pilot the chariot of culture and drive its horses toward the heavens rather than into the abyss (Nietzsche 1967, 94).

The Russian revaluation of myth-making undertaken at the turn of the century was a major part of the cultural program which practitioners and proponents of religious symbolism and religious philosophy were committed to advancing in common. For those whose focus was on myth-making in the eastern world, Nietzsche's reinvention of Greek antiquity was an incitement, as many would later attest, to their own best efforts at understanding how myth had once been made and at making new myths themselves. But Nietzsche's example was only one of several goads urging the religiously inclined of the time to inquire into the nature of myth. Of equal importance were the cognate interests that many among them took in the history of ideas that myth was thought to encode, in the psychology of creation that myth was believed to embody, and in the ancient connection known to exist — at least in the religions of the Greek and Russian East — between myth-making and the making of icons. Beyond these interests, there was also a signal notion of overriding importance which guided the religious thinkers and poets at every turn in the road. This was the idea, widely accepted, that, when taken together, myth, metaphor, symbol, ritual act, and visual image represent a unity which imitates the order of the cosmos, the order within which spirit and matter are always in motion — mingling and interchanging like the elements in archaic cosmologies — in a ceaseless rhythm of merger and distinction. It was as a development of this notion that the gods and heroes of Greek myth came to have such ambiguous meaning in the language of figures common to symbolism and religious philosophy,[2] a language derived from Greek religions and ever at work in works of the period. This language was even put to work, in however unlikely a fashion, to build Bely's *Petersburg*, a serio-comic novel of ideas that despite its idiosyncrasies is as Greek and as religious as are the figures it employs.

The religions of Greece that Bely knew best were both its most modern and its most ancient. Its most modern, Eastern Orthodoxy, he knew from the world of worship around him and from the religious thinkers and theologians with whom he had kept company for years, Nikolai Berdyaev and Sergei Bulgakov being the chief among them. Its most ancient he knew most accurately and in the greatest detail from his sometime friend and antagonist, Vyacheslav Ivanov, whose body of work on the religion of Dionysus remains important even today for Russian scholars of the archaic Greek world.[3] There is little mystery about what first attracted Bely to these two religions with their distinct but overlapping mythologies and iconographies. And indeed there need be none since he tells us himself that it was his early acquaintance with Nietzsche's *Birth of Tragedy* and his personal acquaintance with Vladimir Solovyov that originally kindled his interest. Taken together with the arguments they embodied, Nietzsche's recreated Apollo and Dionysus and Solovyov's reinvigorated Sophia, the Wisdom of God — a figure through whom the philosopher sought to resurrect the oldest Aphrodite, the Wisdom of Zeus (White 1992, 49–55) — suggested to Bely, as well as to others, how the ancient practice of making myth might be renewed in order to shape the modern world of thought and feeling and to forge a future of new meaning.

Immediately, the myth which Bely made with the gods he had borrowed, at least in outline, from Nietzsche and Solovyov — Apollo, Dionysus, Sophia, and Aphrodite — he made in concert with others. As he himself was the first to point out in his commentary on the essays collected in *Symbolism*, he assimilated Nietzsche's unique vision of Greek antiquity with the help of Ivanov's *Hellenic Religion of the Suffering God* (Bely 1969a, 458, 541). He also took in Solovyov's transformed goddess of wisdom, beauty, generation, and unity in sober company, especially as that company included religious philosophers of the stature of Berdyaev and Bulgakov. But what Bely finally did with his borrowed gods, after following the lead of religious philosophy and marrying archaic Greek myth and ritual to Graeco-Russian liturgy, theology, and iconography, was to create a world of meaning that was entirely his own. By the time he had completed *Petersburg,* and had completely refigured Apollo, Dionysus, Aphrodite, and Sophia, the Orthodox among his admirers could only wonder at his private understanding of their common practice of mixing gods (Bely 1969a, 523) and mingling myths. Such was the case with both Ivanov and Berdyaev, each of whom published a review of the novel while still in the grip of astonishment.

In his review in 1916, Ivanov responded to *Petersburg* as if it were an oracle of Apollo or Zeus, and Bely the frenzied woman, through whom the god had issued his word. He described the book as a dream in the Greek sense, in that it might portend either good or ill, and he voiced suspicion that its delirious dreamer only thought he knew its meaning. He called this dream an inspiration of Terror, adding a new category of divine possession to those already established in Plato's *Phaedrus*, that is, to the possessed clairvoyance of Apollo, the mystic rites and *katharsis* of Dionysus, the madness that the Muses inspire, and possession by Eros and Aphrodite. Capturing Bely's Terror in Bely's own images, Ivanov pictured it rushing along the streets of the city like the senator's black carriage; rearing up like the outline of

Falconet's famous statue; clattering into the senator's second space like the unicorn of the family emblem; blazing up in the damp autumn night like the folds of the blood-red domino; winking like the light of the Flying Dutchman's schooner; and finally becoming the bomb — the metallic Erinys or Fury, he called it — that the senator's son feels he has swallowed. In addition to Terror itself, Ivanov thought he sensed Terror's Furies or Erinyes, figures of an ancient family curse and the spirits of blood vengeance, haunting the whole of the novel. These spirits seemed to him to attend the senator, his son, the terrorist, and the double agent; to inhabit the grimy restaurant, the garret, the diplomatic carriage, and Lippanchenko's shoreside rooms; and to take several shapes. These shapes included the Mongolian faces materializing on Dudkin's wall at night, the Mongolian Kronos who appears to Nikolai Apollonovich as he drowses over the bomb, a painting of the Flying Dutchman's flotilla, and Angel Peri's volcanic landscapes.

At a loss to place *Petersburg* in any canonical genre, Ivanov characterized it as an act of creation *sui generis*. An epic of fiery phantasms written in a style of pure dynamism, it danced along dizzyingly as its author sought to picture astral or supersensible reality. The pages of *Petersburg* impressed him, Ivanov said, as the fruit of creative suffering; this was suffering of the same kind as Greek theogonic myth imagined the cosmos to have experienced in the beginning when beauty (Aphrodite) and ugliness (the Erinyes) first emerged from an *agon* between father and son. To Ivanov's mind the statue of the Bronze Horseman was the novel's leading character, and he said that *Petersburg* read as if Bely had suffered the blows of the Horseman's bronze hooves directly in his own astral body. Although a mere dream and illusion, the novel showed, Ivanov thought, that Bely had wrestled with the mystery of Russia's destiny and her fiery heart of being, and Ivanov judged it an achievement that would live forever, not only as a part of the literary heritage, but also as an image of the Russian spirit. To sum up his experience both in hearing it read and in reading it himself, Ivanov quoted from the tragic poet Aeschylus, citing lines spoken by Orestes, the matricide who kills by order of Apollo. Just after he has done Apollo's bidding and murdered his mother in retribution for her murder of his father, and just as the dark-robed Furies materialize before him, Orestes cries out in fear: "My mind's horses have spirited its chariot away. Terror excites its song within and my heart dances to the piping of its awful tune" (Ivanov 1971–87, 4:623).[4]

When Berdyaev reviewed *Petersburg* in 1918, he chose to emphasize the story's mythological dimensions as well. Observing how the myths of modern Russian history coincide with the literary image of the modern Russian capital, he suggested that Bely's apparent tale of two cities (the senator, he notes, sees two spaces) brought to a fitting end the world of double focus that had been founded with Pushkin's "Bronze Horseman." Fathered by a hero whom history had made larger than life, signified by a statue that myth had made animate and vengeful, the catastrophic city was now memorialized in *Petersburg*, its final days pictured in their cosmic aspect by a "literary cubist" (Berdyaev 1986, 200), Picasso's equal in power and effect. Like Picasso, Berdyaev said, Bely sees and conveys more ugliness and terror than beauty. There is no consolation in his vision, no *katharsis* in his work. His art bodies forth his own chaos and the whirling motion of his soul, just as Nikolai Apollonovich's red domino symbolizes the chaos and motion of his novel. Submerged in a nightmare that Berdyaev thought would terrorize his readers too, Bely seemed to him to show once more that he loved Russia to the point of annihilation and believed in her rebirth only through her destruction. Berdyaev agreed with Ivanov that the Bronze Horseman was the dominant presence in the story and that the ancient Turanian represented the principle of disorder, disruption, and catastrophe within Bely's novel, his imagined city, the real Russia, and the larger western world. As Ivanov had put it, so did Berdyaev: Bely's Turanian — the Mongolian Kronos — was the very image of an ancient family curse, the poison that still circulates in the veins of European culture, living in the blood and defiling it.

Similarly to Ivanov, Berdyaev felt that Bely's radical new style and its rhythm were especially well suited to the tale he had to tell. Berdyaev described this style as a whirlwind of words leading to catastrophe, and said that it gives the reader the impression of religious frenzy, of a flagellant moving in a circular motion. Quoting from the novel he characterized its atmosphere as "the fabric of the Furies" (1986, 200), an image of terror and strife that he then associated with the Bronze Horseman and with what he called the Horseman's astral double. Within this atmosphere of age-old terror he also situated the Ableukhovs, father and son, whose relationship to one another and to their surroundings seemed to him to reveal the nature of the novel's strange new rhythm. He said that this rhythm arose from Bely's conducting the cosmic rhythm of creation directly into his writing and that it was made visible, like the Furies to Orestes in Aeschylus, whenever father and son merged with one another or whenever either of them merged with the objects of his thought (as Apollon Apollonovich did with the stars and mathematics in his second space). In its entirety, Berdyaev considered *Petersburg* to be a kind of visionary historiography that bordered on genuine theurgy, although Bely, he insisted, was himself no theurgist. And he considered its overall mythological and religious import to consist in this: that it summed up in myth the immediate past over which Peter the Great had loomed, and pointed the way to the redemptive future by imagining the reunion of the created world with its creator. This hope of reuniting the disjointed histories of God and humankind was one that religious thinkers like Ivanov and Berdyaev expected to be accomplished through the agency of suffering Russia, knew to be part of the notion of theurgy,[5] and figured with poetic and iconographic images of Aphrodite and Sophia.

As Berdyaev and Ivanov touched on similar points in their separate reviews, each was seeking to make prominent the assumptions about myth-making and the act of creation which were common to symbolist theory, to religious philosophy, and to *Petersburg*. These assumptions rested on Solovyov's speculations about the unity of myth-making and philosophy in ancient Greece, especially as this unity presented itself to view in the oldest theogonies and cosmogonies. In Berdyaev's case, these speculations rested most particularly on the ceaseless exchange in Heraclitus's cosmogonic scheme where everything is always in motion — primary matter and motive force together — circulating up and down, coming from and returning to the elemental fire. Solovyov had discussed this unity many times in the course of exploring various philosophical topics beginning with his earliest published work, "The Mythological Process in Ancient Paganism," and continuing through to essays as late as "Plato's Living Drama" (1898). But he took the occasion of reviewing Sergei Trubetskoy's *Metaphysics in Ancient Greece* in 1890 to express himself most succinctly on a few key points. After commending Trubetskoy for approaching Greek religion and philosophy from the perspective of the Greeks themselves — hard to accomplish at so distant a remove and hard to represent to a modern audience, he says, without perverting the material — Solovyov singles out those aspects of Trubetskoy's work that accord with his own investigations and conclusions.

Like Trubetskoy, Solovyov believed that the original and unbroken connection between Greek religion and philosophy is most clearly in evidence when the ancient theogonies and the cosmogonies of the Presocratics are compared. When this is done, the links between popular religious myth and the teachings of the oldest philosophy are thrown into relief, making it easier to see that the two were almost one in antiquity. To illustrate this point, Solovyov recounts what Trubetskoy had outlined of the teachings of the philosopher Parmenides about the original act of creation, or about primary matter and the motive force. Parmenides supposed that in the beginning everything came to be from the coupling of the active principle, Day, and the passive principle, Night, an act governed by Necessity, the progenitor of Eros. Like Trubetskoy, Solovyov thought that this theogonic story revealed one of the constants of Greek speculation, something that was unvarying from the most archaic poetry down to Aristotle and Platonism. He thought it showed the basic dualism of the active, formative, masculine principle of divinity and the passive principle of unformed matter or potentiality.[6] As another example of how closely knit Greek religious and philosophical thinking seemed to be, Solovyov recounted the remarks of the philosopher Empedocles about the origins and motion of the cosmos as Trubetskoy had recorded them. Empedocles observed, Solovyov notes, that there are two elemental forces governing every theogony, Love, or Aphrodite, and Strife. He also observed that the motive force in theogonies was always Eros, and that the theogonic process involves Love continuously gathering the whole of matter into a single universal body and Strife continuously tearing the body apart.[7]

In addition to looking carefully at the theogonies and cosmogonies in which Aphrodite, Eros, and the virgin warrior Athene first appear, Solovyov had also examined the unity of myth-making and philosophy that was still visible in Plato's dialogues. As he did this he paid particular attention to Plato's myth of the charioteer and the two horses in the *Phaedrus*, to his myth of the androgyne, to the story of Aphrodite Pandemos and Aphrodite Urania, to Diotima's discourse in the *Symposium*, to the myth of the true earth in the *Phaedo*, and, finally, to the eschatological myth of Er in the *Republic*. As Solovyov then used these myths in his own work, particularly in *The Meaning of Love* and *The Lectures on Godmanhood*, he developed patterns of image and metaphor that Ivanov, Berdyaev, and Bely would later elaborate into a common figural language although each would shade it with his own emphases. These patterns all involve schemes of doubling and may take several forms, the least exceptional of which from the point of view of Platonic or Neoplatonic thought is expressed in the myth of the true earth where the sensible world echoes the intelligible, however faintly. The figures of doubling can also take the form of mirror images, or of merger and distinction of the kind implied when Solovyov relates Plato's myth of the androgyne — and especially its concluding remark that "love is the name of the desire and pursuit of the whole" — to his own belief that God has possessed a feminine aspect from all eternity, an eternal feminine like the wise Sophia whose incarnation it is yet the purpose of history to realize.[8] Finally, and of the richest consequence for symbolist theory and religious philosophy, these figures can take shape in the pattern of ascent and descent signified with Diotima's ladder, with the two Aphrodites, and with the Phaedran charioteer in particular. This pattern of "up and down" is represented in Plato, in language that is understood to allude to Heraclitus, as a kind of battle. It is "a simultaneous two way flux" (West 1971, 122) occurring within the fiery element that issues in thunderbolts, whirlwinds, and starry light, and which is known, according to the oldest philosophy, by many names, including Zeus, Dionysus, the Erinyes, Aphrodite, and the Wise.

As Solovyov connected his speculations about the nature of Greek myth-making with his reconsiderations of Orthodox theology he wove together significant Greek mythological images, including the images of starry light, robes and veils, ladders of ascent, wrestling, and chariots and teams with corresponding images in Byzantine and Russian iconography. He then figured the forms of thought that emerged — including the surprising notion that sexual love redeems — with the names Aphrodite and Sophia, and gave birth to a universe of discourse that was steered by three assumptions. The first of these was the supposition that the act of creation, an act that always prefigures the end of the world, is primarily a religious problem. The second was the supposition that each act of creation is governed by the rhythm of the archaic gods Love, or Aphrodite, and Strife, who are already coupled in a constant process of gathering the world into a single body and then dismembering it when they first appear in theogonic poetry and cosmogonic thought. And the third supposition was that the act of recreation, the act of transfiguration that was yet to occur under the aegis of Sophia and, because of the practice of theurgy,[9] would repeat whatever events had taken place in the beginning of time.

Among the uses that Berdyaev made of these assumptions, one of the most significant was his employment of them to undergird a major part of *The Meaning of History*. In this work they form the basis for his contention that human history continually experiences periods of catastrophe and disintegration and periods of renewed unity, or is continuously gathered together and torn apart, because it is impelled by the same motion as governs the history of the heavens. Berdyaev likens this motion to the Heraclitean fire going up and down, an image of dynamism that he says paints a truer picture of God than does the image of an unmoved mover. The force behind this motion, or the motive force, he says, is the mysterious and tragic love that God the Father and Son have for one another from all eternity. This love is expressed in an act of violence at the beginning of time when God's inner self becomes the outer world and is made to resemble, or takes shape as, the sufferings and beauty of his Son. But when Berdyaev speaks of the catastrophe that marked the start of the world he is not referring to the Greek theogonic conflicts of Ouranos, Kronos, and Zeus, to their acts of castration, ingestion, overthrowal and imprisonment; indeed, he insists that the Greeks knew as little of catastrophe as he believes they knew of eschatology. Instead, what he means for his readers to imagine is a rupture between fathers and children and the yearning for reunion that follows it, a pattern he symbolizes with Sophia, with Christ, and with Jacob the God-wrestler, in particular.

Berdyaev spoke of the historical reality that these images convey as something comparable to the world figured in popular myth, as a concrete unity that is not of a material order but which is founded and transformed in memory. He also spoke of the experience of history as a tragic drama that begins and ends in catastrophe; this is the condition which leads him to call history apocalyptic, namely that the end is revealed in the beginning. Berdyaev further claimed that apocalyptic speculation clothed in symbols is the peculiar province of Russian thought, and as special evidence of this he pointed to Solovyov. But while Solovyov had certainly said that the unity embracing the material world is not a material unity (1966–70, 7:54), and had written that ancient dramas and the histories they record always end where they begin, in tragic catastrophe (1966–70, 9:212), he had never gone as far in making claims for the operation of memory in the construction of history as Berdyaev did when he proposed that in its myths Christian history preserves a memory of an original state of freedom rather than of necessity, and that it associates this state of freedom with human destiny. This belief of Berdyaev's about the operation of memory in the unfolding of history was much closer to Ivanov's thinking about Dionysus, ecstasy, and the role of memory in tragedy, a similarity that is seen in miniature in their respective reviews of Bely's *Petersburg*.

Ivanov employed the same assumptions as Berdyaev did — assumptions accompanying the belief that philosophy, myth-making, history, and poetry were almost indistinguishable in the archaic world — as he explored the nature of Greek tragedy, paying particular heed to the structure of its myths in relation to the character of its heroes. Arguing that tragedy had been an art of memory, Ivanov proposed that what it remembered was Dionysus, the god of popular myth, who embodied both the primordial unity of the cosmos in the fiery heart of being and also the world's more recent dispersal. He first made this proposal in *The Hellenic Religion of the Suffering God* where, by virtue of the form he gave it, he established an equivalence between the expression of Dionysus' worship, whether in tragedy or ritual, and Platonic *anamnesis*, the doctrine that knowledge is an act of remembrance, the same teaching that Berdyaev recommends to historiographers in *The Meaning of History*. This proposal and its form are as basic to Ivanov's thinking about religion in the ancient world as they are central to his expectations of religious renewal in the modern world. And in later works they more often than not are conflated and assumed together, rather than restated as the basis for discussing myth and symbolism. Such is the case, for example, with the essay "Nietzsche and Dionysus," with the essay "The Symbolism of Aesthetic Principles" which he dedicated to Bely, and with his review of Bely's *Petersburg*. Not insignificantly either for his own theory or for *Petersburg*, Bely had written an introduction to *The Hellenic Religion* when the articles were being prepared for republication as a book.

Ivanov's main argument in *The Hellenic Religion* begins to unfold as he considers the aspect of Greek divinity which is absent from the Roman experience and so is not an obvious part of the modern inheritance. This is the aspect of suffering, both of gods and heroes,[10] which he says the Greeks understood to be an inseparable part of creation, just as they understood creation to be an act of sacrifice; Dionysus was the name they gave to the suffering and to the sacrifice. The Romans, whom he describes as steady in the whirlwind of emotion, whose own gods he says were motionless, freed the ever-moving Dionysus and his frenzied female companions from the bloody past and origins that seemed too foreign to them. They freed them from their associations in myth with regicide, parricide, matricide, and infanticide, and from their expression of the unified mysticism, violence, and eros of the sexual principle in orgiastic religion. The Roman view — embodied in jolly Bacchus and his cheerful bacchants — ignores the ugly, bloody, generative wrestling and fighting among the gods that occurs in the beginning of time in theogonic myth and is mirrored in the human world in tragedy. This mirroring can be seen, for example, in the ancient family curse that afflicts the house of Atreus and impels the action of the *Oresteia*. This curse has its remote origin in a contest between two brothers for a throne and supreme power but more immediately arises from a banquet at which one brother serves the other the latter's own dismembered children. The Romans thus obscure from view the god Ouranos who is castrated by his son Kronos in his pursuit of supremacy; Kronos who dethrones his father and swallows his own children; and Zeus who usurps his father Kronos's throne and imprisons him in Tartarus.

But this Roman view is now being overturned, Ivanov continues, thanks to the many investigations of the Greek world conducted since the late eighteenth century and thanks most recently to Nietzsche's *Birth of Tragedy*, a revolutionary work which is at its most valuable when it suggests that Dionysus, the suffering god of regeneration, exists outside time and can return or recur. Dionysus has not been and ceased to be, his name is not a dead letter, but the signification of something real and of something "more real": he is the experience of crossing the boundary between time and timelessness, between the sensible world and the intelligible, the experience of transformation itself. "Many are the forms of the god," Ivanov says, quoting the *Bacchae* to figure Dionysus as the god of ever-modulating images. Ivanov credits Nietzsche with urging him to look closely at the psychological economy of Greek religious thought, but as he summarizes the dynamic named with the phrase Apollo and Dionysus, he does so in his own terms rather than in terms of what he deems to be Nietzsche's aesthetic abstractions. Viewed from the perspective of Ivanov's psychology of crea-

tion, Dionysian intoxication becomes an affective state within which the
boundaries of the self are obliterated and a sense of merging with the
fundamental principle of being, the principle of unity, is experienced in all
its joy and terror. Ivanov agrees with Nietzsche that this experience would
destroy one completely were it not for the dream vision of Apollo that
resolves the ecstatic act of stepping out of oneself, of self-alienation within
oneself, in the reflected life of the natural world and in the phantasmal world
of tragedy. As a whole, this state of metaphysical merging unites Dionysian
or ecstatic aimlessness with the aims of the cosmos in its entirety and with
the spirit of the suffering world. To Ivanov's way of thinking, what Nietzsche
points us toward in the end is the two-part understanding that suffering and
its raptures were basic to the ancient Greek psyche and that the robe and veil
of Beauty — now known by the religious-minded poets and thinkers as
Aphrodite and Sophia — saved the world once before by saving the Greeks
from anything which the modern world knows as pessimism.

   In its most general outline, Ivanov organizes *The Hellenic Religion* to
reveal the same complex of word and deed which Classicists today still
consider fundamental to the discussion of Greek religion. And he does this
with a comparable aim, directing attention to what is now described as "the
deep structure of catastrophe, guilt, and atonement" (Burkert 1985, 241) still
visible in the myths that inform the cult festivals of Dionysus and Demeter,
in the ritual acts performed at these festivals, and in the symbols that emerge
from the festivals and coincide with the images of tragedy, notably the
bloody stories of Dionysus' arrival and return and of Orestes's defilement
and *katharsis*. These stories are among the myths regularly represented in
Greek vase painting as well, evidence from which Ivanov often cites alongside the tales he retells. Condensed to their elemental details and collocated
for the purposes of painting, these stories collide and compress to form an
image like the poetic echo — the picture of Orestes, the possessed charioteer,
whose ungovernable mind is likened to his ungovernable horses — that
Ivanov employs to considerable effect in *The Hellenic Religion*. As he uses
it here and uses it again in his review of *Petersburg*, this echo is meant to
point backwards from the myth-making of Plato's *Phaedrus* through the
myth-making of tragedy toward the more archaic notion that Dionysus — or
his double, Zeus — is present in every act of ascent or descent, that in
wrestling with the god, in whatever form he takes, one merges with him,
however temporarily.

   This kind of compressed myth-making can be seen at work, for example,
on a vase now housed in the Hermitage[11] that depicts two stories of significance in the annual Dionysian Anthesteria, of significance to Ivanov's
argument, and later of significance for the figures and argument of Bely's

Petersburg. Near the top of this vase and inside the throat there appear four boats with dolphin-shaped sterns and boar-shaped bows. These recall the ship-chariot of the Anthesteria festival which Dionysus pilots when he returns, and as they here combine theriomorphic forms of Dionysus (dolphin) and Artemis (boar) — the goddess Ivanov identifies as Dionysus' eternal feminine — they suggest the image which dominates the exterior of the vase as well. This is the image of the sacred marriage of Dionysus and Ariadne, an event that has been described as "closer to sacrifice than sensual pleasure."[12] This marriage has also been likened to the "death marriage"[13] of Persephone and Hades as well as to the coupling of Semele and Zeus in which Dionysus' mother is reduced to ashes when Zeus appears to her in the form of a thunderbolt.[14] Sacred or profane, marriage is often represented iconographically with a chariot procession, and here "marriage" is one of at least two meanings that issue from the interior image, the procession of the Dionysian ship-chariots. The exterior of the vase shows Ariadne robed and veiled for her union with the god, her veil covered with the stylized rosettes that prefigure two related images in later Byzantine and Russian iconography, the starry veil of theogonic Night and the starry Intercessory Veil of the Theotokos ("Pokrov").[15] Ariadne is understood to be posed in the bridal gesture of unveiling (Hedreen 1992, 36) as she stands opposite Dionysus here. He holds his emblematic drinking horn and the couple are surrounded by satyrs and dancing maenads who are clad in ritual garments resembling leopard skins. As all of these painted images later find a place in *Petersburg*, Bely's readers can expect to come across theriomorphic forms like Apollon Apollonovich's eagle, a sacrificial marriage and its renewal in a chariot ride, a ship chariot, a leopard skin, and a theogonic robe of dragons and stars worn by the Mongolian Kronos.

In its more specific detail, *The Hellenic Religion* explores the mythical background, the world of meaning, and the kind of experience associated with a small group of technical terms drawn from the vocabulary of scholarship about Greek religion, each of which will later feature in Ivanov's theory and criticism. Again not incidentally, they will also appear in Bely's theory and criticism and will be used to figure the story of *Petersburg*. These terms include *theomachia* ("bogoborstvo") which is used directly or by implication to characterize three essential acts associated with "the grace that comes by violence" (*Agam.*, 181–82),[16] namely, Pentheus fighting or wrestling with Dionysus in the *Bacchae*, Cassandra wrestling with Apollo in the *Agamemnon*, and Zeus toppling Kronos in the *Agamemnon*. They also include *orgia*, the basic definition of which Ivanov adopts from Wilamowitz and elaborates to mean active participation in the worship of Dionysus and Demeter involving the entire community equally in bearing and making sacrifice (1904–05,

1:117); *ekstasis* which he says is best evidenced in the *Bacchae*, and in its later Neoplatonist usage names the means of cognizing;[17] mysticism, or the primary archaic experience of merging with god that includes the blood sacrifice of which Semele, in her sacred marriage with Zeus, is an emblem; and *agon* ("bor'ba"), a term whose popularity in this context Classicists today continue to attribute to Nietzsche (Burkert 1985, 105).

Ivanov also uses *The Hellenic Religion* to develop religious philosophy's pattern of doubling into his own notion of double vision, fixing its outlines with images drawn from the well-known dressing scene of the *Bacchae*. In this scene, Pentheus, king of Thebes, is robed like a maenad and readied for death just as Agamemnon, king of Mycenae, had been robed for death in the *Oresteia*; Cassandra had foreseen that Agamemnon would be so robed and Orestes remembers him having been robed just moments before the ungovernable chariot of his own mind veers off course. Pentheus sees double almost as soon as Dionysus has finished disguising him as a maenad, ritually dressing him in women's robes. Or, as Dionysus insists, Pentheus now sees correctly: he sees two suns, two Thebes, and Dionysus in two forms, both as the Stranger who offers to satisfy his prurience by taking him to spy on the women he now mimics and also as a bull. Pentheus' mother, the maenad Agave, suffers double vision as well when she catches sight of her son in his disguise and sees another theriomorph of Dionysus, a lion. Once she and her sisters have dismembered Pentheus at Dionysus' urging, she then impales his head — severed like the oracular head of Orpheus, an image Ivanov calls "an icon" (1904–05, 6: 206) — on her thyrsus and returns to the city in triumph to display her trophy; she sees the head of a lion, while everyone else sees her son. Another kind of double vision is embedded in the structure of the play, in the twin stories of Aktaion being torn apart by his dogs and of Pentheus being torn apart by his mother and her sisters, the one recounted to foreshadow the other and the two together strongly suggesting, as Ivanov argues throughout *The Hellenic Religion*, that Dionysus and Artemis are one and the same.[18] Finally, double vision — or the tension of double nature — is implied in the *Bacchae* in the image of a house divided against itself. To avenge his mother's honor and to make Pentheus honor him as a god, Dionysus brings about the destruction of what he, Pentheus, Aktaion, Semele, and Agave are all part of: the line of descent issuing from Aphrodite's daughter, Harmonia, and dragon-slaying Cadmus, the line of the house of Thebes.

It was, then, these studied perspectives on myth-making in the writing of history and in the creation of tragedy which encouraged Berdyaev and Ivanov to review *Petersburg* as they did. And it would be difficult to consider their approaches unfairly applied since Bely was himself working with companion notions when he wrote the novel. In his essays Bely had already discussed what was to become the novel's shaping force, what he called the rhythm and collision of images in tragedy (1969b, 86). This rhythm was effectively the rhythm of Love and Strife, the inseparably merged generative pair which in Bely's construction comes to resemble Dionysus and Aphrodite more than it does Dionysus and Apollo.[19] It was a rhythm that he proposed to set and keep in motion through the structured deformation of images, a dynamic technique of his own devising that followed from his understanding of the nature of Dionysus, as well as from his familiarity with the way stories are told in icon and vase painting. Again in his theory Bely had already explained how he would create and animate the newly made myth of *Petersburg* just as ancient theurgy had reputedly animated statues. This was to be done by treating the text, the act of creation it embodied, and the world of meaning it generated, like the suffering god. Specifically this practice involved dismembering competing systems of meaning; scattering significant images from these systems of meaning throughout the text; and then gathering the dispersed images of different systems together, bringing the competing systems into collision to generate a new world of meaning. How Bely accomplishes this in *Petersburg* with competing systems of Greek and Russian myth, in terms of the act of creation, and in order to depict the beginning and the end can be seen in the novel's early pages and in the characterization of the elder Ableukhov.

Apollon Apollonovich riding in his chariot or astral body[20] — in his carriage emblazoned with the family crest of a unicorn goring a knight — was the first image to materialize when Bely conceived the novel. The senator thus became the locus for connecting the story's various levels, the character through whom the web of mythological allusion to Russian history, to Greek tragedy, and to Greek philosophy was woven. Furthermore, Apollon Apollonovich became, or at least was made to seem, the figure within whose consciousness the whole world of the novel takes shape. The idea that the whole story is fathered by the thinking of a single character is suggested at many points and in many ways throughout *Petersburg*. Among these is the association that Bely makes between an attribute with which he endows Apollon Apollonovich, a scene from Pushkin's legend of the founding and fate of Petersburg, and events involving Zeus and Athene that occurred when the cosmos began. In Greek epic, Zeus is known by various epithets — as the son of Kronos, the father of men and gods, the cloud gatherer, and the hurler of thunderbolts — and it was by way of these epithets that the customary depictions of him arose in ancient iconography. One such standard of iconography becomes particularly important for the symbolism of Petersburg as a whole: this is the figure of Zeus giving birth to the virgin warrior Athene from his head[21] after swallowing her mother Metis, or Wisdom. Both of these events — the swallowing and the birth — are chronicled in Hesiod's *Theogony*.

   Giving birth from his head is also how Pushkin's mythical Peter the Great is supposed to have engendered the city that bears his name: Peter had only to give it thought and his martial capital, the most intentional city in the world, leapt to life from the gathering mists and gloom. Thus, as Bely sets the stage for the act of creation that the myth-making of his novel is intended to embody, and as he sets it against the backdrop of the city that had once sprung full-formed from the head of its demiurge, he gives Apollon Apollonovich generative powers comparable to those of Zeus in the *Theogony* and Peter in the epic of his eponymous city. Just by thinking, Apollon Apollonovich gives birth to his son, to his house, to the stranger who embodies the piping of Terror's tune, and to the shadowy double agents. "Out of his head flowed goddesses and genii" (Bely 1978, 20), the creations of his thought that contest his rule just as the overmastered elements contest Peter's creation in "The Bronze Horseman" and as fathers and sons contend with one another in Greek myth. In the beginning, according to Hesiod, Kronos separates the merged bodies of his parents and deposes his father, the starry heavens, by castrating him, an act which simultaneously generates beauty and revenge, or Aphrodite and the dark-robed Furies. Kronos's son Zeus then wars against and overthrows him and subsequently gives birth, in acts that myth considers equivalent to castration (Burkert 1985, 165), to Athene and Dionysus.[22] As part of his novel's design, Bely associates Apollon Apollonovich through epithets and imagery with both Zeus and Kronos and so links him twice with the act of violence that is also an act of creation. This generative act of violence is even embedded in the family emblem, the unicorn goring a knight, since goring is also considered an image of castration in Greek myth (Burkert 1979, 108). And, as we saw earlier when we first observed the family emblem fixed on the family home, thoughts and memories of generative violence in the house of Ableukhov merge the images of father and son and link them to wife, mother, carriage, robe, and bomb.

   To make Apollon Apollonovich the cause of generation and appearance in the world of *Petersburg* Bely conjoins distinct mythological systems, bringing them into collision at the point where they share detail; this is the method, consistently employed throughout the novel, by which he gives his ideas concrete form and his symbols their superabundance. In creating his mythical, god-like senator he draws on epithets from the Greek epics of Homer and Hesiod and elaborates these into metaphor, image, symbol, and myth, a practice which he explains in the essay "The Magic of Words." At the same time, he draws from the literary legends attending the birth of modern Russia to set his myth (and within his myth, a statue of immense importance in the Russian historical imagination) in motion. As he manipulates the details that he selects from Greek epic and those that are most resonant in the mythology of modern Russia, Bely parallels what Ivanov had accomplished with his conjunction of the Phaedran charioteer and the Aeschylean figure of Orestes: through the optic of the legendary act of creation which symbolizes the engendering of modern Russia, Bely focuses on a more remote act of creation that signifies Zeus triumphant. In so doing he implies two things of importance for the reading of *Petersburg*. First, he implies that what is common to these two myths of generation is also primary in the original cosmogonic act; this common heritage is the complex of theomachy, agon, eros, violence, and revolt that is also key to the story of *Petersburg*. Second, in keeping with the understanding in religious philosophy that the original cosmogonic act prefigures the end, he implies that the generative catastrophes which have been memorialized in myth will recur during the time of transfiguration that his art and modern Russia are about to usher in.

That Bely should choose to give the god-like character who governs appearance in *Petersburg* the name Apollon Apollonovich is the result of his adding to the mythologies just mentioned more characterizing detail from other competing worlds of meaning, including those of Nietzsche, of Solovyov, and of the Bible. The allusion most often recognized is to the world of meaning that Nietzsche creates in *The Birth of Tragedy*, his free reinvention of ancient Greece and his refiguration of the gods Apollo and Dionysus. As Nietzsche recreates him, the Apollo of epic tradition becomes a more rightful father of the Olympians than Zeus (Nietzsche 1967, 170–71). He comes to be associated with that aspect of tragedy which is "simple, transparent, and beautiful" and as a result of this transformation comes to be like "a bright image projected on a dark wall" (1967, 67). Having assigned him rule of the realm of appearance, Nietzsche makes his Apollo stand in relation to his Dionysus as the rapturous vision of God stands in relation to the suffering martyr (1967, 42): this remade Apollo is redemptive illusion (1967, 99). Nietzsche's Apollo is also the necessary condition for the appearance of Dionysus on stage in tragedy (1967,66), and as such he overlaps in purpose with the Graeco-Russian Theotokos of religious philosophy, a figure associated with Aphrodite and Sophia. The Theotokos is also an instrument of redemption and the necessary condition for the appearance of divinity both in the world of nature and in the world of art. Like Apollo, the shining or radiant one who is figured in myth and iconography as the sun's charioteer, the radiant Theotokos counts the name "the fiery chariot" among her many epithets.

It is probably no accident, then, that Apollon Apollonovich, who is associated through imagery with Zeus, Kronos, Apollo, and the Theotokos, and who is both father and mother to the Athene-like world of *Petersburg*, is characterized at key points by various figures of brilliance and by the contemplation of brilliance in his chariot. Alone in his black lacquered carriage with its emblazoned image of generative violence Apollon Apollonovich contemplates the brilliance of the stars, the same stars as were themselves, according to the myths of Hesiod and Plato, the first gods made visible in the original act of creation. These stars are also, according to Plato and to his Neoplatonist elaborators, the chariots of the gods and the chariots — or astral bodies — of souls that, like Orestes, struggle with ungovernable horses to follow the gods through the beauty of the heavens to a further realm, to the realm of Ideas and to the heart of the Wisdom of Zeus where Love and Strife abide together in fiery unity. Not incidentally, these stars also symbolize the Platonic rhythm of *anamnesis*, of the soul's remembering and forgetting what it had glimpsed in its generative astral chariot ride, and what it will return to in the end.

Nor is the robe imagery of *Petersburg* likely to be accidental, since both Apollon Apollonovich and Nikolai Apollonovich are dressed in world-engendering garments when they appear in one another's dreams and when they merge in the dream sequence called "The Last Judgement." When Nikolai Apollonovich enters his father's dream of the star-filled second space wearing his red domino, and when Apollon Apollonovich appears in his son's dream as the Mongolian Kronos whose robe of smokey-sapphire with miniature gold dragons becomes the starry sky and his son's study, each is attired in ways that hark back to heroic and theogonic epic.[23] These garments also call to mind the world-creating robe of starry light that Bely's fictional Nietzsche wears in the essay "The Phoenix" (Bely 1969b, 152ff.), an image that imitates the star-strewn robes and veils of Byzantine and Russian iconography adorning theogonic Night, the Theotokos, and Sophia the Wisdom of God. The robe worn by this fictional Nietzsche spreads across the heavens like an airy sail and is associated with fire, knowledge, wisdom, mirror images, dreams within dreams, wrestling, and torment; in other words, it is associated with the figures that define Dionysus, Apollo, Aphrodite, and Sophia as Bely has mixed and mingled them.

The interwoven dreams, the robes worn in them, and the identical dream images of disembodied or severed heads that Apollon Apollonovich and Nikolai Apollonovich have of one another not only unite the two of them but link them further to the terrorist Dudkin. Dudkin, too, sees faces on severed heads materialize in the night. These faces appear to him in the shape of saffron light projected on a dark wall and in the same room as hangs his icon of St. Seraphim of Sarov; sometimes the faces even wink at him, like the light on the Flying Dutchman's schooner. Dudkin also sees double; in effect, he sees both world-creating robes when he delivers the bomb to the senator's son and encounters the senator as well. As Dudkin arrives, Nikolai Apollonovich receives him in the Bukhara dressing gown that, in his own dream, the senator's son will liken to the starry robe of the Mongolian Kronos. And just as Apollon Apollonovich intrudes upon them, Dudkin glimpses the red domino as well. In the story's longest arc of antique imagery, and almost in conclusion, it will also turn out to be the case that it is Dudkin who connects the stargazing Apollon Apollonovich with the avatars of Peter the Great, including the cloud-gathering Flying Dutchman and the wonder-working statue which comes to life, the Bronze Horseman. For it is Dudkin who, in the beginning, senses the ominous presence of Apollon Apollonovich soaring above his emblem-bearing carriage, visible only vaguely as a disembodied head. This mystical vision occurs at the same time as the Flying Dutchman first sails his airy schooner through the clouds and just as the terrorist, his bomb, and the senator's carriage are about to collide. And it is Dudkin who, in the end, is driven on to commit what might be described as a mirror-like act of parricide while the Bronze Horseman looms in the sky in the shape of a enrobed body and while, at the same time, the Flying Dutchman approaches the shore in his astral schooner, imitating the mythical return of Dionysus in his ship-chariot.

In the case of the Ableukhovs it would be hard to find a single innocent antique image, or any mythical story element naively introduced. But in the double-focused imitation of Greek myth-making that Bely has consciously crafted in *Petersburg*, in his many-layered application of symbols borrowed from ancient and modern religion, few figures developed so allusive a density as did Apollon Apollonovich. By imagistic design, by extension of that design through the images entailing his wife and son, and by the interweaving of these same images in the plot of political terror, Apollon Apollonovich enacts Bely's version of the argument common to religious symbolism and religious philosophy about the creative and culturally cohesive force of religious myth. Matter and motive force together, Apollon Apollonovich is always circulating in a ceaseless rhythm of merger and distinction. In his carriage and in his second space he ascends to the starry heavens and then descends again, remembering and forgetting everything as he does. In the course of his astral journeys, which he prepares for in ritual ways, Apollon Apollonovich experiences and then forgets a dream vision of himself as a star that blows apart and is gathered together again. He also forgets his dream knowledge of how the family emblem describes a sacrificial marriage, and how this emblem of agonistic generation is related to the red domino and to ungovernable horses, to Russia's past and future.

But although he has forgotten what he has glimpsed in his moments of ecstatic ascent, Apollon Apollonovich still has the power to bring what is buried in memory to life. And what he brings to life, from the very moment when Dudkin, his son, and his house first escape from his head, is the most archaic of memories. This is the memory of violent beginnings — of the cosmos, of modern Russia, and of the Ableukhovs — a memory that is fixed in Peter's rectilinear streets, that circulates in Dudkin's veins like a virus, and that is emblazoned on the senator's house and carriage. In keeping with key notions in religious philosophy as Bely re-imagined them, this memory is also a prophecy of catastrophic and violent renewal, the kind of renewal envisioned in the apostrophe which speaks itself in the presence of Dudkin and the Bronze Horseman, and addresses the ungovernable steed that is Russia (1978, 64). Garbed as a mythical tale of fathers and sons, this memory is lived in a rhythm of love and strife, or in the motivating presence of starry-veiled Aphrodite and the dark-robed Furies. It is also intertwined with, and mirrored in, the drama that Dudkin and Lippanchenko play through to the end under the spectral eye of Peter the Great. These two stories of fathers and sons are knitted together in *Petersburg* in images adopted from myth and iconography which have been designed to recall the original acts of creating the world and the city, as well as to give figural shape to the religious notion of cultural renewal current in the Silver Age (namely, that what happened in the beginning will happen in the end and will herald universal transfiguration). What occurs in the beginning of time among the gods, in the beginning of modern Russian history with the founding of Peter's city, in the beginning of *Petersburg* with Apollon Apollonovich, and in the beginning of the end for the house of Ableukhov with a sacrificial marriage and its violent spawn, is generative catastrophe. As Bely restructures Nietzsche, Ivanov, Solovyov, and religious philosophy to say together, this catastrophe is destined to recur in the end when the "eternal," in the figure of Dionysus and Aphrodite (or Sophia), returns. Taking his Greek sources and the force of belief they presuppose seriously, even as he treats them lightly in the pyrotechnics and parody of *Petersburg*, Bely constructs his "religious tragedy of the suffering resurrection" with metaphors, symbols, and visual images, like the chariots, robes, and stars considered here. And as it has been among the aims of this article to argue, he does this in order to mingle philosophy, poetry, history, and myth in his own act of creation and according to the rules that he himself has written for the theurgic practice of *mifotvorchestvo*.

NOTES

1. In the estimate of one Classicist, Nietzsche's theory of tragedy as it is presented in *The Birth of Tragedy* "contains the essence of his whole metaphysic." Appraising Nietzsche's command of the relevant Greek texts, Hugh Lloyd-Jones also observes that "in building his philosophy Nietzsche used not so much the doctrines of any individual ancient thinkers ... as the religious and ethical attitude held generally in Greece down to the fifth century, and expressed with variations, by many Greek poets, historians, and thinkers." For the full text of this evaluation see Lloyd-Jones (1982, 165–81).

2. The figures of Heracles, Orpheus, Apollo Musagetes, and Apollo driving the chariot of the sun are noteworthy examples of this development. Each was translated into the Russian lexicon with its full range of images and attendant meanings — Greek, Roman, and Byzantine — still in force. For a detailed description of this process see White 1992, 36–104.

3. As concerns the value of his work to scholars at the turn of the century, Vasily Rudich has recently noted that when Ivanov first lectured on the religion of the suffering god in Paris in 1903 "no one doubted ... that he was indeed the leading specialist on Dionysian worship" (Rudich 1986, 277). For an attestation to the enduring importance of Ivanov's classical scholarship, see the complete text of Rudich's "Vyacheslav Ivanov and Classical Antiquity" in *Vyacheslav Ivanov: Poet, Critic, and Philosopher* (Rudich, 1986).

4. Unless otherwise indicated, translations are mine.

5. Among the descriptions of theurgy to which Ivanov and Berdyaev both subscribed was Evgeny Trubetskoy's literal definition of it as the continuous action of "realizing God's work on earth" (1911, 84). In the lives of individuals and in whole societies, this action creates a state in which the earth ascends to the heavens, the heavens descend to earth, and divine wisdom is given bodily form. See also note 9.

6. Solovyov had himself argued in his earliest work that feminine deities are the material cause of appearance and that the first of them, the sky god's consort, Aphrodite Urania, is the principle of multiplicity (1966–70, 1:11). Later he was to represent Urania's (Beauty's) visibility as the robe and veil of the starry sky (1966–70, 6:48), an image that recalls the beginning of creation in Pherecydes's theogony when the sky god Zas (Zeus) gives his bride Chthonie a robe he has woven as a wedding gift, itself the very image of the earth she becomes when her name is changed to Ge (West 1971, 10 ff.)

7. Andrei Bely acknowledges having made use of Trubetskoy on Parmenides; see Bely (1969a, 495). For Bely's own recounting of the beginnings and ends of several different theogonies — stories of generation and stories of Dionysus — see, for example, Bely (1969a, 521–23, 540–41).

8. Solovyov dedicated a section of his 1898 essay on Auguste Comte to discussing the Russian iconographic program for Sophia, the Wisdom of God, as a model

for understanding the process of cosmic merging and distinction (1966–70, 9:173–93).

9. The term theurgy is often encountered but seldom explained or defined in studies devoted to Russian religious culture at the turn of the century. For Solovyov's explanation of its Greek philosophical, as opposed to its magical, meaning see his article on the Neoplatonist philosopher Proclus, originally contributed to the Brockhaus and Efron encyclopedia (1966–70, 10:483–86). In a posthumous tribute to Solovyov, Evgeny Trubetskoy (1911, 84) offered his definition of its modern Russian meaning (see note 5). For a discussion of how Bely incorporates both of these definitions into his work see White 1992, 72–104.

10. According to Jasper Griffin, the hero of Greek myth is unique in the world of ancient mythology (1988, 73) and the tragedies in which he appears are always at home with suffering: with physical agony, madness, incest, murder within families, with "extreme and naked violence" (1984, 77–85).

11. Part of the collection since 1862. See Gorbunova (1983, 86–90) for photographic reproductions.

12. This phrase is Walter Burkert's (1985, 109), but Ivanov expresses the same idea when he says that mystical marriage or union with the god is the analogue of sacrifice in Dionysian religion (1904–05, 6:189).

13. Again Burkert's phrase (1985, 243). This conjunction of sex and death recalls the Heraclitean fragment that Solovyov had quoted first in "The Mythological Process in Ancient Paganism" (1966–70, 1:21) and then in *The Meaning of Love* (1966–70, 7:32): "Dionysos and Hades, one and the same."

14. The first sacred marriage, recorded in theogonies and the source of the world of appearance, united Earth and her son Ouranos, the starry heavens. As a result of her marriage to Dionysus, Ariadne is immortalized as a constellation, a starry crown.

15. For a reproduction of the manuscript image of Night see Buslaev (1908, 1:117). For discussion of the relationship between this image and the "Pokrov," see Kondakov (1899, 70). For Bely's most literal use of the "Pokrov" in the story line of *Petersburg* see p. 273 of the text and p. 253 of the notes ("counting the days, etc.").

16. For the significance that Hugh Lloyd-Jones ascribes to this phrase in this translation see his Sather lectures on ancient religion entitled *The Justice of Zeus* (Lloyd-Jones 1971, 86ff.).

17. In his commentary on *Symbolism*, Bely discusses ecstasy as the precondition for the act of creation that, in the governing formula of his theory, precedes the act of cognition (1969a, 515–16).

18. The stories of Aktaion and Pentheus also appear together in vase painting. See, for example, Boardman 1975, plates 28, 335.2.

19. No matter what he calls the pair, this is a figure he often uses in discussions of theurgy. In addition to calling it Apollo and Dionysus, he also calls it the

"Woman Clothed with the Sun and the Beast," the "Phoenix and the Sphinx," and "Beauty and Terror."

20. For a brief review of the origins in classical Greek philosophy of the Neoplatonic notion of the astral body, especially for its representation as the soul's chariot made of stars which is acquired in the act of descent and discarded in the act of ascent, see E.R. Dodds's appendix II in Proclus 1963, 312–21.

21. See e.g. Boardman 1974, plate 62 and *Homeric Hymn* 28 (Homer 1973, 79).

22. For the iconography of Zeus bearing these gods from his thigh see Arafat 1990, plates 7, 10.

23. At fateful moments in the *Iliad*, both Helen (3.125–28) and Andromache (22.440–41) — the latter, according to Ivanov, the literary image of a genuine maenad — sit weaving red robes that tell the story of the Trojan war in pictures. See also note 6 above.

WORKS CITED

Aeschylus. 1957. *Agamemnon*. Edited with introduction and commentary by J.D. Denniston and Denys Page. Oxford: Clarendon Press.

_____. 1986. *Choephori*. Edited by Sir D.L. Page with introduction and commentary by A.F. Garvie. Oxford: Clarendon Press.

Arafat, K.W. 1990. *Classical Zeus: A Study in Art and Literature*. New York: Oxford University Press.

Bely, Andrei. 1969a. *Simbolizm*. Munich: Fink.

_____. 1969b. *Arabeski*. Munich: Fink.

_____. 1978. *Petersburg*. Translated, annotated, and introduced by Robert Maguire and John Malmstad. Bloomington: Indiana University Press.

Berdyaev, Nikolai. 1986. "An Astral Novel: Some Thoughts on Andrei Bely's *Petersburg*." *The Noise of Change*. Ed. Stanley Rabinowitz. Ann Arbor: Ardis, 197–204.

Boardman, John. 1974. *Athenian Black Figure Vases: a Handbook*. London: Thames and Hudson.

_____. 1975. *Athenian Red Figure Vases: The Archaic Period, a Handbook*. London: Thames and Hudson.

Burkert, Walter. 1985. *Greek Religion*. Translated by John Raffan. Cambridge: Harvard University Press.

_____. 1979. *Structure and History in Greek Mythology and Ritual*. Berkeley: University of California Press.

Buslaev, F.I. 1908. *Sochineniya*. Vol 1. St. Petersburg: [np].

MARY JO WHITE

Euripides. 1960. *Bacchae*. Edited with introduction and commentary by E.R. Dodds. Second Ed. Oxford: Clarendon Press.

Gorbunova, K.S. 1983. *Chernofigurnye Atticheskie Vazy v Ermitazhe*. Leningrad: Iskusstvo.

Griffin, Jasper. 1988. "Greek Myth and Hesiod." *The Oxford History of the Classical World*. Ed. by John Boardman, Jasper Griffin, and Oswyn Murray. Oxford: Oxford University Press, 72–92.

_____. 1986. *The Mirror of Myth: Classical Themes and Variations*. London: Faber and Faber.

Hedreen, Guy Michael. 1992. *Silens in Attic Black-Figure Vase Painting: Myth and Performance*. Ann Arbor: University of Michigan Press.

Homer. 1961. *The Iliad of Homer*. Translated with introduction by Richmond Lattimore. Chicago: University of Chicago Press.

_____. 1973. *The Homeric Hymns*. Translated by Thelma Sargent. New York: Norton.

Ivanov, Vyacheslav. 1971–87. *Sobranie sochinenii*. 4 vols. Brussels: Foyer Oriental Chretien.

_____. 1904–05. "Ellinskaya religiya stradayushchego boga." *Novy Put'*, No. 1–3, 5, 8–9; *Voprosy Zhizni*, No. 6–7.

Kondakov, N.K. and I.I. Tolstoi. 1899. *Russkiya drevnosti v pamiatnikakh isskustva*. Issue 6. St. Petersburg: A. Benke.

Lloyd-Jones, Hugh. 1982. *Blood for the Ghosts: Classical Influences in the Nineteenth and Twentieth Centuries*. London: Duckworth.

_____. 1971. *The Justice of Zeus*. Berkeley: University of California Press.

Nietzsche, Friedrich. 1967. *The Birth of Tragedy*. Translated with commentary by Walter Kaufmann. New York: Vintage.

Proclus. 1963. *Elements of Theology*. A revised text with translation, introduction, and commentary by E. R. Dodds. Second Ed. Oxford: Clarendon Press.

Rudich, Vasily. 1986. "Vyacheslav Ivanov and Classical Antiquity." *Vyacheslav Ivanov, Poet, Critic, and Philosopher*. Ed. Robert Louis Jackson and Lowry Nelson, Jr. New Haven: Yale Center for International and Area Studies, 275–89.

Solovyov, V.S. 1966–70. *Sobranie Sochinenii*. 12 vols. Brussels: Zhizn' s Bogom.

Trubetskoy, Evgeny. 1911. "Vladimir Solovyov i ego delo." *Sbornik pervy o Vladimire Solovyove*. Moscow: Put', 75–95.

West, M.L. 1971. *The Role of Greek Antiquity in Russian Symbolist Theory*. Oxford: Clarendon Press.

White, Mary Jo. 1992. *The Role of Greek Antiquity in Russian Symbolist Theory*. Ph.D. Diss.: University of Washington.

HELLENISM, CULTURE AND CHRISTIANITY: THE CASE OF VYACHESLAV IVANOV AND HIS "PALINODE" OF 1927

Pamela Davidson, University of London

Нет в Европе другой культуры, кроме эллинской (1907)[1]

Ужели я тебя, Эллада, разлюбил? (1927)[2]

     ... Был духу мил
Отказ суровый Палинодий:
Прочь от языческих угодий
Он замысл творческий стремил. (1944)[3]

Several features of Vyacheslav Ivanov's lifelong interest in classical antiquity are typical of his age and were shared by a number of his contemporaries. Like Faddei Zelinsky, he invested his scholarly interest in classical studies with the belief that a renaissance of Slavonic culture could only be achieved through a return to its Greek sources.[4] As in the case of Innokenty Annensky, his profound erudition in classical matters was an integral part of his poetic practice.[5] However, his contribution was unique in one respect: he sought to integrate both these worlds (classical scholarship and poetry) into a Christian world-view.[6] His example therefore provides a particularly interesting avenue for exploring the problematic interrelationship between Hellenism, culture and Christianity at the turn of the century. In this paper we shall first consider the question from a general point of view, in terms of Ivanov's background and through the eyes of his contemporaries, and then focus on one particular key text, the poem of 1927, "Palinodiya" ("Palinode"), in which the poet attempts to provide a retrospective clarification of the development of his relationship to the cultural heritage of classical antiquity.[7]

1. IVANOV'S APPROACH TO CLASSICAL ANTIQUITY

1.1. Sources of Ivanov's syncretic view

Certain aspects of Ivanov's upbringing and education played a vital role in equipping him with the basic elements of his syncretic outlook. His education prepared him for a career as a classical philologist. He first worked on Roman antiquity, writing his dissertation in Latin on legal aspects of the ancient Roman system of taxation (Ivanov 1910a); then, under the influence of Nietzsche, he switched to the study of Greek antiquity, specializing in the study of the cult of Dionysus (Ivanov 1904a, 1905, 1923).[8] The religious intuitions first developed by his mother in his early childhood were later revived by his readings of Dostoevsky and Western mystics, by his encounters with Vladimir Solovyov and by the desire to overcome Nietzsche through developing a religious interpretation of Dionysus. Finally, the discovery of his poetic vocation was initiated by meeting Lidiya Zinov'eva-Annibal, and subsequently approved by Vladimir Solovyov.[9] These three elements combined to create a situation in which Ivanov sought to find support for his mystical intuitions in classical antiquity, and to express these in his poetry.

Had he been of a different temperament, these various strands might well have remained compartmentalized, each confined to a separate area. But the syncretic, integrating drive in his personality was very strong, and led him to search for ways of reconciling disparate elements within the framework of a harmonious religious world-view. An extreme example of this tendency can be found in his essay of 1918, "Nash yazyk" ("Our Language"), in which he argued that the Russian language received the sacred imprint of the Greek religious spirit via Byzantium, thereby establishing the linguistic medium of his poetic tradition as the carrier of a Christian religious spirit which was, in turn, related back to its sources in Hellenic culture (Ivanov 1971–, 4: 673–80).

1.2. Tensions between Christianity and classical culture

At this point, it is worth pausing to consider whether there was in fact any difficulty in reconciling these various strands, firstly from the point of view of traditional Christian theology, and secondly, in the eyes of Ivanov and his contemporaries. Early Christian writings contain much discussion, the intensity of which has now been lost, of the possibility of reconciling the pagan culture of antiquity with the new religion of revelation. The Judaic tradition had traditionally been inimical to pagan influences, regarding these at worst as a source of idol worship, and at best as a pointless distraction from religious pursuits. This attitude was initially inherited by the early Church. With the gradual change of orientation and growth of the mission to the gentiles, however, the problem of reconciling the two traditions became more acute. A significant step was taken with Paul's decision that the gentiles need not keep the Mosaic law. Nevertheless, the tension continued to be perceived as fundamental by many early Christian thinkers. Two examples are worth mentioning in this context, those of St. Jerome and St. Augustine, particularly in view of the fact that, as we shall see later, Ivanov felt a special affinity with these two figures at the time of writing his "Palinode."

In a famous dream of self-indictment, St. Jerome (c. 342–420) accused himself of loving his pagan literature more than Christian writings ("Ciceronianus es, non Christianus"). He then embarked on a period of ascetic withdrawal as a hermit in the Syrian desert in order to cure himself of this sinful tendency. While there he taught himself Hebrew and later sought to bridge the gap between the two traditions by translating the Hebrew scriptures into Latin (Cross 1978, 731–32).

The *Confessions* of St. Augustine (354–430) are peppered with similar worries. Born of a pagan father and Christian mother, St. Augustine went through several periods of crisis and oscillation between the two traditions during his lifetime. The opening books of his major work, *The City of God*, are almost entirely devoted to proving the superiority of Christianity over Greek and Roman paganism; the emotional intensity of the tone adopted in this series of vehement invectives forcefully conveys the topical urgency of the subject (Augustine 1945, 1: 1–111). Some years later, shortly before his death, he wrote his *Retractions* in which he reassessed his past literary work from the point of view of his later Christian convictions (Brown 1967, 428–31).

In the middle ages, the line of demarcation was still clearly drawn by Dante who firmly excluded pagans from the sphere of Christian revelation. In post-Renaissance humanist culture, however, the tension was considerably relaxed, and the turn of the century in Russia was generally characterized by an all-embracing tendency towards cultural syncretism. This reflected the fact that Christianity, although an offshoot of Judaism, took root in the soil of pagan Greco-Roman culture, and accordingly absorbed many aspects of Hellenic culture into its religious tradition.

1.3. Contemporary responses to Ivanov's syncretic view

Despite this blurring of traditional distinctions, Ivanov's attempt to build a bridge between pagan culture and Christianity was nevertheless perceived as an issue for public debate as soon as his views reached a wider audience. In Paris, in 1903, he gave a course of lectures on the religion of Dionysus, arguing that the Greek god was a prototype or forerunner of Christ, whose cult offered a certain method or psychological parallel to that of Jesus (1904a, 1905). Soon after the text of these lectures began to appear in *Novy put'*, Merezhkovsky published a polemical article entitled "Za ili protiv?" ("For or Against"), which was printed in the same issue as one of Ivanov's lectures. In the context of a general attempt to clarify the religious position of the Symbolist writers contributing to *Vesy*, Merezhkovsky questioned Ivanov's faith in Dionysus as a living God of salvation, and asked why he should turn to masks when the "Face" has already been revealed.

> Маски нужны тем, кому еще не открылось Лицо. Но к чему маски, когда уже есть Лицо? К чему Дионис «*многоименный*», когда «нет под небесами другого имени, кроме *одного* которым надлежало бы спастись?» Или Вяч. Иванов еще не знает этого Имени, еще не видел этого Лица? (1904, 270)[10]

Merezhkovsky concluded his article by quoting the Biblical verse "Kto ne za menya, tot protiv menya" ("He that is not with me is against me," Matt. 12:30), hoping thereby to elicit a clear response to his charge. However, his prediction that Ivanov would avoid giving a direct answer turned out to be correct.

Ivanov's rejoinder, written in the form of a poem "*'Litso — ili maska'?*" ("'Face — or Mask'?") and published in the next issue, did not go beyond reaffirming that Christ appears in many guises to those who seek him. After evoking a series of these appearances ("*liki*") it concludes with a final stanza, clearly designed to reinforce the link between Christ, Dionysus and Orpheus; the image of Orpheus was evidently introduced to extend the Dionysiac parallel into the realm of poetry and art:

Ты, Сущий, — не всегда ль? и, Тайный, — не везде ли, —
И в гроздьях жертвенных, и в белом сне лилей?
Ты — глас улыбчивый младенческой свирели;
Ты — скалы движущий Орфей. (1904b, 165; 1971–, 2: 265)[11]

Ivanov refused to draw a rigid line of demarcation between Christian revelation and Hellenic prefiguration; while not confusing or identifying them in any way, he would not admit the need to exclude the first, arguing that certain aspects of the mystical essence of Christianity were present in pagan cults which predated it in time, but anticipated it in spirit. His critics were not convinced, however; they remained uneasy about the blurring of the dividing line between the revealed truth of religion and cultural phenomena (this, rather than any theological debate between Christianity and paganism, was the heart of the issue). This difference of opinion surfaced at intervals in various guises. The debate conducted among Ivanov, Blok and Bryusov on the pages of *Apollon* in 1910 essentially dealt with the application of the same issue to art; the question of whether there is a firm distinction to be drawn between the spheres of culture and of revelation evolved into the more general question of whether art belongs to the realm of the purely aesthetic or the theurgic.

In 1916, after reading Ivanov's new collection of essays, *Borozdy i mezhi* (*Furrows and Boundaries*), Berdyaev and Shestov both came quite independently to the conclusion that Ivanov's world was not related to the realm of true philosophical or religious inquiry or to reality. Berdyaev took a particularly severe line, arguing that Ivanov's syncretism is false, and that his reconciliation of opposites is illusory, for it operates only on the level of philology, not of ontological revelation.

У него филология незаметно подменяет онтологию ... Боги и герои Греции всегда подменяют для него живые существа нашей жизни и жизни вечной. И всякий дионисизм для него не феномен жизни, нашей и вечной жизни, а феномен греческой культуры, греческой религии и мистики, греческой литературы и искусства. Ему ведомы усложненные откровения культуры, а не простые откровения бытия.... И у него вечно стирается грань между бытием первичным и бытием отраженным. Не слово делается плотью, а плоть делается словом, бытие переходит в слово.[12]

At the end of his article he concludes that Ivanov has no real role to play in the history of Russian Christian thought: "On slishkom prebyvaet v yazycheskoi stikhii i yazycheskoi kul'ture, chtoby bolet' khristianskoi problemoi cheloveka" (1916).[13]

Shestov set Ivanov apart from the mainstream of Russian thought, commenting on his tendency to write about the realm of the possible rather than of the real: "Ego idei i mysli ... ne imeyut rovno nikakoi svyazi s tem, chto prinyato nazyvat' obyknovenno deistvitel'nost'yu" (1916, 81).[14] The philosopher Vladimir Ern upheld the counter argument. He took issue with Shestov's article, and attacked it as an unduly subjective and misleading portrait of Ivanov. Dwelling on the question of Ivanov's relation to Hellenism, he emphasized the radical novelty of his ideas and their fundamental importance for a renaissance of Hellenism in Orthodox Russia (1917, 176). Another religious philosopher, Sergei Bulgakov, while applauding Ivanov's "religious calling" to deepen Christian self-awareness through revealing the Christian significance of the religion of Hellenism, at the same time sounded a note of caution not unrelated to some of the strictures expressed above: "Osobenno velika dlya nego opasnost' esteticheskogo podmena religioznykh tsennostei, nepravogo apollinizma, k kotoromu on inogda byvaet blizhe, chem sam dumaet" (1918, 137–38).[15]

This debate has continued up to the present day, with critics dividing into two camps.[16] On the one hand, there are those who, following Berdyaev and Shestov, repudiate Ivanov's ability to reconcile culture and religion on the level of philosophical truth, and relegate him to a world of purely philological mythopoetry. The problem with this line of argument is that it fails to take into account the seriousness of Ivanov's own Christian convictions and his position as a religious thinker. On the other hand, there are those who view Ivanov's path as an even progression or gradual ascent, leading from Dionysus to Christ, eventually achieving a full synthesis and reconciliation of culture and revelation. This is the line followed in the main by later religious thinkers, such as Schultze (1949), Tyszkiewicz (1950a, 1950b), and Fotiev (1964, 1988).[17] The weakness of this approach is that it tends to gloss over early incompatibilities retrospectively, and cannot accommodate later poems such as "Palinodiya" in which the poet appears to be making a revisionary statement reflecting a changed perception of his orientation.

There was evidently a certain amount of difficulty in reconciling the two traditions. Although, as we have seen, Ivanov rather smoothed over the tension in his reply to Merezhkovsky's article, it did not disappear, but presented itself to him with increasing force over the years. Hints of it can already be seen in some poems of 1915, such as "Razvodnaya" ("Song of Parting") or "Chistilishche" ("Purgatory") (Ivanov 1971–, 3: 541, 548). His most open confrontation with the issue, however, did not come until many years later, in the late 1920s, when he wrote a retrospective poem on the subject, "Palinodiya." This is the best source for reaching a deeper understanding of this question in Ivanov's own terms, and the remainder of this essay will accordingly be devoted to a detailed analysis of this poem's biographical context, textual history and meaning.

2. IVANOV'S "PALINODE"

2.1. Biographical context

"Palinodiya" was written on 14 January 1927, during a period of considerable reorientation in Ivanov's life. In 1924, after four years of largely unbroken poetic silence in Baku,[18] he left Russia and moved to Rome. Upon his arrival he wrote the cycle "Rimskie sonety" ("Roman Sonnets"), describing his return to the eternal city as a spiritual homecoming, and then fell silent once more. In March 1926 he formalized his decision, long in the making, to embrace the Catholic faith, and in the autumn of the same year moved from Rome to Pavia to take up an academic position at the Collegio Borromeo. He spent the latter part of 1926 preparing a series of lectures for the University of Pavia on Russian religious thought; these were delivered in late January 1927, around the same time that "Palinodiya" was composed.[19]

It is clear from even a brief review of these events that a major preoccupation at this time must have been reassessing the relationship between culture and Christianity, and between Russian religious thought and Western Catholicism, following the different paths which the two traditions had taken after departing from their common roots in Hellenic antiquity. This was, for example, the context within which Ivanov presented his lectures, prefacing them with a long introductory preamble on the importance of his theme for the ecumenical union of the churches.[20]

The question of the relationship of the two branches of the Christian tradition to their origins in Judaism is also likely to have been on his mind around this time, following the initiation of his friendship with the German Jewish theologian and philosopher, Martin Buber. In August of the previous year he had received his first letter from Buber, shortly before the publication of a German translation of *Perepiska iz dvukh uglov* (*Correspondence from Two Corners*) in the latter's journal *Die Kreatur*. Buber sent him his German translation of the Old Testament in January 1927 and came to meet him a few months later in March (D. Ivanov 1989; Ivanova 1990, 173–74).

This was therefore a period of relative isolation for Ivanov who had left his children in Rome upon moving to Pavia.[21] It was also a retreat in more

ways than one into a new phase of seclusion and spiritual introspection which
provided him with an opportunity to review his relationship to the religious
and cultural heritage of the past.[22] The fruits of these reflections are presented
on an autobiographical level in the "Palinode" which he wrote at this time.
The significance of this poem as a statement is further increased by the fact
that it was written after a substantial interval of poetic silence. Apart from
"Kamenny dub" ("Stony Oak") written in June 1925, Ivanov wrote no verse
for over two years between the "Roman Sonnets" and the cluster of poems
including "Palinodiya" which were composed within six weeks of each other
at the very end of 1926 and beginning of 1927.[23]

2.2. Textual history

Before we begin to look at the poem itself, it is necessary to make a few
preliminary comments about the texts on which the discussion will be based.
These comprise five unpublished manuscript variants, as well as a number
of published texts, including an early version of the poem in Italian. The
manuscript drafts of the poem are located in Ivanov's archive in Rome. Four
successive versions, ranging from an initial very rough draft to a later more
finished version, occupy three pages in a notebook. The Rome archive also
contains a neat, final version of the poem, written out on a separate sheet of
paper, dated 14 January 1927, and differing only slightly from the published
text.[24]

The first "official" publication of the poem was in *Sovremennye zapiski* in
1937 (Ivanov 1937, 164–65).[25] There are, however, three earlier published
texts of 1930 which should be taken into account, two in the original Russian
and an Italian translation, evidently also prepared by Ivanov. The first two
Russian texts both appeared in articles about Ivanov written by the émigré
scholar and poet, Ilya Golenishchev-Kutuzov. After visiting Ivanov in Rome
during the summers of 1927 and 1928 and hearing some of his recent verse,[26]
Golenishchev-Kutuzov gave a lecture on the poet in Paris in January 1930
which led to the publication of two articles on him later that same year. At
this stage Ivanov did not yet wish to publish his work in the émigré press,
but gave Golenishchev-Kutuzov his unofficial permission to quote a limited
number of his recent poems in his articles.[27]

Golenishchev-Kutuzov chose to quote "Palinodiya" in full in both articles
and a few of the "Roman Sonnets" in the second. The title of his first article,
"Otrechenie ot Dionisa" ("Renunciation of Dionysus"), was inspired by the
"Palinode" and followed a review of Ivanov's book of 1923 on Dionysus
with comments on this poem, interpreted as an act of cathartic renunciation

of Dionysus in favor of the purifying spirit of Western Christianity; it appeared in the daily Paris newspaper *Vozrozhdenie* in July (1930b). The second piece, "Lirika Vyacheslava Ivanova" ("The Lyric Verse of Vyacheslav Ivanov"), was published in *Sovremennye zapiski* (1930a) and consisted of a more general survey of the poet's development, interpreted in a similar vein, in the light of the "Palinode," as a gradual ascent from Bacchic chaos to Roman harmony.

These early texts of 1930 were slightly adapted in the later "official" version of 1937 (the main differences being one change of adjective and an inversion of two phrases in lines 8 and 9). The final version of the poem subsequently included in *Svet vecherny* (*Evening Light*) (Ivanov 1962, 78) represents a synthesis of both earlier texts; it kept the order of the phrases given in the 1937 version, but reverted to the original adjective used in the first published text of 1930.[28]

Another important but little-known source for understanding the poem is the literal Italian translation which was first published in 1930 alongside three other poems by Ivanov in the Catholic journal edited by Giovanni Papini, *Il Frontespizio* (Ivanov 1930), and subsequently reprinted in the 1934 issue of *Il Convegno* devoted to Ivanov (Ivanov 1934). Although the authorship of this translation is not entirely clear, on balance the evidence suggests that it was prepared by Ivanov.[29] It is a very useful source for determining the meaning of the original; it does not seek to reproduce the formal properties of the Russian text and is therefore free to offer a remarkably faithful and literal translation which effectively fulfills the function of an explicatory commentary. Where the syntax of the original Russian is in places compressed to the point of density, the Italian translation offers clarification through the lighter medium of its language and syntax, always clear and lucid.

We give below the text of the canonical Russian version of the poem (Ivanov 1962, 78; 1971–: 3, 558) on which our commentary will be based, followed by the Italian translation (based on the original Russian version of 1930) in its second published version of 1934 (Ivanov 1934) which incorporated a few minor corrections to the first version of 1930.

ПАЛИНОДИЯ

1 И твой гиметский мед ужель меня пресытил?
2 Из рощи миртовой кто твой кумир похитил?
3 Иль в вещем ужасе я сам его разбил?
4 Ужели я тебя, Эллада, разлюбил?
5 Но, духом обнищав, твоей не знал я ласки,
6 И жутки стали мне души недвижной маски,

7   И тел надменных свет, и дум Эвклидов строй.
8   Когда ж, подземных флейт разымчивой игрой
9   В урочный час ожив, личины полой очи
10   Мятежною тоской неукротимой Ночи,
11   Как встарь, исполнились, — я слышал с неба зов:
12   «Покинь, служитель, храм украшенный бесов».
13   И я бежал, и ем в предгорьях Фиваиды
14   Молчанья дикий мед и жесткие акриды.[30]

Palinodia
1   Anche il tuo miele d'Imetto mi ha saziato?
2   Dal bosco di mirti l'idolo tuo chi lo rapi?
3   Oppure per sacro orrore io stesso lo spezzai?
4   Forse, o Ellade, non ti amo più?
5   Ma, divenuto povero di spirito, non conobbi più le tue carezze;
6   e cominciarono a incutermi paura le facce dell'anima tua immutevole,
7   dei corpi altieri la limpidezza e dei pensieri l'ordine euclideo.
8   Quando poi, in ora fatidica, coll'inebriante suono
9   di flauti sotterranei risvegliandosi, gli occhi della maschera vuota
10   d'una bramosia ribelle dell'indomita Notte,
11   come in tempi remoti, si riempirono, — io udii dal cielo la voce:
12   "Lascia, o neòcoro, il tempio ornato di dèmoni…"
13   Ed io fuggii, e mangio, sui pendii della Tebaide,
14   del silenzio il miele selvatico e le coriacee locuste.

2.3. Connotations of the title

The title which Ivanov has chosen for his poem is of significance and deserves our attention. The Greek noun "palinoidia" (the same form occurs in Latin), usually translated as a "palinode" or "recantation," most commonly refers to an ode or song in which the author retracts an earlier statement.[31] It was taken up in a religious sense by the early Church fathers to signal their revocation of previously espoused pagan cultural values (in a spirit similar to that of St. Augustine's *Retractions*, mentioned above) and occurs in liturgical usage as a more general expression of repentance from sin (Lampe, 1961). In literature the form enjoyed a revival after the Renaissance, particularly in France and Italy. As a recognized literary term, it passed into the main European languages (for example the French phrase "chanter la palinodie," derived from the Latin "palinodiam canere," is fairly common), but not, as the evidence would suggest, into the Russian literary tradition which retained the term sanctioned by Biblical usage, "otrechenie" ("renunciation").[32]

Ivanov's choice of this term as his title therefore frames the poem's statement explicitly within the classical tradition and immediately invites the question: what exactly is the author retracting? The opening lines indicate that it is Hellenic culture. This is confirmed by the final manuscript version of the poem in which the main title, "Ellada" ("Hellas"), was followed by a subtitle in brackets "(palinodiya)" ["(palinode)"].[33] Before exploring the nature of this revocation any further, however, one should point out from the outset its somewhat paradoxical aspect. The fact that the term "palinodiya" is so unusual in the Russian language creates a certain irony or ambiguity: the apparent renunciation of the classical tradition is couched in terminology which refers the reader to this very tradition and depends on it for its meaning. This ambivalence is also latent in the second, less common, meaning of the term "palinodiya" which in both Greek and Latin carries an additional sense of a song of repetition or refrain.[34] As we shall see, this potential ambiguity is to some extent deliberate and reflects the delicate balance which the poet is trying to achieve in redefining his approach to classical antiquity.

2.4. Analysis of the poem

The poem follows a closely knit structure. It consists of seven rhyming couplets written in iambic hexameters with a fixed medial caesura. In Russia this form was very frequent in eighteenth- and early nineteenth-century verse where it predominated in tragedy and in epic; the meter, regarded as the Russian equivalent of the alexandrine, was traditionally associated with lofty sentiments or philosophical reflection in poetry. The first two couplets pose a question to which the rest of the poem articulates an indirect response: the poet asks himself whether it can really be true that he has fallen out of love with Hellas? This opening question is built up to gradually and with an element of suspense. Hellas is only named directly in the fourth line — in fact the critic Adamovich took the view that the whole poem was written just for the effect of this particular line (1938).[35] In this context it is interesting to note that in its very first manuscript draft the poem began with this line.[36]

The opening "i" ("and," "also," "even") suggests a continuing debate in the poet's mind, which is struggling to make sense of a growing sense of disenchantment with previous enthusiasms (this comes across more forcefully in the Italian translation which renders "i" as "anche" — "also" or "even"). The use of "tvoi" ("your") suggests the intimacy and closeness of a past relationship, while the relentless succession of one-line questions all ending in verbs (the last two are in the first person and refer directly to the narrator) betray the poet's confusion and uncertainty over his role: is he the initiator or the passive victim of the new state of affairs? Furthermore, the repeated use of "uzheli" ("really") to frame the opening and closing questions conveys a measure of incredulity, a certain unwillingness or reluctance to accept what the evidence would suggest.[37] The terms of reference introduced in the first two couplets already indicate a partial answer to the question raised. Before being named directly in the final line, Hellas is first identified through two images, honey and a smashed or stolen idol. What exactly is meant by these images, and what is their inner connection?

Honey is used by Ivanov as an image of poetry or culture, occasionally, in certain contexts, with a slightly negative connotation, suggesting an overly cloying or illusory sweetness.[38] In a poem of 1915 entitled "Chistilishche" ("Purgatory"), he referred to the fact that every pleasure of the past had been honey on the lips but wormwood inside:

> Лишь ныне я понял, святая Пощада,
> Что каждая лет миновавших услада
> В устах была мед, а во чреве полынь (1971–, 3: 548)[39]

In 1920, in the course of his epistolary debate with Ivanov, Mikhail Gershenzon used honey as an image for his friend's poetic style, reflecting the burden of an oversaturated and oppressive culture from which he wished to escape: "Ya upyus' gustym myodom vashikh stikhov, no i snova ispytayu znakomoe shchemyashchee chuvstvo" (Ivanov 1971–, 3: 387).[40]

Hymettus was famous for its marble as well as for its honey, and was also the site of a temple devoted to the cult of Zeus. These associations prepare for the second aspect of Hellas mentioned, the "kumir" ("idol") of the next line, and further developed in the "khram" ("temple") of line 12. Here it is important to note that Ivanov is deliberately drawing on Biblical imagery in order to set Hellenic culture within a Judæo-Christian perspective and to establish a link between its alluring sweetness and the dangers of idol worship. The Biblical commandment prohibiting idolatry ("Ne delai sebe kumir" — "Thou shalt not make unto thee any graven image," Exod. 20:4) is developed in several scriptural passages which call upon Israel to uproot all traces of pagan cults from its midst. One could cite as an example the following description of the attempts of Josiah, the son of David, to cleanse Israel of all idol worship and foreign cults: "i reznye i litye *kumiry* izlomal i *razbil* v prakh," "i *kumiry razbil* v prakh" ("and the carved *images*, and the molten images, he *broke* in pieces, and made dust of them," "and he had *beaten* the graven *images* into powder," 2 Chr. 34:4, 7; my emphasis).

In various other passages these idols are associated, as in Ivanov's poem, with sacred groves. The prophet Micah exhorts Israel with the following threats: "istreblyu istukanov tvoikh i *kumirov* iz sredy tvoei, i ne budesh' bolee poklonyat'sya izdeliyam ruk tvoikh. Iskorenyu iz sredy tvoei svyash-chennye *roshchi* tvoi" ("Thy graven images also will I cut off, and thy standing *images* out of the midst of thee, and thou shalt no more worship the work of thine hands. And I will pluck up thy *groves* out of the midst of thee," Mic. 5:13–14; my emphasis).

By echoing these terms in his poem through phrases such as "iz roshchi mirtovoi" ("from the grove of myrtles"), "kumir" ("idol," "image"), "razbil" ("broke"),[41] Ivanov suggests a link between culture and idol worship. He had already done this in his correspondence with Gershenzon, where he refers to the need to absorb the vital spirit of other cultures by visiting their idols and bringing sacrifices at their altars (1971–, 3: 397).[42] There, however, the image was positive; in "Palinodiya," written seven years later, it acquired a negative connotation, connected with the poet's reappraisal of his relationship with the cultural heritage of classical antiquity.

* * *

The opening question, posed with such force, is not in fact fully resolved in the rest of the poem. The remaining five couplets present a condensed review of the poet's spiritual past; they outline the three stages which have led up to the present retreat into silence, but make no wider statement on the extent or permanence of this withdrawal.

Here it is important to grasp the elusive significance of the opening conjunction "but," which introduces the second section of the poem ("no," translated in the English version of the poem as "yet"). Within the overall scheme of the poem, this word carries a great deal of weight and appears to suggest the following: it might appear (from the first four lines) that the poet has lost all feeling for Hellenism, but this is not the case; past circumstances (detailed in lines 5 to 12) have brought him to the present state of silence and withdrawal, yet this does not necessarily mean that his attachment to Hellenism has disappeared; it simply signals that it has gone "underground," following a temporary withdrawal from outward verbal expression.

The circumstances which have led up to the poet's present retreat fall into three stages. An earlier phase of disenchantment was interrupted by a re-newal of the attraction, which was then in turn broken off by a voice commanding him to resist the call and to withdraw into silence. The first

stage of alienation is described as one of "poverty of spirit." The loss of an
intimate relationship with Hellenism led to a perception of Greek culture as
a series of masks screening an immutable soul, and associated with its
rational, intellectual aspects. In the first four manuscript versions of the
poem, these dead masks of Hellenic culture were referred to as "tvoi pustye
maski" ("your empty masks"); in the last manuscript version the phrase
"strastei nedvizhnykh maski" ("the masks of immutable passions") was
crossed out and replaced with the final "dushi nedvizhnoi maski" ("the
masks of your immutable soul").[43]

The term "maski" ("masks") was generally used by Ivanov to refer to the
various outward manifestations of the Dionysiac spirit in Hellenic culture (as
in the poem "'Litso — ili maska'?" discussed above), or to its renaissance in
early twentieth-century Russian culture (as in his essay of 1904, "Novye
maski" — "New Masks"). Following this line of interpretation, it is possible
to read this section of the poem in terms of the polarity between Apollo and
Dionysus which was so fundamental to Ivanov's thought. The poet's sense
of distance from Hellas at this stage may have resulted from his loss of
contact with the dark Dionysiac forces which underlie and give meaning to
the Apollonian mask of light, order and culture.

There is also a hint at the Luciferian aspect of the Apollonian dimension.
This was the sense in which Golenishchev-Kutuzov understood the reference
to the "tel nadmennykh svet" ("the light of lofty bodies"): a reading which
may well have been based on conversations he had with Ivanov in the
summers of 1927 and 1928.[44] Lucifer (meaning "light-bringing") was used
to refer to the morning star or the planet Venus; it was also regarded as the
proper name of the rebel archangel whose fall from heaven was supposed to
be referred to in Isaiah 14:12. The Luciferian aspect of the soul's refusal to
recognize its dependence on the spiritual was associated by Ivanov with the
impulse towards Apollonian creation, and regarded as the main basis of the
whole of human culture; this was a theme which was particularly dominant
in his essays of the immediately pre-revolutionary period, to which this part
of the poem may be referring on an autobiographical level.[45]

* * *

Lines 8 to 11 introduce the second stage in the poet's development (the
Italian translation renders "kogda zh" — "when then" — more explicitly as
"quando poi"). The importance of the change of orientation introduced in this
section is underscored by the striking split between the syntax and the
rhyming scheme at this point; the full stop at the end of line 7 breaks the unity
of the couplet defined by the rhyming scheme, and effectively splits the poem

into two equal halves. The eyes of the hollow mask (the unmoving mask of Hellas described in line 6) revived and filled once more ("kak vstar'" — as in olden times, in the poet's earlier years) with the restless longing of indomitable Night. The capitalization of "Night," in line with the reading suggested above, alludes to the Dionysiac spirit, forever reviving after cyclical periods of stagnation or death. The Apollonian mask was about to be reinfused with its life-giving Dionysiac content. The intoxicating sound of the subterranean flutes which accompanied this process of revival indirectly evokes the renewal of the poetic impulse,[46] represented by Orpheus who enchanted the underworld and brought the dead back to life through the magic of his music.[47]

In Ivanov's terms, this would previously have signalled a period of spiritual renewal, and have been embraced as a positive change. However, on this occasion, just as the new mood was developing, the poet heard a call from the heavens. The abrupt suddenness of this intervention is underlined by the dash which coincides with the caesura and breaks line 11 at its midway point. The call to flee from the temple of idols returns us to the Biblical imagery introduced in the first lines of the poem, reinforcing the link between the bewitching appeal of culture or poetry (sweet as honey, intoxicating as the maddening music of subterranean flutes) and idolatry. The poet's response to this summons is to withdraw into silence and isolation. He flees to the foothills of the Thebaid, a region of the upper Nile valley (named after the ancient Egyptian city of Thebes), which was much favored from the third century onwards by early Christians seeking refuge from the pagan world; subsequently it came to be regarded as the cradle of the monastic, ascetic tradition.[48]

The significance of the idea of the Thebaid in Ivanov's spiritual development can be traced back to a much earlier period in his life. In his autobiographical poem, *Mladenchestvo* (*Infancy*), written mainly in 1913 and completed in 1918, he described an episode from his childhood which subsequently remained engraved in his memory; a monk appeared to him in a night-time vision, the purpose of which was apparently to impress on him, a future "beglets" ("fugitive") and "bludny syn" ("prodigal son"), that in later life he should always remember "o rodimoi Fivaide" ("about the native Thebaid").[49] Thus the Thebaid stands as an image of an ideal state of ascetic purity of spirit, to which the poet should aspire throughout life — an injunction which lies at the root of "Palinodiya."[50]

In this later poem, Ivanov finds that attempts to match the early ideal of spiritual purity now entail a withdrawal from the temptations of culture. Hence the contrast between the honey of Hymettus of the first line, representing the alluring sweetness of culture, and the "diky myod" ("wild honey") of the final line. The reference to the diet of St. John the Baptist in the wilderness suggests that asceticism or a retreat from artistic expression is a necessary preparation for spiritual growth and revelation.[51]

2.5. The "Palinode" and Pushkin

This final section of "Palinodiya" develops an aspect of Pushkin's well-known poem of 1826, "Prorok" ("The Prophet"). The Biblical source of Pushkin's poem (Isa. 6) describes the purification of Isaiah in preparation for his mission of prophecy to the people. By applying these terms to the description of the poet's calling, Pushkin establishes spiritual purity as a prerequisite of poetic activity, and poetic discourse as a sacred God-given form of language. For this reason the poem became one of the key texts most frequently cited by the Symbolists in support of their view of the theurgic power of art.

One can compare lines 11 and 12 of Ivanov's poem with the end of Pushkin's poem:

> Как труп в пустыне я лежал,
> И Бога глас ко мне воззвал:
> «Восстань, пророк, и виждь, и внемли,
> Исполнись волею моей,
> И, обходя моря и земли,
> Глаголом жги сердца людей.»[52]

Syntactically, lexically and metrically, there are many features in common. In Ivanov's poem as in Pushkin's, the call from heaven opens with a disyllabic imperative ("Pokin'," "Abandon"), and the verb "ispolnit'sya" ("to be filled") is also echoed. These similarities underline both poets' shared view of the poetic vocation as a form of spiritual calling, requiring the highest standards of purity and dedication.

However, there is an important difference in the way Ivanov develops the analogy. Whereas Pushkin's prophet is called upon to travel among the people and to set their hearts on fire with the Word, Ivanov's protagonist is charged with a different mission. His geographical space is not a journey over land and sea, but a retreat to the foothills of the Thebaid, and his spiritual tool is silence rather than speech. Both these changes indicate a withdrawal from the outgoing impulse of creativity in favor of an inward act of spiritual contemplation, the "poslushanie molchaniya" ("obedience of silence") characteristic of the poet in the 1920s.

Here Ivanov is developing an aspect of Pushkin's "Prorok," latent in other parts of the poem and closely in tune with the original Biblical theme of spiritual purification. The opening line of Pushkin's poem, "Dukhovnoi zhazhdoyu tomim..." ("Tormented by spiritual thirst...") was precisely the state which gave rise to Ivanov's "Palinodiya." Furthermore, Pushkin's poet, like the prophet Isaiah, submits to the removal of his tongue, described by three negative epithets, "greshny..., prazdnoslovny i lukavy" ("sinful..., given to idle speech and deceitful"). This awareness of the potentially sinful nature of human discourse is shared by both poets. The difference is that in Ivanov's poem the poet no longer claims the gift of prophetic speech.

The same point is illustrated by Ivanov's allusion to another poem by Pushkin, "Poet" ("The Poet"), written after a return to Mikhailovskoe in August 1827. Ivanov's response to the call to withdraw, "I ya bezhal, i em... / Molchan'ya diky myod" ("And I ran, and eat... / The wild honey of silence") echoes the conclusion of this poem, "Bezhit on, diky i surovy" ("He runs, wild and austere"). In both poems the renewal of inspiration is linked to the desire to withdraw, but whereas Pushkin's poet retreats to the burgeoning sounds of incipient creative activity, Ivanov's protagonist retires to unbroken silence. This preoccupation with the value of silence is reflected on the notebook pages of the first manuscript version of "Palinodiya"; at the top of the opposite page which carries a draft of a poem written at the same time, "Sobaki" ("Dogs"), Ivanov has scribbled the words "Silentsium luchshe" ("Silentium is better").[53]

January 1927, the month when "Palinodiya" was written, marked the ninetieth anniversary of Pushkin's death. Pushkin and his view of the poetic calling were evidently much on Ivanov's mind at this time. A few weeks after completing his "Palinode," on 10 February 1927, he commemorated this anniversary with the poem "Poeziya" ("Poetry"), later retitled "Yazyk" ("Language") (Ivanov 1971–, 3: 567). This profound meditation on the relationship between earth, poetry and language is linked to "Palinodiya" through its theme and reminiscences of the same Pushkinian texts.[54] Both poems are connected to Ivanov's view of Pushkin as a poet of "dukhovnoe trezvenie" ("spiritual sobriety") (Ivanov 1971–, 4: 342), a state of mind not far from that which informs the "Palinode."[55]

In this connection, it is interesting to note that in the final manuscript version of "Palinodiya" the text of the poem is followed by a fragment from Pushkin copied out in Ivanov's hand. The lines quoted are taken from Pushkin's unfinished drama of 1835, "Stseny iz rytsarskikh vremyon" ("Scenes from Knightly Times"), where they are sung in a mood of cheerful defiance by peasant scythe-men engaged in cutting down the grass. The fragment, as quoted by Ivanov, reads as follows:

Ходит вó поле коса,
Золотая полоса
Вслед за ней ложится.
Ой, ходи моя коса!
Сердце веселится.[56]

This manuscript copy of the poem may have been the one which Ivanov sent to his children in Rome. If so, the quotation from Pushkin may have been intended for them as a humorous postscript to his own poem, serving as a lighthearted counterpoint to the gravity of its subject and tone. Pushkin's trochaics convey a sense of almost childlike gaiety (accentuated by Ivanov's addition of an exclamation mark) at the decisive action of the scythe, levelling the grass which once grew in the field, a mischievous delight which the poet seems by implication to extend to his own decisive act of inner reorientation, leading to the creation of new spaces and of a new point of departure.[57]

3. CONCLUSION

It remains to relate the "Palinode" back to some of the general questions posed at the beginning of this essay, to determine exactly what, in the final analysis, Ivanov was recanting in his "Palinode," and to consider what relation this statement bore to his spiritual and poetic development as a whole. It is clear that the poem is not to be interpreted literally as a rejection of Hellenism, construed as a pagan, religious system. Ivanov never placed his faith in Greek religion in the same way as he did in Christianity; Dionysus was a precedent and a fruitful analogy, but never a substitute for Christian revelation. For Ivanov, Hellenism, apostrophized as "Hellas" in the "Palinode," was a synonym of culture, of the cultural tradition which stretched from Greece through Rome to modern Europe. In an early essay of 1907 he wrote of the "edinaya na dolgie veka sredizemnaya kul'tura; imya ei — ellinstvo. Net v Evrope drugoi kul'tury, krome ellinskoi, podchinivshei sebe latinstvo i donyne zhivoi v latinstve" (Ivanov 1971–, 3: 69–70).[58]

Why, then, if Ivanov intended by Hellenism to refer to the cultural tradition which it engendered, did he choose to couch his apparent rejection of this tradition in terms which belong to the language of idol worship? Clearly, he is using the latter as a metaphor for a certain attitude to culture from which he wishes to dissociate himself. Culture is likened to a form of idol worship in so far as it is man-made and can become an end in itself, an alternative form of religion, distracting the soul from higher pursuits and its ultimate goal. Ivanov referred to this facet of culture as its Luciferian aspect.[59] We saw above that this aspect was hinted at in "Palinodiya" through the images of line 6. The following extract from Ivanov's introduction to his essay of 1916 on Dostoevsky provides further clarification:

> действие в человеке люциферических энергий ... составляет естествен-
> ную в этом мире подоснову всей исторической культуры, языческой
> по сей день, и по истине первородный грех ее (ибо культура лишь
> отдельными частями «крещена» и только в редких случаях «во Христа
> облекается» ...). (1971–, 3: 250)[60]

Ivanov continues to demonstrate that the Luciferian aspect of culture is not necessarily fatal for humans on an ontological level, provided that they strive continuously to overcome the stagnation of set forms through the creation of new dynamic ones. Culture is thus defined as a process of eternal movement ("beg"). Considered in this light, the "Palinode" would appear to be describing a retreat from the need for such constant movement, a withdrawal from culture into the respite of silence. The poet is not engaging in any final rejection of culture, he is merely stepping back in order to redefine his approach more completely within a Christian context. To achieve this change of balance, he must first go through a period of temporary withdrawal and purification.[61] This reading links up with the interpretation which Deschartes gives to the poem in a succinct and penetrating note: "Pereotsenivaya svoyo prezhnee dukhovnoe sostoyanie, V.I. v 1927 g. napisal 'Palinodiyu', chtoby posle kratkogo otkaza ot gumanizma obresti ego v dukhe khristianstva, kak 'Docta Pietas'"[62] (Ivanov 1962, 216; 1971–, 3: 860). Following this line of interpretation, Ivanov's poem can be seen to combine both the meanings of the title discussed earlier: it is primarily a palinode of recantation, but can also be read as a palinodic refrain, for the rejection of Hellenism is but a step on the way to its renewed discovery.

In this sense "Palinodiya" can be regarded as a personal, poetic development of the concise formulation found in *Perepiska iz dvukh uglov*: "Mozhno stat' nishchim v dukhe, ne vovse zabyv samoe uchyonost'" (Ivanov 1971–, 3: 396).[63] Poverty of spirit as a positive attribute on the spiritual level does not necessarily require a rejection of Hellenic culture, but it does necessitate a profound inner reorientation and a refusal to invest culture with the characteristics of idol worship.

In this aspect of the "Palinode," Ivanov was consciously emulating the spirit of the early Church fathers, particularly St. Jerome and St. Augustine, whose contribution to the debate between Christianity and classical culture was briefly touched upon in the opening section of this essay. Both figures are referred to by Deschartes in connection with the "Palinode." In an early biographical sketch of Ivanov published in 1934, she cites a letter written by Ivanov in 1925 in which he stated that he felt a special sense of spiritual affinity with St. Augustine and regarded him as exerting a beneficial influence on his life. This feeling was strengthened during the years in Pavia, which, as Deschartes points out, was the burial-place of St. Augustine (Deschartes 1934, 407–08).[64] Golenishchev-Kutuzov's account of his meetings with Ivanov in 1927 and 1928 confirms the same point: "V.I. lived in great isolation. He was full of resignation. His favorite book was St. Augustine's *De civitate Dei*" (1935, 102).

* * *

Many years later, Ivanov provided a retrospective commentary on his "Palinode" in a poem of 1944, "S tekh por kak putnik u kresta…" ("Since the Time When the Pilgrim by the Cross…") (Ivanov 1971–, 3: 624). The first three stanzas of this revealing poetic autobiography are worth quoting as the stages which they outline correspond closely to those described in the "Palinode":

> С тех пор как путник у креста
> Пел "De Profundis", — , и печали,
> И гимнам чужды, одичали
> В безлирной засухе уста.
>
> Благословенный, вожделенный
> Я вновь увидел Вечный Град,
> И римским водометам в лад
> Взыграл родник запечатленный.
>
> Не на́долго. Был духу мил
> Отказ суровый Палинодий:
> Прочь от языческих угодий
> Он замысл творческий стремил.[65]

The chronological stages of the poet's spiritual and poetic development are mapped out as follows. Since the time of the writing of the cycle "De Profundis Amavi," broken off by the death of his third wife, Vera, in August 1920, the poet embarked on a period of "bezlirnaya zasukha" ("parched of verse"), bereft of both emotional and poetic inspiration. This corresponds to the phase of spiritual poverty described in lines 5–7 of "Palinodiya." When the poet arrived in Rome in 1924, the source ("rodnik") of poetic inspiration was unlocked once more, leading to the imagery of water released through fountains characteristic of the "Roman Sonnets" written at this time. This stage corresponds to the revival brought about by the music of the subterranean flutes referred to in lines 8–11 of the "Palinode."

This outpouring did not last for long, however. The third stanza of the poem directly takes up the word "palinodiya" in order to comment on the period of the poet's life with which that poem is concerned. The important point to note here is that the move away from pagan pleasures, associated with spiritual growth, is initiated by the soul's "zamysl tvorchesky" ("creative design"); the poet's spiritual development as a Christian was clearly inextricably linked to his creative development as an artist.

In this respect "Palinodiya" is a vivid illustration and confirmation of a point which the critic and philosopher Fedor Stepun put very well in his essay of 1936: Ivanov derived all his ideas from the analysis of his own creative work and poetry (Stepun 1936, 232).[66] "Palinodiya" is not an abstract theological statement. It stems from the poet's reflective meditation on the course of his own creative path, which interprets the period of poetic silence which descended on him in the 1920s as a positive step in the context of his spiritual development as a whole. One could go beyond this and add that Ivanov's frame of reference in the "Palinode," although autobiographical in the first instance, is in fact wider in scope and extends beyond the purely personal. The Pushkinian sub-text of the poem adds a broader historical dimension and suggests that Ivanov is making a more general statement about the future of Russian and European culture in its relation to Christianity. He is advocating the need to strive for a new balance between spiritual purity and artistic expression, to reach art through the spiritual rather than the spiritual through art, as the theurgic symbolists had once set out to do. In this Ivanov was shifting the balance back from the philological to the ontological, from culture to religion.[67]

NOTES

1. "There is no other culture in Europe, apart from Hellenic culture" (Ivanov 1971–, 3: 69–70). Unless otherwise stated, all translations are mine.
2. "Have I really, Hellas, stopped loving you?" (Ivanov 1971, 3: 553).
3. "... The soul found pleasure in / The stern denial of Palinodes: / Away from pagan pleasures / It sped its creative design" (Ivanov 1971, 3: 624).
4. For an outline of Zelinsky's approach to classical antiquity, see Zelinsky, 1903. The main focus of his essay on Ivanov (Zielinsky 1934) was the latter's role as a pioneer of the Slavonic renaissance. In 1933 Ivanov wrote a poem entitled

"Drugu gumanistu" in which he addressed Zelinsky as a fellow humanist with whom he had conspired "Daby v yuneishem plemeni zavetom / Zhil Dionisa novy svet" ("In order that amongst the youngest tribe through this testament / The new light of Dionysus should shine" Ivanov 1971–, 3: 530–31).

5. The relationship between classical antiquity and poetry was the subject of some polemical dispute between both poets. Annensky was critical of Ivanov's use of classical references and myth in his poetry (Annensky 1909). In the following year, Ivanov published his essay on Annensky's poetry (1910b). For a comparative study of both poets' approaches to classical tragedy and conflicting views of the function of the chorus, see Kelly, 1989.

6. In this respect Merezhkovsky provides the closest parallel (significantly, it was largely through his agency that Ivanov made his entrée into St. Petersburg literary circles). An aspect of his disagreement with Ivanov over the relationship of Christianity to classical antiquity will be discussed below.

7. The author would like to thank both the British Academy and the Leverhulme Trust whose generous support of research for a complete annotated bibliography of critical literature about Ivanov has facilitated work on this essay.

8. A book form edition of Ivanov's early lectures on Dionysus (1904a, 1905) was planned by the Sabashnikov publishing-house but perished in a fire in 1917. In Baku Ivanov published a further study of Dionysus (1923). He worked on correcting a German translation of this later work in the 1930s, but did not succeed in completing the revision (two chapters of the German text were published in *Castrum Peregrini* in 1961 in Heft 48 and in 1985 in Heft 168–69). For an analytic review of Ivanov's approach to classical antiquity, see Rudich, 1986. A summary of the formation of Ivanov's classical and Christian outlook is given in Davidson 1989, 25–33.

9. For Ivanov's own account of these events, see his "Avtobiograficheskoe pis'mo" (1971–, 2: 11–12, 14, 18–20).

10. "Masks are needed by those to whom the Face has not yet been revealed. But what is the point of masks when the Face already exists? What is the point of Dionysus of '*many names*' when 'there is none other name under heaven apart from *one* whereby we must be saved'? Or does Vyach. Ivanov not yet know this Name, has he not yet seen this Face?." Merezhkovsky's comments were related to Ivanov's essay "Poet i chern'," published in *Vesy*, 1904, no. 3. In the passage cited, he quotes from Acts 4:12, substituting "krome odnogo" ("apart from one") for "dannogo chelovekam" ("given among men"). All citations from the Bible in English are given according to the Authorized Version of King James.

11. "You, Who Exists, — are you not always present? and, Mysterious One, — not everywhere,— / In both the sacrificial clusters, and in the white sleep of lilies? / You are the smiling voice of the youthful reed-pipe; / You are Orpheus, mover of cliffs." Cited as in the original 1904 publication, to which Ivanov appended a note, relating images from the poem to New Testament sources and explaining that Orpheus was a common symbol of Christ in early Christian art.

12. "In his world philology imperceptibly replaces ontology.... For him, the gods and heroes of ancient Greece always take the place of the living creatures of our life and of eternal life. And for him any sort of Dionysianism is not a phenomenon of life, of our life and of eternal life, but a phenomenon of Greek culture, of Greek religion and mysticism, of Greek literature and art. He is familiar with the complex revelations of culture, but not with the simple revelations of existence.... And in his world the dividing-line between primary existence and reflected existence is constantly eroded. It is not the word which becomes flesh, but the flesh which becomes word, existence is transformed into word."

13. "He is too much immersed in the pagan element and in pagan culture to worry about the Christian problem of man." This essay is reprinted in Berdyaev, 1989, 3: 516–28, but with an incorrect reference to the newspaper issue of its original publication.

14. "His ideas and thoughts ... have absolutely no connection with what is normally called reality."

15. "A particularly great danger for him is the substitution of aesthetic values for religious ones, of an incorrect Apollonianism to which he is at times closer than he himself thinks" (from Bulgakov's essay of 1916 on *Borozdy i mezhi*, "Sny Gei"). In an earlier essay, "Khristianstvo i mifologiya," Bulgakov specifically addressed the question of the distinction between Christianity as a revealed religion and other forms of religious experience outside the sphere of revelation; in this context he praised Ivanov's deep insights into the mysteries of Hellenism and the creation of myth, relating his views to Schelling's understanding of the mythological process as a path to revelation (1918, 191–93).

16. Discussion of this question at a recent international symposium on Ivanov (University of Geneva, June 1992) erupted into a heated debate as to whether the cult of Dionysus was practiced in the present day as a live religious rite or not.

17. Schultze's essay, reprinted in several different versions between 1944 and 1950, sets out to demonstrate that Ivanov is a pure Christian, not tainted by the Dionysus phase, superseded at an early stage. A similar approach is taken by Tyszkiewicz. Fotiev describes Ivanov's development in terms of a progression from culture to religion, from Dionysus to Christ.

18. In August 1922 Ivanov wrote to Sologub "Ne vypuskaite iz ruk Vashei divnoi liry. Moya razbita" ("Do not let your magnificent lyre out of your hands. Mine is broken"). In December 1923, his step-son Sergei Shvarsalon explained Ivanov's silence to A.D. Skaldin in a letter: "Zdes′ V.I. drugoi; posle vsego, chto s nim bylo, on oblechyon poslushaniem molchaniya.... Poslushanie ne tol′ko v molchanii poeticheskom, no ochen′ gluboko" ("Here V.I. is different; after everything which has happened to him he is shrouded in the obedience of silence.... This obedience is not just in poetic silence, but goes very deep") (Lavrov, 1976: 149–50).

19. For an account of Ivanov's life in Pavia see O. Deschartes's introduction to the poet's collected works (Ivanov 1971–, 1: 175–76), and the memoirs of his daughter (Ivanova, 1990, 163–82), including valuable extracts from the letters Ivanov wrote to his children at this time. Details of the lectures and their dates are in Ivanova, 1990, 171–72.

20. See Ivanov's letter of 29 January 1927 (Ivanova 1990, 171–72).

21. "Otyezd v Paviyu byl pervoi razlukoi" ("The move to Pavia was the first separation") (Ivanova 1990, 164).

22. These aspects are indirectly reflected in Golenishchev-Kutuzov's letters to Ivanov. On 28 August 1928, he evoked the atmosphere of Ivanov's seclusion by recalling the "gor′koe blagoukhan′e bibliotechnoi Tebaidy" ("bitter fragrance of a bookish Thebaid"), quoting obliquely from "Palinodiya." Later on 3 February 1935 (not realising that Ivanov had by this time already left Pavia), he wrote "Chto vy pishete v Vashem velikolepnom uedinenii, napominayushchem pustynnichestvo Petrarki?" ("What are you writing in your magnificent solitude, reminiscent of Petrarch's hermetic seclusion?") (Shishkin 1989, 490, 514).

23. These were "Notturno" and "Pchela" (31 December 1926), and in 1927 "Kot vorozhei" (7 January), "Sobaki" (12 January), "Palinodiya" (14 January) and "Yazyk" (10 February). See Deschartes's notes to the poems of *Svet vecherny* (Ivanov 1971–, 3: 829, 839, 842, 843, 846) and Ivanova, 1990, 174, 176.

24. RAI (Rimsky arkhiv Vyacheslava Ivanova) (Rome archive of Vyacheslav Ivanov), MS, Tetrad′ 13, l. 6 ob., l. 7, l. 8 ob. (Notebook 13, leaf 6 verso, leaf 7 verso, leaf 8 recto); MS, Papka III (Folder III). I am grateful to Dimitry Ivanov and Andrei Shishkin for kindly supplying me with copies of these manuscript versions. The first notebook version (leaf 6 verso) is untitled and consists of two drafts of the first four lines of the poem, beginning with the line "Uzheli ya tebya, Ellada, razlyubil…" ("Have I really, Hellas, stopped loving you?…"), and continuing through until line 11 of the poem in its published form. It is followed on leaf 7 recto by a rough draft of Ivanov's poem "Sobaki." Neither text carries a title or date. The second and third versions (both on leaf 7 verso) correspond to lines 1–12 of the published poem. Both versions are untitled and begin with the same line as the final published text ("I tvoi gimetsky myod uzhel′ menya presytil?" "Have I really become sated with your honey from Hymettus?"). The fourth version (leaf 8 recto) is the first to carry a title ("Palinodiya") and date (14 January 1927); it is also the first to cover the complete text of the poem. In its overall structure and imagery it is substantially the same as the final published text; there are, however, several significant differences of phraseology and imagery. The final manuscript version of the poem is on a separate sheet, filed in RAI, Papka III (Folder III), containing miscellaneous original manuscript versions of poems by Ivanov. This may have been the copy of the poem which Ivanov sent to his children in Rome. It is almost identical to the published version, with only very few differences of which the most significant is the title, "Ellada," followed by a subtitle in brackets

"(palinodiya)." The text is dated 14 January 1927, and is followed by a five-line fragment quoted from Pushkin's "Stseny iz rytsarskikh vremyon."

25. The poem was published alongside five others ("Kot-vorozhei," "Slovo — plot'," later renamed "Yazyk," "Polden'," "Mitropolit Filipp" and "Novodevichy monastyr'"). Deschartes's note to the poem on its subsequent publication in *Svet vecherny* states: "Poyavilos' vpervye v Sovremennykh Zapiskakh, 1937, LXV" but does not mention the earlier published texts of 1930 (Ivanov 1962, 199, and 1971–, 3: 842).

26. These dates are given in Golenishchev-Kutuzov 1935, 102. I am grateful to Alexis Klimoff for kindly translating excerpts of the article for me. Further aspects of Ivanov's friendship and correspondence with Golenishchev-Kutuzov (1905–69) are covered in D.V. Ivanov 1982 (this article deals with the preface which Ivanov wrote in Pavia in 1931 for Golenishchev-Kutuzov's book of verse, *Pamyat'*, Paris, 1935) and in Shishkin 1988 and 1989 (the 1989 essay is a fuller version of the previous one, including the complete text of the correspondence from 1928 to 1937 with introduction and notes).

27. See Golenishchev-Kutuzov's letter to Ivanov of 31 March 1930, and Ivanov's reply of 24 April 1930 (Shishkin 1989, 494–99).

28. For the purposes of comparison the translations given below reproduce the word order of the original as closely as possible. The key differences in lines 8 and 9 are in italics:

— 1930 texts:

Kogda-zh, *v urochny chas, razymchivoi* igroi
Podzemnykh fleit ozhiv, lichiny poloi ochi

When, then, *at the fated hour*, having revived *through the intoxicating* sound
Of subterranean flutes, the eyes of the hollow mask

— 1937 text:

Kogda-zh, *podzemnykh fleit bezumyashchei* igroi
V urochny chas ozhiv, lichiny poloi ochi

When, then, having revived *through the maddening* sound of *subterranean flutes*
At the fated hour, the eyes of the hollow mask

— 1962 *Svet vecherny* text:

Kogda-zh, *podzemnykh fleit razymchivoi* igroi
V urochny chas ozhiv, lichiny poloi ochi

When, then, having revived *through the intoxicating* sound *of subterranean flutes*
At the fated hour, the eyes of the hollow mask

"Palinodiya" was included in the fifth section of *Svet vecherny*, after the two opening poems "Bezbozhie" and "Bogopoznanie," and immediately before "Sobaki" and "Vecherya lyubvi." This version was reprinted in the collected works (Ivanov 1971–, 3: 553).

29. The 1930 Italian versions of four poems by Ivanov were prefaced by a brief note by Papini without, however, any reference to the authorship of the translations. When Ivanov included "Palinodiya" in a letter to Metner of 18 December 1930

(GBL f. 167, k. 14, ed. khr. 10), he mentioned that an Italian translation had appeared in *Il Frontespizio* in 1930, but did not refer to it as his own (I would like to thank Michael Wachtel for drawing my attention to this point). On the other hand, since Papini knew no Russian, it would seem likely that Ivanov provided him with the translation. It was described as his a few years later, when reprinted with several other translations in *Il Convegno*; the Italian versions of "Palinodiya" and of two Roman sonnets were followed by the note "Traduzioni di Venceslao Ivanov"; this attribution was echoed on the title page and in a bibliographical note on p. 413. Another factor pointing to Ivanov's authorship of the translation is the fact that the Italian word "neòcoro" chosen to translate "sluzhitel'" ("devotee") in line 12 occurs in its Russian form "neokhor" ("one who sweeps a temple," "verger," from the Greek "neokoros") in the fourth manuscript version of the poem as one of the deleted variants of "sluzhitel'" (see note 24). However, Deschartes's note to the "Roman Sonnets" (Ivanov 1971–, 3: 849) suggests that Papini may in fact have had a hand in at least some of these translations. These conflicting indications are resolved by the account of Papini's role given by Lo Gatto. He records that Ivanov provided literal Italian versions of his poems from which Papini prepared verse translations of the "Roman Sonnets" for *Il Frontespizio*; Papini's verse translations appeared anonymously, however, as he knew no Russian and did not therefore wish to be named as the translator. Lo Gatto further notes that Ivanov's original literal versions were later published in *Il Convegno* (Lo Gatto 1971, 281). For further details of Ivanov's relations with Papini and his journal, see Ivanova 1990, 181.

30. A translation of this poem appeared in Rannit 1972, 285–86, but is too loose for the purposes of this essay. The following literal translation has taken into account the interpretation of certain passages in the Italian version.

   Palinode
1 Have I really become sated with your honey from Hymettus?
2 Who carried off your idol from the grove of myrtles?
3 Or did I break it myself in prophetic terror?
4 Have I really, Hellas, stopped loving you?
5 Yet, impoverished in spirit, I no longer knew your caresses,
6 And began to find awesome the masks of your immutable soul,
7 And the light of lofty bodies and the Euclidean structure of thoughts.
8 When, then, the eyes of the hollow mask, having revived at the fated hour
9 Through the intoxicating sound of subterranean flutes,
10 Filled once more, as in olden times,
11 With the restless longing of indomitable Night, — I heard a call from the heavens:
12 "Abandon, devotee, the ornate temple of demons."
13 And I fled, and eat in the foothills of the Thebaid
14 The wild honey of silence and tough locusts.

31. The noun comes from the Greek verb "palinoideo," meaning "to recant what has been said in an ode," or generally "to recant." It was first derived from an ode in which the Greek poet Stesichorus apologized for his earlier attack on Helen

of Troy. Plato recounts in the *Phaedrus* (243 A–B) that Stesichorus was struck blind after his first attack, but subsequently cured after composing a palinode.

32. The term "palinodiya" is not listed in Dal' or in any of the standard academic dictionaries. In Russian, apart from being used to refer to classical examples of the genre, it is best known as the title of an early seventeenth-century polemical work by archimandrite Zakhariya Kopystensky, offering an erudite defense of the Russian Orthodox faith against Catholicism and the Uniate creed (*Entsiklopedichesky slovar'* 1897, 631; *Polny pravoslavny bogoslovsky entsiklopedichesky slovar'* 1913, 1748).

33. RAI, Papka III (Folder III). See note 24.

34. The dual sense stems from two meanings of the Greek prefix "palin": "on the contrary, reversely," with an implication of opposition, and "again, once more," referring to repetition in time. In both Greek and Latin, the term "palinodia" derives its most common meaning of "retraction" from the first of these meanings, but following the second meaning it can also refer to a "refrain," a song taken up again, without any idea of opposition or contrast. Hence the term "palinodic," used to denote two systems of corresponding form in verse.

35. "Dlya etoi stroki vsyo stikhotvorenie kak budto i napisano i vsyo ono eyo 'obramlyaet'" ("It is as if the whole poem were written just for this line for which it serves as a 'frame'"). Adamovich's view that the rest of the poem adds no further significance to this line is, however, rather a distortion and ignores the subtlety of the argument.

36. RAI, Tetrad' 13, l. 6 ob. (Notebook 13, leaf 6 verso). See note 24.

37. The force of "uzhel'" is lost in Italian which lacks such a word and renders it more weakly and tentatively as "forse."

38. In the first manuscript version of "Palinodiya," the phrase "sladchaishy myod" ("sweetest honey") was used. RAI, Tetrad' 13, l. 6 ob. (Notebook 13, leaf 6 verso). See note 24.

39. "Only now have I understood, O holy Mercy, / That every sweet pleasure of years gone by / On the lips was honey, but in the womb was wormwood." The images recall Lucretius (quoted by Ivanov in the critical essays of *Po zvyozdam*), whose Epicurean philosophical message (wormwood) was conveyed by poetry (honey) (1.936–8).

40. "I will drink in the thick honey of your verse, but will experience once more the familiar aching sensation."

41. The key role of these images is reflected in the fact that they are present from the earliest manuscript versions of the poem through all its various drafts. The first version includes the phrases "siyayushchy kumir" ("shining idol") and "iz roshch moikh" ("from my groves"); in the third version the last phrase is changed to "iz roshch torzhestvennykh" ("from the solemn groves"). RAI, Tetrad' 13, l. 6 ob., l. 8 (Notebook 13, leaf 6 verso, leaf 8 recto). See note 24.

42. "budem prokhodit' mimo beschislennykh altarei i *kumirov* monumental'noi *kul'tury*, chastiyu lezhashchikh v zapustenii, chastiyu obnovlyonnykh i zanovo *ukrashennykh*, svoenravno ostanavlivayas' i zhertvuya na zabytykh mestakh" ("we shall pass by the countless altars and *idols* of monumental *culture*, some of them lying in neglect, others restored and newly *ornate*, pausing at our fancy and bringing sacrifices at forgotten places") (my emphasis).

43. RAI, Tetrad' 13, l. 6 ob., l. 7 ob., l. 8 (Notebook 13, leaf 6 verso, leaf 7 verso, leaf 8 recto); MS, Papka III (Folder III). See note 24.

44. "I esli on v svoei Palinodii otkazalsya ot dionisovykh tainstv, on ne otverg Apollona (stikhi: 'i tel nadmennykh svet i dum Evklidov stroi' — otrazhayut siyan'e ne dnevnogo boga, no vechernego Lyutsifera)" ("And if in his Palinode he turned away from the mysteries of Dionysus, he did not reject Apollo [the lines: 'and the light of lofty bodies and the Euclidean structure of thoughts' reflect the shining not of a daytime god, but of the evening Lucifer])" (Golenishchev-Kutuzov 1930a, 469).

45. This point is more fully explained in the concluding section of this essay.

46. In the published Russian versions of 1930 and 1962, the sound of the flutes is described by the adjective "razymchivy" ("intoxicating"). According to Dal', this adjective is derived from the verb "raznimat', raznyat'" or "razymat', razyyat'," meaning "to take apart into pieces"; in the expression "razymchivy sosed" it refers to a neighbor who breaks up all quarrels. When applied to drink, it acquires the meaning of "strong," "intoxicating," "exciting," "sharp." Pushkin used it in this sense in his poem of 1826, "K Yazykovu," to compare the source of his friend's poetic inspiration to a strong, intoxicating drink. Ivanov's use of the adjective follows Pushkin in linking the image of intoxication to the source of poetic inspiration. In 1937 he changed the adjective back to "bezumyashchy" ("maddening," from "bezumit'," "to drive a person mad, to deprive someone of their senses"); this was in fact the original adjective used in all five manuscript versions of the poem (see note 24). In *Svet vecherny* he reverted to "razymchivy." Both adjectives, like the Italian translation "inebriante suono," evoke the link with Dionysus, the god of intoxication, ecstasy and righteous madness.

47. For the links between Orpheus, Dionysus, and the figure of the poet, see "'Litso ili maska'?" the early poem of 1904 discussed above, "Orfei rasterzanny" (Ivanov 1971–, 1, 801–04) and "Ad Rosam," a later poem serving as the prologue to the fifth book of *Cor Ardens*, "Rosarium" (1971–, 2: 449–50).

48. According to St. Jerome, the first ascetic in the region was St. Paul of Thebes (c. 230–341), widely regarded as the earliest Christian hermit (Cross 1978, 1053, 1357).

49. "Ikonu l' krotkuyu svoyu / V dushe myatezhnoi i bezdomnoi / Khotel navek otpechatlet', / Chtob znal beglets, o chyom zhalet', — / Chtob o rodimoi Fivaide, / ... / Vospomnil v den' svoi, bludnyi syn?" *Mladenchestvo* XXXVII–XXXVIII (Ivanov 1971–, 1: 249).

50. In the fourth notebook manuscript version of the poem the phrase "v pustyne Fivaidy" ("in the desert of the Thebaid") was first introduced, then crossed out and replaced by "v predgor'yakh Fivaidy" ("in the foothills of the Thebaid"). While the use of the word "pustynya" ("desert") recalls the perception of this period of Ivanov's life as a type of spiritual Thebaid or "pustynnichestvo" ("hermitic seclusion") (see note 22), its replacement by "predgor'ya" ("foothills") emphasizes its positive function as a preparatory stage on the path of spiritual ascent. RAI, Tetrad' 13, l. 8 (Notebook 13, leaf 8 recto; see note 24).

51. For the link between the diet of St. John the Baptist and repentance see Mark 1:4, 6: "Yavilsya Ioann, krestya v pustyne i propoveduya kreshchenie pokayaniya dlya proshcheniya grekhov.... Ioann zhe ... el akridy i diky myod" ("John did baptize in the wilderness and preach the baptism of repentance for the remission of sins.... And John ... did eat locusts and wild honey").

52. "Like a corpse I lay in the desert. / And the voice of God called out to me: / 'Arise, o prophet, see and hear, / Be filled with my will / Go forth over land and sea, / And set the hearts of men on fire with your Word'" (translation from Obolensky 1965, 93).

53. RAI, Tetrad' 13, l. 7 recto (Notebook 13, leaf 7 recto). See note 24.

54. This poem was first published together with "Palinodiya" (Ivanov 1937, 165–66). For a detailed analysis, see Venclova, 1986.

55. "Pushkin ne byl 'mistikom', osobenno v sovremennom smysle etogo nerazborchivo upotreblyaemogo slova. Kak 'ottsy-pustynniki', on predpochital dukhovnomu khmelyu dukhovnoe trezvenie" ("Pushkin was not a 'mystic,' especially in the contemporary meaning of this incomprehensibly used word. Like the 'hermit-fathers' he preferred spiritual sobriety to spiritual intoxication"). From the essay of 1937, "Dva mayaka," a Russian version (with notable variations) of the Italian lecture published in the same year under the title "Gli aspetti del bello e del bene nella poesia del Pushkin."

56. "The scythe swings in the field, / The golden strip / In its wake lies down. / O, swing my scythe! / The heart is merry." RAI, Papka III (Folder III). See note 24. Ivanov was evidently quoting from memory, for he has substituted "zolotaya" ("golden") for Pushkin's "zelenáya" ("green") and added an exclamation mark at the end of the fourth line.

57. Such a humorous postscript would have been in keeping with Ivanov's character. His son, Dimitry Ivanov, informs me that "Palinodiya" was the subject of several family jokes, particularly with regard to the poet's diet of tough locusts.

58. "for many centuries a single Mediterranean culture; the name of which is Hellenism. There is no other culture in Europe, apart from Hellenic culture which subordinated the Latin world to itself and lives on to this very day in the Latin world."

59. "Lyutsifer, tvoryashchy kul'turu, — kakoyu my donyne eyo znaem" ("Lucifer, creating culture — as we know it to this day") (1971–, 3: 251).

60. "the operation within man of Luciferian energies ... constitutes the natural foundation in this world of the *entire culture of history, pagan to this day* (for culture has only been 'christened' in certain parts and only in rare instances 'puts on Christ')" (my emphasis). The last words paraphrase the Biblical verse "vse vy, vo Khrista krestivshiesya, 'vo Khrista obleklis'" ("as many of you as have been baptized into Christ have put on Christ") (Gal. 3:27).

61. This point was not always understood by Ivanov's contemporaries. Lidiya Ivanova records the outraged response of a former pupil of Ivanov's from Baku, Kseniya Kolobova. Upon receiving a copy of the "Palinode," on 16 November 1927 she wrote an indignant letter to Ivanov demanding an explanation for what she perceived as a total betrayal of Hellas. Lidiya Ivanova comments that her view was erroneous (1990, 176).

62. "Reappraising his earlier spiritual state, V.I. in 1927 wrote a 'Palinode' in order to rediscover humanism, after a brief rejection of it, in the spirit of Christianity, as a 'Docta Pietas.'"

63. "One can become poor in spirit without in the least forgetting one's learning." These words are echoed in line 5 of "Palinodiya" in the phrase "obnishchav dukhom" ("impoverished in spirit").

64. These points were later amplified, incorporating additional reference to St. Jerome, in Deschartes's introduction to the poet's collected works (Ivanov 1971–, 1: 175–76). Rannit's comments on the "Palinode" closely follow Deschartes's interpretation (1972).

65. "Since the time when the pilgrim by the cross / Sang 'De Profundis', — and lips foreign to sorrow / And to songs, / Grew wild, parched of verse. / The blessed, the longed for / Eternal City I saw again, / And in tune with the Roman fountains / The sealed source began to play. / But not for long. The soul found pleasure in / The stern denial of Palinodes: / Away from pagan pleasures / It sped its creative design." See Deschartes's note on this poem (Ivanov 1971–, 3: 860).

66. "Vyacheslav Ivanov nikogda ne pisal statei opredelyonno khristianskogo bogoslovskogo soderzhaniya. Iskhodnaya tochka zreniya vsekh razmyshlenii poeta — analiz sobstvennogo tvorchestva" ("Vyacheslav Ivanov never wrote essays with a specifically Christian theological content. The point of departure for all the poet's reflections was the analysis of his own art") (Stepun 1936, 232).

67. In connection with this shift of balance it is interesting to quote the later observation (first published in 1937) of the Russian religious philosopher, Georgii Florovsky. Commenting on Ivanov's creation of a new Christian myth in the light of the Dionysian religion, he wrote: "U nego eto skoree esteticheskaya skhema, chem religioznaya, no imenno religioznaya zhazhda i utolyaetsya zdes' esteticheskimi poddelkami.... To i bylo glavnoi opasnost'yu 'simvolizma', chto religiya zdes' prevrashchalas' v iskusstvo, pochti chto v igru, i v dukhovnuyu real'nost' nadeyalis' prorvat'sya pristupom poeticheskogo

vdokhnoveniya, minuya molitvenny podvig (slishkom mnogo grez i malo trezveniya)" ("In his case it was more of an aesthetic design, than a religious one, but it was a specifically religious thirst which satisfied itself with these aesthetic fabrications.... This was the main danger of 'symbolism': religion turned into art, almost into a game, and they hoped to break through into spiritual reality in a fit of poetic inspiration, bypassing the feat of prayer [too many dreams and not enough sobriety]") (1981, 458). Ivanov's "Palinodiya" derived from a recognition of this danger and conscious move towards greater spiritual sobriety. This move can also be linked with the earlier comments quoted above of contemporaries as varied as Merezhkovsky, Berdyaev, Shestov and Bulgakov.

WORKS CITED

Adamovich, Georgii. 1938. Review of *Sovremennye zapiski*, Kniga 65. *Poslednie novosti*, no. 6144, 20 January: 3.

Annensky, In. 1909. "O sovremennom lirizme." *Apollon*, no. 1 (October): 12–42 (first pagination).

Augustine, Saint. 1945. *The City of God (De Civitate Dei)*. Translated by John Healey. Edited by R.V.G. Tasker. Introduction by Ernest Barker. 2 vols. London: J.M. Dent.

Berdyaev, Nikolai. 1916. "Ocharovaniya otrazhyonnykh kul'tur." *Birzhevye vedomosti*, Utrenny vypusk, no. 15833, 30 September, 2–3.

_____. 1989. *Tipy religioznoi mysli v Rossii. Sobranie sochinenii*, Vol. 3, Paris: YMCA-Press.

Brown, Peter. 1967. *Augustine of Hippo: A Biography*. London: Faber and Faber.

Bulgakov, Sergei. 1918. *Tikhie dumy: Iz statei 1911–15 gg*. Moscow: Izdanie G.A. Lemana i S.I. Sakharova.

Cross, F.L. and E.A. Livingstone, Eds. 1978. *The Oxford Dictionary of the Christian Church*. 2nd ed. Oxford: Oxford University Press.

Davidson, Pamela. 1989. *The Poetic Imagination of Vyacheslav Ivanov: A Russian Symbolist's Perception of Dante*. Cambridge: Cambridge University Press.

Deschartes, O. 1934. "Cenni biografici." *Il Convegno*, Anno XIV, no. 8–12: 384–408.

Entsiklopedichesky slovar'. 1897. Vol. 22a. St. Petersburg: F.A. Brokgauz, I.A. Efron.

Ern, V. 1917. "O velikolepii i skeptitsizme (K kharakteristike adogmatizma)." *Khristianskaya mysl'* (Kiev), March–April: 163–86.

Florovsky, Georgii. 1981. *Puti russkogo bogosloviya*. Second edition. Paris: YMCA-Press.

Fotiev, K. 1964. "Ierarkhiya blagogoveniya: (Zametki o tvorchestve Vyacheslava Ivanova." *Grani*, no. 55: 222–28.

_____. 1988. "'Dionis i pradionisiistvo' v svete noveishikh izyskanii." In Kul'tura i pamyat'. *Trety mezhdunarodny simpozium, posvyashchyonny Vyacheslavu Ivanovu.* Edited by Fausto Malcovati. *Zapiski fakul'teta literatury i filosofii Paviiskogo universiteta*, no. 45. Vol. 2, *Doklady na russkom yazyke*. Florence: La Nuova Italia Editrice, 163–70.

Golenishchev-Kutuzov, Ilya. 1930a. "Lirika Vyacheslava Ivanova." *Sovremennye zapiski* 63: 463–71.

_____. 1930b. "Otrechenie ot Dionisa: Vyacheslav Ivanov." *Vozrozhdenie*, no. 1857, 3 July: 3–4.

_____. 1935. "Dostojevski i Vjacheslav Ivanov." *Srpski knizhevni glasnik* (Belgrade), Nova serija XLVI, Br. 2, 16 September, 100–09.

Ivanov, D.V. 1982. "Vyacheslav Ivanov i Ilya Golenishchev-Kutuzov." In *Russica — 81: Literaturny sbornik*. New York: Russica, 379–87.

_____. 1989. "Martin Buber i Vyacheslav Ivanov." In *Russian Literature and History*. Edited by Wolf Moskovich, Jonathan Fraenkel, Victor Levin, Samuel Shvarzband, Jerusalem: Hebrew University of Jerusalem, 151–54.

Ivanov, Vyacheslav. 1904a. "Ellinskaya religiya stradayushchego boga: Opyt religiozno-istoricheskoi kharakteristiki." *Novy put'* 1 (January): 110–34; 2 (February): 48–78; 3 (March): 38–61; 5 (May): 28–40; 8 (August): 17–26; 9 (September): 47–70.

_____. 1904b. "'Litso — ili maska'?" *Novy put'* 10 (October): 165.

_____. 1905. "Religiya Dionisa: Eyo proiskhozhdenie i vliyaniya." *Voprosy zhizni* 6 (June): 185–220; 7 (July): 122–48.

_____. 1910a. *De societatibus vectigalium publicorum populi romani. Zapiski Klassicheskogo Otdeleniya Imperatorskogo Arkheologicheskogo Obshchestva*, vol. VI, Prilozhenie. St. Petersburg.

_____. 1910b. "O poezii I.F. Annenskogo." *Apollon*, no. 4 (January): 16–24 (second pagination).

_____. 1923. *Dionis i pradionisiistvo*. Baku.

_____. 1930. "Il Paradiso terrestre," "Palinodia," "Regina Viarum," "Monte Pincio." *Il Frontespizio*, September, VIII: 5.

_____. 1934. "Palinodia." *Il Convegno*, Anno XIV, no. 8–12: 368.

_____. 1937. "Palinodiya." *Sovremennye zapiski* 65: 164–65.

_____. 1962. *Svet vecherny*. With an introduction by Sir Maurice Bowra and commentary by O. Deschartes. Edited by Dimitri Ivanov. Oxford: Clarendon Press.

_____. 1971–. *Sobranie sochinenii*. Edited by D.V. Ivanov and O. Deschartes. 4 vols. Brussels: Foyer Oriental Chrétien.

Ivanova, Lidiya, 1990. *Vospominaniya: Kniga ob ottse*. Edited by John Malmstad. Paris: Atheneum.

Kelly, Catriona. 1989. "Classical Tragedy and the 'Slavonic Renaissance': The Plays of Vyaceslav Ivanov and Innokentij Annenskij Compared." *Slavic and East European Journal* 33, no. 2: 235–54.

Lampe, G.W.H., Ed. 1961. *A Patristic Greek Lexicon*. Oxford: Clarendon Press.

Lavrov, A.V., Ed. 1976. "Vyacheslav Ivanov. Pis'ma k F. Sologubu i An. N. Chebotarevskoi." *Ezhegodnik rukopisnogo otdela Pushkinskogo doma na 1974 god*. Leningrad: Nauka, 136–50.

Lo Gatto, Ettore. 1971. *Russi in Italia: Dal secolo XVII ad oggi*. Rome: Editori Riuniti.

Merezhkovsky, D. [D.M.]. 1904. "Za ili protiv?" *Novy put'* 9 (September): 268–72.

Obolensky, Dimitri, Ed. 1965. *The Penguin Book of Russian Verse*. Harmondsworth: Penguin Books.

Polny pravoslavny bogoslovsky entsiklopedichesky slovar'. 1913. Vol. 2. St. Petersburg: Izdatel'stvo P.P. Soikina.

Rannit, Aleksis. 1972. "Vyacheslav Ivanov and His *Vespertine Light:* Notes from My Critical Diary of 1966." *Russian Literature Triquarterly* 4 (Fall): 265–88.

Rudich, Vasily. 1986. "Vyacheslav Ivanov and Classical Antiquity." *In Vyacheslav Ivanov: Poet, Critic and Philosopher*. Edited by Robert Louis Jackson and Lowry Nelson, Jr. New Haven: Yale Russian and East European Publications, 275–89.

Schultze, Bernardo. 1949. "Ivanov." In *Pensatori russi di fronte a Cristo: Saggi sul loro atteggiamento verso Cristo, la Chiesa e il Papa*. Biblioteca dell'Oriente Cristiano. Vols. II and III. Florence: Mazza, 253–73.

Shestov, L. 1916. "Vyacheslav Velikolepny: K kharakteristike russkogo upadochnichestva." *Russkaya mysl'* 10: 80–110 (second pagination).

Shishkin, Andrej. 1988. "Vjaceslav Ivanov ed i giovani poeti dell'emigrazione russa: Corrispondenza con I.N. Goleniscev-Kutuzov." In *Cultura e memoria: Atti del terzo Simposio Internazionale dedicato a Vjaceslav Ivanov*. Edited by Fausto Malcovati. Pubblicazioni della Facoltà di lettere e filosofia dell'Università di Pavia, no. 45. Vol. 1, *Testi in italiano, francese, inglese*. Florence: La Nuova Italia Editrice, 211–23.

_____. 1989. "Perepiska V.I. Ivanova i I.N. Golenishcheva-Kutuzova." *Europa Orientalis* 8: 481–526.

Stepun, Fedor. 1936. "Vyacheslav Ivanov." *Sovremennye zapiski* 62: 229–46.

Tyszkiewicz, T. 1950a. "L'ascension spirituelle de Wenceslas Ivanov." *Nouvelle Revue Théologique* (Tournai and Paris), 72, no. 10 (December): 1050–62

_____. 1950b. "Orthodoxie und Humanismus: Wjatscheslaw Iwanows Weg nach Rom." *Wort und Wahrheit* (Vienna), Year 5, no. 6 (June): 431–42.

Venclova, Tomas. 1986. "'Jazyk': An Analysis of the Poem." In *Vyacheslav Ivanov: Poet, Critic and Philosopher*. Edited by Robert Louis Jackson and Lowry Nelson, Jr. New Haven: Yale Russian and East European Publications, 108–22.

Zelinsky, F. 1903. *Drevny mir i my*. Izvlecheno iz Zhurnala Ministerstva Narodnogo Prosveshcheniya za 1903 g. St. Petersburg: Senatskaya tipografiya.

Zielinsky, Taddeo. 1934. "Introduzione all'opera di Venceslao Ivanov." *Il Convegno*, Anno XIV, no. 8–12: 241–51.

SOVIET RUSSIA THROUGH THE LENS OF CLASSICAL ANTIQUITY: AN ANALYSIS OF GRECO-ROMAN ALLUSIONS AND THOUGHT IN THE OEUVRE OF VASILII GROSSMAN

Frank Ellis, University of Leeds

> This makes one deride the stupidity of people who believe that today's authority can destroy tomorrow's memories. On the contrary, repressions of genius increase its prestige. All that tyrannical conquerors, and imitators of their own brutality, achieve is their own disrepute and their victims renown.
>
> Cornelius Tacitus, *Annals* (4:34)

Notwithstanding the very best efforts of the literary commissars and a handful of disgruntled and vociferous anti-Semites, Vasilii Grossman has emerged from the *glasnost'* period of the late eighties as one of the outstanding names of Soviet Russian literature. The Stalingrad epic, *Zhizn' i sud'ba* (*Life and Fate*), and the clinical annihilation of the Lenin cult in *Vsyo techyot* (*Everything Flows*), are literary and philosophical accomplishments of the first magnitude.[1] In his incisive analysis of Soviet ideology and its consequences Grossman stands alongside Pasternak, Bulgakov and Solzhenitsyn.

Until well into the eighties Grossman was largely ignored by Western scholarship. *Vsyo techyot* failed to ignite the kind of scholarly debate that one

would have expected, and many Western publishers were indifferent towards
Zhizn' i sud'ba. Scholarly lack of interest in *Vsyo techyot* when it was first
published in the West is especially startling and baffling. Two factors help to
account for this neglect.

Firstly, there is Grossman's exposition of Russia's millennial history.
Anti-communists could welcome attacks on Lenin and Soviet Russia, but his
evident hostility to the notion of Russia's unique spiritual qualities was
deeply offensive to many émigré writers and publishers. Solzhenitsyn, a
nationalist exile, scourge of the CPSU and Nobel prize-winning author to
boot, was the name who more than any other came to symbolize the hopes
and fears of those struggling for Russia's freedom.

Secondly, left-wing ideologies of various hues still commanded a considerable following in the West. True, Lenin is the focal point of Grossman's
attack on ideology in *Vsyo techyot*, but Hegel and Marx do not escape
censure. So, Grossman, resented by Russian nationalists, dwarfed by the
fame of Solzhenitsyn, and in open dispute with the architects of socialism,
remained in limbo.[2]

However much neglected, *Vsyo techyot* was at least published, unlike
Zhizn' i sud'ba which fell into the hands of the KGB. Throughout *Zhizn' i
sud'ba* Grossman relentlessly draws the parallels between Stalin's Russia
and Hitler's Germany. Both states are linked in a spiral of totalitarian
collusion: the mass murder of Russian peasants adumbrates Eichmann's
Final Solution of the Jewish Question; Hitler's prophylactic removal of the
Röhm faction hints at the Great Terror and the purge of the military; and
towering above both systems is the omnipotent and wise leader, guided by
an infallible ideology.

Such was the substance of the novel that Grossman submitted for publication in 1960. The subsequent drama surrounding the novel is a gripping and
moving tale in its own right. Having read the manuscript, Semen Lipkin, one
of Grossman's lifelong friends, was quite convinced: no Soviet journal
would ever touch *Zhizn' i sud'ba*.[3] The guardians of Soviet literature obviously shared Lipkin's assessment. On 14 February 1961, worried that Grossman might be tempted to send the manuscript abroad, as Pasternak had done
with *Doktor Zhivago* (*Doctor Zhivago*), the KGB arrested all remaining
copies of the novel. Rough drafts, carbon paper and typewriter ribbons were
seized. A letter to Khrushchev and an interview with Suslov, the party's chief
ideologist, failed to secure the release of the manuscripts. In disgrace Grossman fought a bitter battle for literary survival until his death on 14 September
1964.

Apostasy is a theme of abiding intellectual interest. What causes a moderately successful, and by all appearances, conventional writer to tread the lonely and dangerous path towards heresy? For our present theme it is a relevant question. Various answers have been forthcoming.

Many Western scholars, including Grossman specialists, have argued that the war must be seen as the turning point in Grossman's relationship to Soviet power.[4] Further radical reassessments, it is claimed, were forced on the author in the wake of the *Zhdanovshchina*, the state orchestrated Doctors' Plot of 1952–53 and Khrushchev's partial denunciation of Stalin in 1956. The significance of the war and the post-war ideological crackdowns for Grossman needs no disputing. It is my belief, however, that we must turn to the pre-war period, specifically the late thirties, in order to identify the origins of the heretical conclusions expressed in *Zhizn' i sud'ba* and *Vsyo techyot*.

By 1939, Soviet society had been turned upside down. Millions had perished in the collectivization drive. Successive waves of terror had struck at writers and the intelligentsia, the army and the party apparat itself. Society in any meaningful sense had all but ceased to exist. In its place were millions of fragmented groups and individuals, fearful and compliant. Literature in such a repressive climate either fights for its very existence, or falls silent. Many writers were indeed silenced during the Terror. The survivors, where they had not been totally cowed into submission, waged a very unequal battle for artistic integrity.

Much of Grossman's work in this period can be regarded as standard Soviet fare. Glorification of heavy industry, miners, indefatigable shock workers, party activists and civil war veterans are recurring characters and themes. Yet in a number of stories, a long novel and a play written before the war, one can detect a definite unease with the new Soviet Union which had emerged from Stalin's bloody experiment.[5] Classical thinkers, among them, Cornelius Tacitus, Pythagoras of Samos and Heraclitus of Ephesus, in *Stepan Kol'chugin*, a Soviet *Bildungsroman*, and the play, *Esli verit' pifagoreitsam* (*If you Believe the Pythagoreans*), provide the opportunity for Grossman to question, albeit in camouflaged form, the claims of Soviet officialdom.[6]

Greco-Roman civilization and culture are at once a challenge and an opportunity for the founding fathers of Soviet ideology. Hegel, Engels, Marx and Lenin could nod approvingly at the growth of a class struggle in the Greek city. Slavery, too, offered rich pickings for the aetiology of class warfare. Likewise, Roman imperialism could be cited as the historical template for European colonial expansion in the nineteenth century. But the legacy of these two ancient civilizations in law, art, civil administration, science, philosophy and mathematics had to be accounted for within the framework of the emerging philosophy of dialectical materialism. It had to be demonstrated that, flawed as these civilizations were, the engine of history, which would at some unspecified time lead to the classless society, had spluttered into life in the cities of Greece and Rome.

Hence, allusions to classical thinkers are not *per se* subversive of Soviet ideology. Certain figures, such as Aristotle, Democritus, Plato, Archimedes, Epicurus, the Stoics and Heraclitus enjoy considerable standing in the party's analysis of pre-Marxist history.[7] References and allusions could quite reasonably be a confirmation of faith in the established interpretation. Clearly, the choice of writer, historian or philosopher, and context are the key.

References to ancient writers did, however, open up other possibilities. Forced to contend with an all-embracing censorship, Soviet writers, like their Tsarist predecessors, developed and refined certain techniques to circumvent the censor. Use of historical allusions is a tried and tested method. Problems in distant or ancient cultures and civilizations serve as a platform on which to expose, or draw attention to, shortcomings in the writer's own time and society. This, I believe, is Grossman's intention in referring to Tacitus and Pythagoras. By the time Grossman comes to write *Vsyo techyot*, the Tacitean mask has been discarded. Approaching death, and by now totally free from the debilitating influence of Soviet ideology, Grossman is able to embark upon a fearless and remorseless analysis of Soviet society, and its founder Lenin. Truth and the freedom to speculate beyond the limits of party orthodoxy no longer need to be protected by a bodyguard of allusions and Aesopian language.

But that was still to come. Writing before the war, Grossman had to be far more circumspect. Thus, in interpreting the elusive and at times ambiguous tone of *Esli verit' pifagoreitsam*, we need to proceed with caution. The problem is twofold: (i) to what extent do the Pythagoreans serve as an allegory of certain features of Soviet society? (ii) what are the implications, if any, of Pythagorean discoveries and research for Soviet ideology?

The title of Grossman's play would have seemed most unusual, even provocative, to a Soviet reader who throughout the thirties and forties had been fed a diet of socialist-realist novels and odes to Stalin. Curious readers would have been stimulated to find out more about the Pythagoreans (Grossman's intention no doubt). Founded by Pythagoras of Samos, the Pythagorean brotherhood embraced a heady amalgam of mysticism and rationalism. Remote from the common people, they were an intellectual élite, delighting in the pursuit of knowledge, which was not shared with the uninitiated. Membership involved drastic limitations of personal freedom. To quote Walter Burkert: "Everywhere are rules, regulations, and an ascetic zeal for discipline" (1972, 191). Towering above the brothers is the figure of

Pythagoras himself. Few commentators, even if they are skeptical of Pythagorean achievements, doubt the charismatic appeal of the founder. To him
are attributed a number of remarkable happenings which lack any rational
explanation. Thus, he is seen at the same hour, and on the same day in both
Croton and Metapontum; one of his thighs is seen to be made of gold; he is
able to stroke a white eagle; he bites a poisonous snake to death.

The Pythagoreans believed that the master's words and thoughts were
divinely inspired. Such overwhelming and uncontested authority, backed up
by a plethora of taboos and personal restrictions, ensured quite a striking
consensus of opinion and submission to the master. To the outsider accus-
tomed to disagreements and conflict, the degree of unanimity among the
Pythagoreans must have seemed somewhat bewildering. However, at a
fundamental level, Peter Gorman's explanation is convincing: "The idea of
the unity of minds and belongings is ultimately inspired by the mystical
intuition that there is one true interpretation of reality" (1979, 117).

By now, the Pythagoreans and their leader suggest some intriguing parallels. A fiercely guarded, esoteric and jealously interpreted body of knowledge, the belief that there is one true interpretation of reality and the charismatic leader are recognizable features of Soviet reality. The party asserted an
absolute right to be the interpreter of dialectical materialism, the final
exegesis of historical progress and reality. Where disputes did arise they were
solved by recourse to the authority of Lenin, or his disciple Stalin. In the eyes
of their followers, Pythagoras, Lenin and Stalin are the universal geniuses of
their time.

Historical and biographical details in the lives of both Pythagoras and
Lenin strengthen this parallel. Frank Vatai has observed:

> The activists, the exile and the prophet: all three of these postures were
> dictated by the turbulent political events of the sixth and early fifth century in
> Asia Minor. All three postures were adopted by ... Pythagoras of Samos.
> (1984, 34)

So too for Lenin, who was no stranger to political activism and exile before
his final, triumphant emergence as the undisputed prophet and leader of the
world's proletariat.

One further aspect of the Pythagorean school would seem to have some
relevance for Soviet Russia. After Pythagoras died, the school split into two
sects. The Acousmatics, or Pythagorists, preserved the mystical idea of his
teaching, whereas the Mathematicians concentrated on the scientific aspects.[8] Of the two halves the Mathematicians were better grounded in the
teachings of Pythagoras. The Acousmatics had only studied a summary of

the master's works. One is tempted to see the split among the Pythagoreans functioning as an allusion to that which occurred in the Communist Party after Lenin's death. Trotsky, the brilliant theorist, and himself a mathematician, could easily assume the role of the Mathematicians' leader, while Stalin's more mediocre talents in this direction, combined with his pragmatism, invite comparison with what is represented by the Acousmatics.

In *Esli verit' pifagoreitsam* Grossman develops an idea which first appeared in embryonic form in *Stepan Kol'chugin*; namely that historical phenomena are repeated *ad infinitum*. Grossman quotes from Claudius' speech to the Roman Senate as recorded in Tacitus' *Annals*: "Everything, honoured senators, that today is considered old, was once new ... and that which today we affirm with examples, will itself become an example" (Tacitus 1989, 11:24).[9] The title and one of the play's main themes allude to an apocryphal remark made by the Greek teacher, Eudemius, which is quoted by Grossman from Theodore Gomperz, the well-known classical scholar: "If we are to believe the Pythagoreans, I shall once more gossip among you, with this little staff in my hand, and again as now ye will be sitting before me, and likewise will it be with all the rest" (Gomperz 1901, 140).[10] This idea is not unique to the Pythagorean school of philosophy. We find it among the ideas of Anaximander, Heraclitus and Empedocles, and it manifests itself in the modern era in Nietzsche's ideas of eternal recurrence.

Pythagorean ideas on time are not easily reconciled with Lenin's historicism. Marxist–Leninist teleology is predicated on the belief that time is linear. Such an assumption is indispensable for its utopian ideology. Indeed, the same belief in the linear progression of time underpins much of the ethos of Western capitalism. Cyclical time is inimical to both systems. For cyclical time would mean that history was a series of events doomed to be repeated in an endless cycle of millennia. Wars, poverty and famine, afflictions which both political systems claim to be able to surmount, would thus be an ineradicable feature of the human condition. Progress towards a unique and strife-free world would be a mirage.

Furthermore, Pythagorean researches in the field of mathematics led to the important discovery that the root of 2 was irrational. If irrationality inheres in mathematics, the indispensable tool of scientific enquiry, then perhaps skepticism towards scientific communism was not entirely misplaced. Indirectly, Grossman adopts a similar line to that taken by Zamyatin, who in *My* (*We*) cleverly exploited concepts of irrationality to cast doubt upon the advocates of a crude rationalism.[11] Through the Pythagoreans, Grossman suggests that Soviet notions of progress — and consequently the justification for wholesale social engineering irrespective of the human cost — rest on criteria whose scientific and rational status is more apparent than real. If these inferences are correct, then from the standpoint of Soviet orthodoxy certain Pythagorean ideas undoubtedly lead to heresy.

Yet the indictment of heresy cannot be consistently applied. Having made the discovery that the square root of 2 was irrational, the Pythagoreans suppressed it. An even greater doctrinal crisis arose from one of the key Pythagorean concepts: that of the dualism of limited and unlimited. It proved impossible to apply the polarity of odd and even to geometry. The major stumbling block was the reconciliation of unrelated pairs, a problem which was unconvincingly resolved by equating odd numbers with limited, and even with unlimited. Grossman was well aware of this conundrum among the Pythagorean mathematicians. In *Stepan Kol'chugin*, whose final chapters are in many respects the most interesting, and which are contemporaneous with the writing of *Esli verit' pifagoreitsam*, one can locate specific references to the question:

> In Classical Antiquity the Pythagorean school, having discovered the fundamental ratios between figures, worshipped them: "two," "three," and "four." Even corresponds to the unlimited, uneven to the limited, love to an octave. There we are, the mysticism of the numbers! The fascination of numbers! (1951, 340)

Discrepancies between prediction and result in the Pythagorean doctrine of limited and unlimited find a cogent parallel in the disparity between Marxist–Leninist theory and practice (of course such discrepancies are by no means unique to these two systems of thought). Moreover, since the discovery of flaws and inconsistencies originated from within the school itself, Grossman's Pythagorean analogue implies not merely heresy — which while it has negative connotations from the standpoint of orthodoxy, at least suggests intellectual integrity — but hypocrisy and treacherous cynicism. The Party's right to power stems from the claim that it, and it alone, is the moral and intellectual heir to Lenin, that it believes in Lenin's teachings. In Stalin's Russia these considerations are of little consequence. Thus the arch-heretics, if one may apply such a term here, are not those who question the precepts of Marxism–Leninism, but those in authority, who, realizing that it is bankrupt, nevertheless continue to implement it in a form suitable to their needs.

Lenin and subsequent ideologists attack the Pythagoreans because of their number theory, their idealism, or their hostility to change.[12] Differences in philosophy, however, should not distract us from fundamental congruencies in organizational structure and ethos. The fact is that, in their reforming zeal, discipline and tightly knit brotherhood, the Pythagoreans are an effective

model of an organization dedicated to a social experiment. Does Lenin
recognize and resent these similarities? And, if so, may we see this as the real
source of hostility towards the Pythagorean sect? For from this perspective
Lenin and his party appear as just another brotherhood claiming to have
solved the mysteries of being.[13] Despite its pretensions to scientific precision
and rigor, Marxism–Leninism shares many of the flaws which can be identified in Pythagoreanism:

> Pythagorean philosophy is basically mystical and intuitive, rather than scien-
> tific and rationalistic. It is rational because it offers arguments for its mystical
> conclusions and does not rely on faith or credulousness like revealed religion;
> and yet it is irrational or supernatural in its insistence on the reality of the
> unseen as opposed to the visible, whether these invisibles be the music of the
> spheres or the cosmos of divine numbers or the ecstatic vision of the One.
> (Gorman 1979, 3–4)

The main advocate of the cyclical view of time in *Esli verit' pifagoreitsam*
is the ageing engineer Shatovskoi, who throughout the play repeats variations on the following: "All life is subordinated to the great law of circular
time" (Grossman 1946, 75). Having lived through the First World War and
the Revolution, he has ample grounds for viewing the optimism of Varnavitsky, his ideological counterpart, with skepticism. For his part Varnavitsky
rejects Shatovskoi's fatalism. He does not accept that "people are doomed to
repeat the weaknesses and imperfections of past generations.... Our strength
is in movement, our victory is in movement, while we live we go forwards"
(1946, 87). War in Europe vitiates this confident claim. When Grossman was
writing *Esli verit' pifagoreitsam* Russia was not yet at war, but German
military successes in the Mediterranean, and the bombing campaign against
British cities were closely followed in the Soviet Union.
  Shatovskoi regards the war between Britain and Germany as a rerun of
World War One. This would appear to be a conventional stance. From the
official Soviet standpoint the war between Germany and Britain was simply
war between two deadly capitalist rivals. Cyclical time adds a new dimension. If the war is, as Shatovskoi claims, a repetition of World War One, then
this must mean that at some stage Germany and Russia will come to blows.
According to the pattern of World War One, Russia would lose, with all the
consequences that would entail for Stalin's survival. In the relationship
between the two World Wars lurks the inference that Stalin might fall in the
event of a German invasion. At the very least there would seem to be
criticism of Soviet foreign policy in the form of the Molotov–Ribbentrop
pact implied here. This latter point finds some support in Shatovskoi's

statement that "once again Russia stands before a great war" (1946, 75). Grossman seems to have harbored no illusions as to Germany's real intentions. That the play was due to be given a public reading (*chitka*) on 23rd June 1941 is not without some irony.

The arguments between Shatovskoi and Varnavitsky resemble a religious dispute. Here, the theme of belief, referred to in the title, assumes special importance. Shatovskoi does not assert dogmatically the conventions of the Pythagoreans. He views them with healthy skepticism while seeking evidence to support them. His approach is that of the scientist. Acceptance of the Pythagoreans is partially conditioned by his loss of faith in success, which in the context of the play, is synonymous with progress. But it is also the search for explanations which the prophets of Marx and Lenin seem unable to provide.

Belief in progress is the cornerstone of Varnavitsky's political philosophy. His rebuttal of the Pythagoreans raises interesting questions: "But another great ancient philosopher taught that life goes forward in a mighty flood" (1946, 76). Why, one wonders, does Varnavitsky not quote from the copious writings of Marx, Lenin, or even Stalin, in order to make his point? After all, the idea of progress which he advocates is founded on the principles of dialectical materialism, allegedly the highest stage in man's political consciousness. If the idea of forward movement or progress was also expounded on in the ancient world, its modern adherents can hardly claim it to be an original discovery of socialist thought. By referring to an ancient philosopher (most likely Heraclitus), Varnavitsky inadvertently confirms the Pythagorean aphorism, the validity of which he seeks to deny. Ideas as well as physical phenomena repeat themselves.

Varnavitsky refers to the law of forward movement as a "great, stern law," adding that, "nobody in the world believes in it as we do" (1946, 76). Faith is the essence of the doctrine. Varnavitsky offers no verifiable evidence, no scientific proof, to support the existence of a law of forward movement; it cannot be deduced from experience. To quote J.B. Bury, a trenchant critic of these ideas:

> The Progress of humanity belongs to the same order of ideas as Providence or personal immortality. It is true or it is false, and like them it cannot be proved either true or false. Belief in it is an act of faith. (Bury 1928, 4)

Varnavitsky's arguments are highly subjective and betray all the signs of the religious fanatic. Having assumed the existence of a law of forward movement, he deifies it as "great and stern." Epithets such as this belong to a god. But for Varnavitsky this is exactly what progress is. It is, as Bury observes, the new *idolum saeculi* for which no sacrifice is too great (1928, vii). Those who do not believe are heretics or madmen: "Only madmen will get it into their heads that we will tire. Our wisdom resides in motion" (Grossman 1946, 76).

"Wisdom in motion" reflects the strength and weakness of the current philosophy. The relentless forward movement brushes aside all opposition. No rational discussion of the issues is tolerated. All dissent is crushed. In the words of Mikhail Heller, the Plan "became an ethical category, which explained and justified the behaviour of the builders of the new world" (Heller 1988, 71). Yet the longer the process continues, the greater the number of victims. The notion of progress, now married to theories of regeneration, becomes indispensable to stifle their cries, justifying still greater sacrifice. Hence the reason why Shatovskoi calls the flow of life "cruel," not "great" as does Varnavitsky (Grossman 1946, 73). Varnavitsky's obsession with movement and progress reflects the same passionate commitment which we find in Mostovskoi and Krymov, two prominent party members in *Zhizn' i sud'ba*. Passion masks a deep-seated flaw. In the words of Igor Dedkov:

> One must never stop, one must keep moving forwards. They [Krymov and Mostovskoi] burn with faith and enthusiasm, beautiful abstractions inflame their minds. In this circumscribed motion there is a sense of romanticism. At first it seems to be revolutionary. But those who come to their senses, suddenly realize: it is the romanticism of faith, mixed up with fear and the sense of self-preservation. (1988, 237)

Death is the most potent challenge to Varnavitsky's determined enthusiasm. Progress is an abstraction. It is by no means certain that it will attain its goals. Of death there can be no such doubts; it mocks the idea of progress. In the case of Monakhov, Leva's father, death is welcomed. His belief that "Life is not arithmetic. Not everything can be explained" (Grossman 1946, 82), recognizes the mystery of death, and is diametrically opposed to the confidence with which Varnavitsky envisions the present and future. The play's conclusion confirms the paradox of death: Shatovskoi dies at the very moment when he achieves recognition of his work; his parting shot — "is this my death or birth?" (1946, 106) — is a restatement of the Pythagorean belief in the eternal cycle of death and rebirth.

Soviet responses to *Esli verit' pifagoreitsam* were predictably hostile. By far the harshest assessment came from Vladimir Ermilov in *Pravda*. He scorned the idea that the Pythagoreans could be taken seriously, arguing that Grossman "is flirting with a philosophy which is deeply alien to the Soviet people" (Ermilov 1947, 33). One of the main thrusts of Ermilov's invective consisted in the following: "It turns out that the Bolshevik Party with its progressive ideology, with its philosophy of dialectical materialism, does not rule Soviet society" (1947, 38). Ermilov also criticized Grossman on account of the play's title, which he said was "evasively pretentious" (1947, 32). Evasiveness and ambiguity offer significant advantages. But they can be readily exploited by the hostile critic, who is able to ignore, or turn any ambiguities against the author. This Ermilov does in his attack on Grossman's play. Despite Ermilov's manifest hostility — very much in keeping with the ideological rigidity of the *Zhdanovshchina* — he shows a clear grasp of the implications and questions raised in *Esli verit' pifagoreitsam*. An unattributed article in *Znamya* supported Ermilov, but widened the scope of criticism to include the journal's editorial board:

> The editorial board of *Znamya* committed a serious blunder when they published a play which amounts to a major ideological and artistic error for V. Grossman, who worked well during the war. According to the law of contrast this only serves to underline the harm and minimal artistic worth of this pre-war play. (1946, 10: 31)[14]

Unfortunately for Grossman his ideas were linked with Oswald Spengler and Friedrich Nietzsche, "the direct predecessors of Fascism" (Ermilov 1947, 32). Grossman was certainly familiar with some of Nietzsche's ideas as can be seen from *Za pravoe delo* (*For a Just Cause*), but he was no follower. For the present discussion, Spengler is the more important of the two and there appear to be several places in Grossman's art where a definite correlation with Spengler can be identified.

Spengler's main work, *Der Untergang des Abendlandes* was first published in Russian translation in 1923, and his central theme — decline — is implicit in the Pythagorean concept of circular time. Another important motif in Spengler, which is germane to this pre-war play and Grossman's post-war work, is the *Schicksalsidee* or concept of fate. Spengler submits the view that modern science with its reliance on intellectual systems and models is a manifestation of "unconscious hatred against the powers of fate and the unknowable" (1980, 157). One of the main consequences of rationalist and scientific research, he argues, is the belief that mankind is moving towards a definite goal; Varnavitsky clearly subscribes to this belief. Laws confer legitimacy. They provide an apparently scientific basis for progress. But they are not the laws of physics or chemistry, which possess a narrow range of prescription, and can be verified. In fact they are not laws at all. They are suppositions about the development of human societies rather than laws.

Thus teleology is illusory. It is "a caricature of the idea of fate" (Spengler 1980, 157). With some justification, Ermilov asks, why struggle for anything, if everything is beyond our control? Fadeev made a similar point when he criticized Grossman for having written a "harmful play" in which he attempted to accuse the Soviet people of "degeneration and regeneration" (Fadeev 1947, 3).

Western criticism, while less vitriolic, generally has little good to say about Grossman's play. Shimon Markish's evaluation is the most severe: "In my opinion there is nothing worse in Grossman's art than this play. Through and through it is artificial, full of false pathos and pseudo-philosophy" (Markish 1985, 2: 403). Two points need to be stressed. Soviet criticism, whatever it felt about characterization and plot, correctly perceived that the real threat was ideological and philosophical.[15] Grossman's play struck at the very premises of Soviet progress, its inflated optimism and unreasonable dreams. To those who unhesitatingly believed in the "planification" of time (Heller 1988, 66), it was, to paraphrase Mayakovsky, a slap in the face.

Markish's harsh criticism gives way to Gleb Struve's somewhat superficial analysis:

> The play is not devoid of interest, but its "philosophy" is not easily detectable. Its moral seems to be that a good old Liberal of the Tsar's days who swears by Pythagoras is a more valuable individual than a bad Bolshevik who values his material well-being above everything else. (Struve 1971, 351)

Marginally more accurate is the view that the play was attacked "for its exposure of certain aspects of Soviet life and mentality" (Struve 1972, 944). No attempt has been made to consider the relevance of the Pythagorean school, and, thus, to ask why Soviet critics should react in the way in which they did.

It should be noted that Efim Etkind, a scholar thoroughly familiar with Grossman's work, adopts a different approach from both Markish and Struve, and one, which in my opinion, lies much closer to the real nature of *Esli verit' pifagoreitsam*: "The basis of Grossman's play is questioning, doubt, heresy" (Etkind 1986, 180). Grossman, he observes, had the temerity to point out to the Soviet people that "there are other philosophies in the world apart from Marxism–Leninism, and that the theory of progress is not the only possible basis of historical development!" (1986, 180).

The Pythagoreans are not the sole allusion to classical antiquity in the play. Two others can be found, and both are consistent with the subversive themes of the text. In scene V of the play, Leva reads to Shatovskoi from Tacitus' *Annals*.[16] This is an apposite association, since the message of the *Annals* pertains directly to an older generation which experienced the revolution, and to both generations which have been through Stalin's terror, and now stand on the threshold of World War Two. Tacitus offers little support for the Marxist–Leninist view that "wars are a historically transient phenomenon" (Kozlov 1975, 14). Struggle, which for Tacitus did not just mean wars, was a permanent characteristic of human societies. As one Tacitean scholar has put it:

> He [Tacitus] has learnt to see life as a continual struggle between the power-ful, who seek to destroy virtue, and the forces of courage and hope which can be maimed, and in the individual, killed. If this struggle is continual it must in essentials be continually the same. (Walker 1951,195)[17]

The dominant archetype in Tacitus is the tyrant, and one of his central themes is tyranny. Both are most forcibly and eloquently expressed through the figure of Tiberius, who occupies the first hexad of the *Annals*. Intellectual freedom is an obvious casualty in Tiberius' Rome. The historian is especially vulnerable:

> The reigns of Tiberius, Gaius, Claudius, and Nero were described during their lifetimes in fictitious terms, for fear of the consequences; whereas the ac-counts written after their deaths were influenced by still raging animosities. (Tacitus 1989, 1:1)

The case of Aulus Cremutius Cordus who was prosecuted for praising Brutus in his *History*, and for describing Cassius as "the last of the Romans" (Tacitus 1989, 4:30), illustrates the personal dangers. Originality and independence of thought, as in Stalin's Russia, are to be avoided. Fear is corrosive. Mediocrity and grovelling subservience are rewarded, ability persecuted. In Tiberius' Rome or Stalin's Moscow, there is little to choose between the atmosphere of calculated uncertainty and terror which Tacitus describes as follows:

> At Rome there was unprecedented agitation and terror. People behaved se-cretly even to their intimates, avoiding encounters and conversation, shunning the ears of both friends and strangers. Even voiceless, inanimate objects — ceilings and walls — were scanned suspiciously. (Tacitus 1989, 4:66)

> It was, indeed, a horrible feature of the period that leading senators became informers even on trivial matters — some openly, many secretly. Friends and relatives were as much suspect as strangers, old stories as damaging as new. In the Forum, at a dinner-party, remark on any subject might mean prosecu-

tion. Everyone competed for priority in marking down the victim. Sometimes
this was self-defence, but mostly it was a sort of contagion, like an epidemic.
(Tacitus 1989, 5:4)

In addition, as Stalin was to do, Tiberius manipulated the laws relating to
treason (the *Maiestas* Law) to dispose of his political enemies, real or
imagined. This resulted in a number of show trials. One of the most famous
was that of Libo Drusus (16 C.E.), who like Bukharin, Zinoviev and countless others in Stalin's dictatorship, was accused of attempting to overthrow
the government. A new departure — and one that Stalin was to pursue with
the utmost vindictiveness — was to hold the relatives of those condemned
responsible for the actions of the arrestee. Women are "accused of weeping"
(Tacitus 1989, 5:8), and in the aftermath of one massacre Tacitus tells us that
"relatives and friends were forbidden to stand by or lament them, or even
gaze for long" (Tacitus 1989, 5:16).[18] A startling parallel between Tiberius'
and Stalin's main show trials can be seen in the dates. Large numbers of trials
took place in the thirties C.E., particularly 31–33 C.E., and in 37 C.E. One
scholar of Tacitus could easily have been writing about the Stalinist terror,
when he stated: "The total effect is of many little known persons, not sharply
defined, passing rapidly before us in the ranks of the condemned" (Walker
1951, 21).

A Soviet critic has observed: "Nothing is fortuitous in Grossman's volu-
minous and precise prose" (Anninsky 1988, 260). We can readily acknowledge the precision of Grossman's writing in *Esli verit' pifagoreitsam* and
elsewhere. It must also be pointed out, however, that Tacitus is the least
quoted of the three classical thinkers under scrutiny. Apart from the direct
quotation from Claudius' speech given above, the *Annals* are mentioned only
twice in Grossman's *oeuvre*: once in *Esli verit' pifagoreitsam* and once in the
wartime work, *Narod bessmerten (The People Are Immortal)*.[19] So, how does
one counter the criticism that the interpretation of Tacitus in Grossman is
convincing, but one which is based on too little?

We can begin by commenting on the parallels. So closely does Stalin's
abuse of power correspond to Tiberius', so striking and consistent are the
many major and minor parallels that it is difficult to concede the likelihood
of mere coincidence. Reading the main Tiberius chapters with their depress-
ing inventory of treason trials, terror, informers and alleged plots, Grossman
would have been repeatedly confronted — in diluted form to be sure — with
Russia's own agony. For Grossman, writing in 1941, Tiberius' Rome provided the sharpest and most complete image of the tyranny of his own time.[20]

Although post-war research has tended to cast doubt on the portrayal of
Tiberius given by Tacitus, Grossman's allusion to Tacitus coheres with the

manner in which Tacitus has been interpreted over the centuries, a code indicating the presence of tyranny. D.R. Dudley has pointed out that Camille Desmoulins uses Tacitus to mirror the Terror of the Jacobins in his *Le Vieux Cordelier*. Dudley's comments relate to Tacitus in Grossman's play: "The whole episode is thoroughly Tacitean, and a notable example of how Tacitus is seen to be especially relevant in dark and troubled times" (Dudley 1968, 236). Tacitus was, in the words of Milton, "the greatest possible enemy to tyrants" (quoted in Burke 1969, 164).[21] Thus, the mere mention of the *Annals* would be quite sufficient for the reader familiar with Tacitus, and his traditional association with the exposure of tyranny, to draw the necessary conclusions. Grossman's reticence is, therefore, not unusual. Indeed, in view of the nature of the *Annals*, reticence was probably desirable. Copious quotation would only have made Grossman's purpose too clear, and would in turn have incurred considerable risk for the author.

Official Soviet sources cast some light on this question. Successive editions of the *Bol'shaya Sovetskaya Entsiklopediya* (*The Large Soviet Encyclopaedia*) indicate a definite change in attitude towards Tacitus. We find no detailed discussion of Tacitus' historical role as an enemy of tyranny, as for example in the Tsarist *Entsiklopedichesky slovar'* (*Encyclopaedia*), where Châteaubriand, echoing Milton, says that Tacitus is "the people's avenger against tyrants" (quoted in Arsen'ev 1901, 32a: 696). The first edition of the *Bol'shaya Sovetskaya Entsiklopediya* carries a short entry, and the entry in the second edition states that Tacitus "idealised Antiquity, and lauded ancient historical events and laws" (quoted in Vvedensky 1956, 42: 18). By the third edition the emphasis shifts from Tacitus, the conservative historian, to his portrayal of the Roman emperors:

> The images of the emperors in his work are ambivalent. In his portrayal the emperors come across not only as *progressive* [emphasis added] political figures who assert the splendour of the empire, but also as bloody tyrants, who, relying on crude military force, denouncers and cowardly magistrates, crush the state's best people. (quoted in Prokhorov 1976, 25: 306)

"Progressive" is an important word in the lexicon of Marxism–Leninism, reserved for those struggling for the cause of socialism. It is most unusual, therefore, to find Roman emperors being described as "progressive." This defence of the Roman emperors closely follows the reassessment of Stalin's role in Soviet history which asserted itself from the mid-sixties onwards. Stalin's purges are condemned (by some), but they are mitigated by the fact that he guided the Soviet Union to glory, and made it a superpower. The imposition of a neo-Stalinist interpretation of Soviet history on Tacitus'

emperors seeks to place what Stalin inflicted on the Russian people within
the framework of European history. The inference to be drawn is that
Tiberius and Nero were tyrants, but this has not prevented the glories of
Rome from being acknowledged. Likewise the glories of Soviet culture
should not be overshadowed by Stalin's tyranny. Rehabilitating Stalin in
these terms, of course, recognizes the Tiberius/Stalin parallel which, I have
argued, is implicit in Grossman's reference to the *Annals*.

Heraclitus is by far the most important of our three classical thinkers for
Soviet ideology. Marx, Engels, Plekhanov and Lenin see him as one of the
first to recognize the dialectical process of history. Lenin, in his commentary
on Hegel and Lasalle writes that Heraclitus is "one of the founders of
dialecticism" (Lenin 1963, 29: 309).[22] Soviet ideology envisages history
moving towards a specific goal. Yet the author of *panta rhei* identified
change as something continual: it will not cease with the arrival of the
classless society. As Karl Popper has pointed out, Heraclitean thought not
only emphasizes change, but "an inexorable and immutable *law of change*"
(Popper 1973, 13). The problem inherent in "everything flows" was noted by
Plato, who saw change as synonymous with decay. Change was something
to be arrested at all costs. The same problem must eventually confront Soviet
society, hence the reluctance to discuss what will happen when the classless
society arrives. At such a time, change and innovation will pose exactly the
sort of threat which Plato foresaw in the *Republic* and the *Laws*. At this
theoretical point, the end of history as it were, the idea that everything flows
is most unwelcome.[23] In similar fashion it becomes impossible to make
definitive statements about the physical world if everything is in continual
flux. The ideological certainties claimed by Marx and Lenin are a chimera.
Grossman's analysis of Heraclitus follows this unorthodox line.

We encounter the first of many references to Heraclitus in Grossman's
work in scene VI of *Esli verit' pifagoreitsam*.[24] During one of his exegeses
on the theme of circular time, Shatovskoi passes the following comment:
"The years pass, everything changes and nothing changes. Everything
flows!" (Grossman 1946, 96). Shatovskoi's comment is significant for both
Esli verit' pifagoreitsam and the later *Vsyo techyot*. Within the play a paradox
arises: how can history repeat itself, yet admit continual change or flux? The
paradox is resolved by the temporal perspective from which we view change:

> But if one follows this great flow, then it too is subordinated to circular
> motion. Millennia will pass, the earth will flourish, or be held tight in the grip
> of ice, and nothing will have changed, the eternal cycle with its eternal
> measure of sin and good deeds, with its eternal measure of grief and tears,
> this eternal cycle will continue to be completed. (Grossman 1946, 96)

Great advances in science pose no threat for this view. For even if people can change the Earth itself, this is still too narrow a definition of progress. Progress has to be assessed in terms of man's emotional, psychological or moral nature. Only if he advances here can we assert worthwhile progress. The continuing existence of war underlines the point. War is one of the abiding causes of human misery, the final eradication of which has persistently eluded mankind. For Heraclitus, war served as a metaphor of the continual change, which all Utopias fear.[25]

The theme persists in Grossman's post-war prose. Once again Heraclitus is the starting point. In *Za pravoe delo* Mostovskoi, a veteran Bolshevik considers the changes which have taken place since 1917:

> Mostovskoi saw, felt and knew: never in the thousand-year history of Russia had there ever been such a headlong change of events, such a monumental shift in life's strata, as there had been in the last quarter of a century. True, everything flowed and changed in pre-revolutionary times, and a person would not be able to step into the same river twice. But the river flowed so slowly that the people of that time only saw the same river banks. To them Heraclitus's discovery seemed strange and dark. But would any of them living in the Soviet period be surprised by the truth which was discovered by the Greek? These days that truth had moved from the realm of philosophical thought into the perception of reality, which was accessible to scholars and workers. (Grossman 1964, 56)[26]

Mostovskoi's geological metaphor is an anodyne euphemism for the successive blows that struck Soviet society from 1929 onwards. Heraclitus envisaged continual change, even strife and war, as ineradicable features of human societies.[27] But he would undoubtedly have been somewhat surprised to find himself being associated with attempts to legitimate state-sponsored terror and mass murder. The challenge from within the novel to Mostovskoi's vision of progress is brutal and effective. Sofya Levinton, a Jewish doctor, who eventually perishes in the gas chamber, confronts Mostovskoi at the height of the Stalingrad battle:

> Comrade Mostovskoi, you just take a look at these ruins. What kind of faith can there be in the future? Technology progresses, but ethics, morals, humanity do not. This is some kind of stone age. (Grossman 1964, 481)

The increasing importance of Heraclitus for Grossman's post-war thought is evident in the title of *Vsyo techyot*. Indeed, one of the first Western reviewers of *Vsyo techyot* claimed that the influence of Heraclitus was ubiquitous:

The whole book, in fact, is permeated with the metaphysical ideas attributed
to Heraclitus more than 2000 years ago; and while this destroys its literary
quality, it gives it a special historical and philosophical interest. ("Synthesis
with Slaves," 1973, 197)

Two preliminary observations are worth making. Firstly, Grossman's
interest in Heraclitus is far from metaphysical. Secondly, the philosophical–
historical speculations compliment, even enrich, the work's literary qualities,
the synthesis of the two being essential for the development of Grossman's
arguments.[28]

The link between socioeconomic progress and human freedom rests at the
very core of *Vsyo techyot*, and follows logically and demonstrably from the
skepticism and arguments of Shatovskoi and Sofya Levinton. In effect, *Vsyo
techyot* proves to be an extended analysis of the theory and practice of
historical materialism. Further, in the hands of Vasilii Grossman, Heraclitus'
"everything flows" develops into a powerful counter-argument to the attrac-
tions of Utopianism. In short, *Vsyo techyot* may be seen as a summing up of
the entire Soviet experiment and the ideology underpinning it.

The hopes, murderous failures and misery of this period are viewed
through the experience of Ivan Grigorevich, a survivor of Stalin's camps. He
is Grossman's interpreter whose vision and intellectual courage seem quite
out of place among the spineless and malleable Soviet intelligentsia. Several
strands in Ivan's intellectual and ethical outlook suggest a propinquity with
various Heraclitean fragments. Mathematics, physics, classical antiquity and
Parthian civilization are all grist to his mill. Ivan's unceasing quest for
answers to Russia's fate sets him apart from the professional class of the
intelligentsia with their taboos and genuflexion to Party myth. Doctrine
promotes intellectual stasis. For Ivan the pursuit of knowledge, and ultimately wisdom, is a process "without a beginning and end" (Grossman 1974,
88). Thus the dependence of doctrine on a finite body of knowledge is
inimical to unfettered enquiry. This, in turn, leads to a debased language.
Prefacing his painful, moral enquiry into the informers' mentality with "in
the beginning was the word ... truly it was so" (1974, 59), Grossman
recognizes that the corruption of *Logos* is a landmark on the road to tyranny.
Ivan's incarceration stems from his revolt against the lie, the corruption of
Logos, and his determined assertion of intellectual independence. His behaviour is entirely consistent with Heraclitus' view: "Man's character is his fate"
(Kahn 1979, 81).[29]

The influence of Heraclitus is most pronounced in Ivan's reflections on
Russia's history. Time and time again his thoughts turn to the prison trains
moving across the Russian countryside, one of the most pervasive images in

Vsyo techyot. Variations on "everything flows" seem quite deliberate: "The prison train keeps on running and running" (1974, 85), "but the prison train keeps running" (1974, 105), and "this prison camp existence went on and on" (1974, 109). Any doubts we might have are brushed aside in Ivan's modification of Heraclitus' fragment: "To be sure, everything flows, everything changes, you cannot get into the same prison train twice" (1974, 96). Subverting the river metaphor deals a telling blow to Soviet mythology. Russia has not moved from a lower to a higher state, as postulated by Lenin and Stalin. It has instead metamorphosed into a giant prison train. For Grossman the sole criterion of meaningful historical progress is the evolution of human freedom: "The history of peoples is the history of freedom, from less to greater freedom. The history of all life from the amoeba to human beings is the history of freedom, the transition from less freedom to greater freedom" (1974, 203).[30]

With the demise of ideology, quite a different picture of Lenin's place in Russia's history manifests itself. Heraclitus can be felt here in two ways. To begin with, the fanaticism and absolute intolerance of dissent are recurring phenomena in Russia's intellectual and religious landscape. Persecution of religious heretics in defence of Russian Orthodoxy or Peter the Great's imposition of reform irrespective of the human cost are obvious antecedents. Grossman has no difficulty in placing Lenin alongside an established pattern of Russian autocrats. Then there is the style of Grossman's analysis of Lenin which frequently suggests the river metaphor. It is, however, no bubbling brook. Grossman's river is wide, deep and slow-moving. But the glacial slowness is unstoppable and remorseless and more than a match for Lenin's, and his apologists's, defenses. It is here, if anywhere in the grim catalogue of *Vsyo techyot*, that one can draw some hope for Russia's lot. The very fact that Grossman rises to such heights in *Vsyo techyot* bears ample witness that no tyranny of the body, mind and spirit lasts forever. Equally, no tyranny can totally eradicate the idea of freedom.

Tacitus, Pythagoras and Heraclitus fulfil specific, yet overlapping, functions in Grossman's analysis of totalitarianism. Tacitus is the scourge of tyranny whose *Annals* go some way to portraying Russia's own terrible suffering. For that reason they were, I think, a source of comfort for Grossman. Informers, bloody purges, perversion of justice and attacks on intellectual freedom were not invented by Stalin. They are possibilities inherent in the growth of certain organized communities wherever they may be. Russia is not alone in her madness. Others have trodden the same path.

If the *Annals* are a recognizable pattern of Stalin's mayhem then the Pythagoreans are the fraternal ancestors of Lenin's supposedly new model party. Pythagoras and his sect do indeed suggest an analogue of the infallible

Soviet leader (be he Lenin or Stalin), an all-embracing epistemology and a collectivist ethos hostile to heresy. There are inconsistencies which muddy the waters, but the parallels stand. Moreover, their implications for Soviet ideology did not pass unnoticed.

Despite the claims of Marx, Engels and Lenin, Heraclitus remains aloof from Soviet ideology. At some stage the question of what will happen when historical materialism has run its course must be confronted. Heraclitus offers no help. Having peered into this particular abyss, the Soviet leadership abandons the Great Plan. Consolidating its own power base, it becomes reactionary, no longer retaining the ideological justification for the exercise of power. Similar conclusions can be drawn and applied to the Pythagoreans in the aftermath of the discovery of irrationality.

The empire which Grossman sought to examine through the legacy of an illustrious trio of classical thinkers no longer exists. However, on the threshold of the twenty-first century, with the open society still not universally accepted, we cannot say with complete conviction that Tacitus, Pythagoras and Heraclitus have lost all meaning for our time.

NOTES

1. I would like to thank Roger Brock, School of Classics, University of Leeds, for reading this article and making several valuable suggestions. After it was smuggled out of the Soviet Union, *Zhizn' i sud'ba* was eventually published in Switzerland by *L'Age d'Homme* in 1980. The first Soviet version appeared in the journal *Oktyabr'*, vols. 1–4 (1988). *Vsyo techyot* was first published in 1970 by Possev-Verlag. Its publication in *Oktyabr'*, 6 (1989): 30–108 marked the high point of *glasnost'* in literature.

2. An unnamed reviewer of *Everything Flows* commented: "the whole book leaves an impression of artistic confusion mixed with intellectual conviction of a disturbing kind" ("Synthesis with Slaves," *Times Literary Supplement* 23 Feb. 1973: 197). There is no discussion of Lenin's role in laying the foundations for Stalin, or the significance of attacking Lenin after so many years of deification in Soviet literature. Equally superficial is Elaine Feinstein's review in *The Times* some thirteen years later. Feinstein fails to realize, or simply ignores, Grossman's demolition of Lenin. Nor does she comment on Grossman's bold analysis of the traditional role ascribed to Dostoevsky in the history of Russian thought (Elaine Feinstein, "Will Russia Ever be Free? Maybe Never," *The Times* 27 Nov. 1986: 17).

3. Lipkin provides a detailed account of events before and after the novel's arrest in *Stalingrad Vasiliya Grossmana* (*The Stalingrad of Vasilii Grossman*) (Ann

Arbor, Michigan: Ardis, 1986). Additional details concerning the arrest can be found in David Fel'dman ("Do i posle aresta," *Literaturnaya Rossiya* 11 Nov. 1988: 16–17).

4. In the words of Shimon Markish: "I believe that the path towards the duel with Soviet power began for Grossman on 22nd June 1941" (Shimon Markish, *Na evreiskie temy, Vasilii Grossman*, 2 vols., Jerusalem and New York: Biblioteka Aliya, Sifrit-Aliyah, 1985: 376.). Unless otherwise stated, all translations from primary and secondary sources are mine.

5. Other key works of the pre-war period are: *Los'* (*The Elk*); *Molodaya i staraya* (*The Young and the Old*); and *Neskol'ko pechal'nykh dnei* (*Several Sad Days*).

6. *Esli verit' pifagoreitsam* was written before the war, but not published until 1946.

7. A good introduction to Marx's reading of classical authors is given in G.E.M. de Ste. Croix, *The Class Struggle in the Ancient Greek World: From the Archaic Age to the Arab Conquests* (London: Duckworth, 1981). Cf. Manfred Kliem, ed. *Karl Marx, Friedrich Engels über Kunst und Literatur in zwei Bänden* (Berlin: Dietz Verlag, 1967). Another useful reference work is *Karl Marx, Friedrich Engels, Über Geschichte der Philosophie (Ausgewählte Texte)* (Leipzig: Reclam, 1983). Lenin conducts a wide ranging discussion of classical thinkers in the "Filosofksie tetradi" ("Philosophical Notebooks") (*Polnoe sobranie sochinenii*, 5th ed. vol. 29 (Moscow: Gosudarstvennoe izdatel'stvo politicheskoi literatury, 1963)).

8. Burkert notes: "The *mathematici* claimed that their studies were no more than the explication of the doctrine of Pythagoras, and that "everything came from him." This principle, which seems to have been accepted in the day of Xenocrates, emanates from a completely unhistorical point of view, close to that of myth. What seems important and desirable, takes the form of a quasi-historical assertion: in the beginning there was Pythagoras" (1972, 208).

9. Quoted in *Stepan Kol'chugin* (Grossman 1951, 596).

10. Quoted in Grossman *Esli verit' pifagoreitsam* (1946, 73). According to Markish the Russian translation of Gomperz appeared between 1911 and 1913 and enjoyed considerable popularity (1985, 2: 404). G.S. Kirk and J.E. Raven offer a slightly different translation to the one quoted from Gomperz. Cf. *The Pre-Socratic Philosophers. A Critical Study With a Selection of Texts* (Cambridge: Cambridge UP, 1957) 223. This text was my primary source of information on the Pythagoreans, in particular the discussion of limit and unlimit.

11. Whether by design or coincidence Zamyatin's One State recalls a number of features of the Pythagorean sect. First and foremost is the One State's obsession with mathematics, even to the extent that all inhabitants are known by numbers, not names. The irrational number (the square root of minus 1) poses precisely the sort of doctrinal crisis for the One State which confronts the Pythagoreans. 2×2 is revered as is the number 1. The Pythagorean devotion to the psychogonic

cube with its recurring 6 finds an echo in the One State's Plaza of the Cube (scene of ritual execution), surrounded by 66 concentric circles. Praising the music of the One State, D-503 cites, among others, Pythagoras as a criterion of excellence: "the full-toned, squarely-massive passages of the Pythagorean theorem.... What grandeur! What irrevocable regularity!" (*My*, trans. Bernard Guerney, Harmondsworth: Penguin Books, 1980, 34). Last, but by no means least, is the set of rules, the Table of Commandments, which lays down rigid guidelines for sex, exercise, drinking (alcohol and tobacco are strictly forbidden) and eating.

12. In his "Filosofskie tetradi" Lenin expresses hostility to Pythagorean number theory and the implications of their doctrines for dialectical materialism (Lenin 1963, 29: 223–24). To the Pythagorean doctrine of the transmigration of souls, Lenin adds the note: "The connection of the rudiments of scientific thought and fantasy à la religion and mythology. And these days! The very same connection, but the proportion of science and mythology is different" (Lenin 1923, 29: 225). Accompanying editorial remarks describe the Pythagoreans as "a reactionary, political and religious–philosophical union" (Lenin 1923, 29: 648).

13. The characteristic features of the sect are clearly identified by Leszek Kolakowski: "Unflagging vigilance over its own meticulous boundary lines is an essential characteristic of every social group that can be called a 'sect' — constant control to assure precise and unambiguous criteria differentiating it from the entire outside world. These criteria are of various sorts: ideological, organizational, traditional, ritualistic; and the greater their number, pettiness, and variety, the more advanced the ossification of the sect" (1969, 118).

14. The editor of *Znamya*, V. Vishnevsky, admitted that he had made a mistake in permitting publication of this "philosophically failed play" (quoted in Bocharov 1990, 163).

15. The censor, commenting on the Pythagorean theme, said that "from the censor's point of view all this is completely unacceptable" (quoted in Bocharov 1990, 96).

16. Grossman would have been familiar with Pythagoras from his studies of mathematics. Heraclitus' name would have cropped up in the compulsory courses in scientific communism and dialectical materialism. Tacitus was held in high esteem by Corneille, Montesquieu, Racine, Voltaire and Rousseau as a defender of freedom, and it may well be that Grossman first encountered Tacitus through his mother who was a teacher of French.

17. The cyclical idea can also be found in the *Annals*: "Or perhaps not only the seasons but everything else, social history included, moves in cycles" (Tacitus 1989, 3:55).

18. In citing the many parallels between Tiberius and Stalin I have concentrated on those which, I believe, would have seemed the most compelling to Grossman in the thirties. The show trials, the use of informers, exile and intellectual persecution are the obvious ones. However, there are many more which repeatedly bring

Stalin to mind. Tacitus' Tiberius is clearly a master of deception and dissimulation which is used to great effect. Likewise Tiberius, while demanding servility, despises those who throw themselves at his feet. Tiberius' fear of the charismatic Germanicus, and the military generally, are prescient of Stalin's fears about able commanders such as Tukhachevsky and political rivals such as Kirov.

19. Vasilii Grossman, *Gody Voiny* (*The War Years*) (Moscow: Ob"edinenie gosudarstvennykh izdatel'stv, 1946) 31.

20. So, too, for Mikhail Bulgakov in whose *Master and Margarita* the Rome/Moscow and Tiberius/Stalin parallels are quite explicit.

21. Burke's concluding remarks are especially relevant to Tacitus in Grossman: "In the twentieth century too, Tacitus has his uses; for despotism has come round a third time.... In Eastern Europe, a Tacitean mask has sometimes been useful to writers prepared to take more risks than Lipsius" (Burke 1969, 170). It is worth noting that the volume in which Burke's essay is published is dedicated to the people of Czechoslovakia. In the introduction to his translation of Tacitus, Michael Grant quotes André Chénier's remark on Tacitus: "The utterance of his name turns tyrants pale" (Tacitus 1989, 24).

22. Cf. Lenin's "Konspekt knigi Lassalya 'Filosofiya Geraklita tyomnogo iz Efesa'" (Summary of Lasalle's book, *The Philosophy of Heraclitus the Elusive of Ephesus*, Lenin 1963: 29, 303–15).

23. J.B. Bury's comments neatly summarize the advantages and disadvantages of appropriating Heraclitus: "His [Heraclitus'] influence was both subversive and conservative, according as one took hold of the doctrine of flux or the fixed law of the world" (Bury 1975, 199).

24. A likely source for Heraclitus was *Antichnaya filosofiya* (*The Philosophy of Antiquity*), which Grossman refers to in the play (1946, 72). He mentions no author. However, a work of the same title, edited by G.F. Aleksandrov, was published in Moscow in 1940. This book may well have included some discussion of Tacitus. An early Russian edition of the fragments is V. Nilender, *Geraklit efessky* (*Heraclitus of Ephesus*) (Moscow: 1910). Further sources are S. Trubetsky, *Metafizika v drevnei Gretsii* (*Metaphysics in Ancient Greece*) (Moscow: 1890); M.I. Mandes, *Ogon' i dusha v uchenii Geraklita* (*The Fire and the Soul in the Teaching of Heraclitusy*) (Odessa: 1912); A.O. Makovel'sky, *Dosokratniki* (*The Pre-Socratics*) vol. 1. (Kazan': 1914); M.A. Dynnik, Dialektika Geraklita efesskogo (*The Dialectics of Heraclitus of Ephesus*) (Moscow: 1929); and *Ocherk istorii filosofii klassicheskoi Gretsii* (*An Essay on the History of the Philosophy of Classical Greece*) (Moscow: 1936); and in the post-war period A.O. Makovel'sky, *Materialisty drevnei Gretsii* (*The Materialists of Ancient Greece*) (Moscow: 1955). Some mention must also be made of the fascinating and detailed study of Pushkin and Heraclitus in M. Gershenzon, *Gol'fstrem* (*The Gulfstream*, Moscow: Izdatel'stvo Shipovnik, 1922). In his introduction he states: "two points on the line of the flood: they will be Heraclitus and Pushkin" (introduction, no pagination). *Esli verit' pifagoreitsam*

and *Vsyo techyot* are not the only works in which Grossman quotes Heraclitus. Direct quotation can also be found in *Za pravoe delo* (Grossman 1964, 56) and the post-war *rasskaz*, "Na vechnom pokoe" ("At Eternal rest") in the collection *Neskol'ko pechal'nykh dnei*, Moscow: Sovremennik, 1989: 429.

25. Cf. fragment LXXXIII: "War is father of all and king of all: and some he has shown as gods, others men; some he has made slaves, others free" (quoted in Kahn 1979, 67; all fragments are taken from Kahn). In the essay "O dialekticheskom i istoricheskom materializme" ("Concerning dialectical and historical materialism") Stalin leaves us in no doubt as to what is meant by the dialectical concept of progress: ... the dialectical method believes that the process of development should not be understood as something which describes a circle, not as a simple repetition of what has passed, but as forward movement, as movement along a rising line, as the transition from an old, quantitative state towards a new one, as development from the simple to the complex, from the lower to the higher (Stalin 1945, 537). Grossman offers no support for this in his play.

26. *Za pravoe delo* was first published in *Novy mir*, in vols. 7–10 (1952). Soon after it was published the party press unleashed a vicious campaign against phantom Jewish conspirators (the so-called Doctors' Plot). Grossman and his novel were targeted along with the hapless doctors. Detailed accounts of the campaign against Grossman can be found in the combined work, Semen Lipkin, *Zhizn' i sud'ba Vasiliya Grossmana* (*The Life and Fate of Vasilii Grossman*) and Anna Berzer, *Proshchanie* (*Farewell*) (Moscow: Kniga, 1990). In their subsequent criticism of *Za Pravoe delo* Fadeev and Tvardovsky accused Grossman of returning to the same ideas developed in *Esli verit' pifagoreitsam* (Berzer 1990, 186–216).

27. Fragment LXXXIII for example, about which Lenin remains silent in his "Filosofskie tetradi" (Lenin 1963, 29: 233–37).

28. After publication in the Soviet Union critics made every effort to split Grossman's synthesis of literature and analysis of ideology. Vodolazov claimed that *Vsyo techyot* "is not a scholarly treatise, but an artistic creation and should be viewed and assessed according to the laws of art" (Vodolazov 1989, 9).

29. Fragment CXIV. Grossman makes a similar point in *Esli verit' pifagoreitsam*. Semenov argues that "both life and fate are the individual's" (Grossman 1946, 97).

30. This would appear to be a conscious rebuke of Stalin's crude historicism.

WORKS CITED

Anninskii, L. 1988. "Mirozdan'e Vasiliya Grossmana." *Druzhba' narodov* 10: 253–63.

Arsen'ev, K.K. Ed. 1901. "Tatsit." *Entsiklopedichesky slovar'* vol. 32a. St. Petersburg: Brockhaus-Efron, 692–96.

Berzer, Anna and Semen Lipkin. 1990. *Zhizn' i sud'ba Vasiliya Grossmana* and *Proshchanie.* Moscow: Kniga.

Bocharov, Anatolii. 1990. *Vasilii Grossman. Zhizn', Sud'ba Tvorchestvo.* Moscow: Sovetskii pisatel'.

Burke, P. 1969. "Tacitism" in T. A. Dorey, Ed. *Tacitus. Studies in Latin Literature and its Influence.* London: Routledge and Kegan Paul, 149–71.

Burkert, Walter. 1972. *Lore and Science in Ancient Pythagoreanism.* Trans. Edwin L. Minar, Cambridge: Harvard University Press.

Bury, J.B. 1928. *The Idea of Progress. An Enquiry into Its Origins and Growth.* London: Macmillan.

_____ and R. Meiggs. 1975. *A History of Greece to the Death of Alexander the Great.* 4th Ed. London: Macmillan.

Dedkov, Igor'. 1988. "Zhizn' protiv sud'by." *Novy mir* 11: 229–41.

Dudley, D.R. 1968. *The World of Tacitus.* London: Secker and Warburg.

Ermilov, Vladimir. 1947. "Vrednaya p'esa." *Samaya demokraticheskaya literatura mira. Stat'i 1946–47 gg.* Moscow: Izdatel'stvo literaturnaya gazeta: 32–39.

Etkind, Efim. 1986. "1946 god: Krushenie nadezhd." *Vremya i my* 89: 173–85.

Fadeev, Aleksandr. 1947. "O literaturno-khudozhestvennykh zhurnalakh." *Pravda* 2 February: 3.

Feinstein, Elaine. 1986. "Will Russia Ever be Free? Maybe Never." *The Times* 27 November: 17.

Gomperz, Theodor. 1901. *Greek Thinkers. A History of Ancient Philosophy.* vol. 1. Trans. L. Magnus. London: John Murray.

Gorman, Peter. 1979. *Pythagoras: A Life.* London: Routledge and Kegan Paul.

Grossman, Vasilii. 1946. "Esli verit' pifagoreitsam." *Znamya* 7: 68–107.

_____. 1951. *Stepan Kol'chugin.* Moscow: Sovetskii pisatel'.

_____. 1964. *Za pravoe delo.* Moscow: Sovetskii pisatel'.

_____. 1974. *Vsyo techyot.* 2nd Ed. Frankfurt am Main: Possev-Verlag.

_____. 1989. *Neskol'ko pechal"nykh dnei. Povesti i Rasskazy.* Moscow: Sovremennik.

Heller, Mikhail. 1988. *Cogs in the Soviet Wheel. The Formation of Soviet Man.* Trans. David Floyd, London: Collins.

Kahn, Charles H. 1979. *The Art and Thought of Heraclitus*. Cambridge: University Press.

Kolakowski, Leszek. 1969. *Marxism and Beyond. On Historical Understanding and Individual Responsibility*. Trans. Jane Zielonko Peel, London: Pall Mall Press.

Kozlov, V.G. and A.S. Milovidov, Eds. 1975. *The Philosophical Heritage of V.I. Lenin and Problems of Contemporary War*. Trans. United States Air Force. In the series *Soviet Military Thought*. Vol. 5. Washington: U.S. Government Printing Office.

Lenin, V.I. 1963. *Polnoe Sobranie Sochinenii*, 5th Ed. Vol. 29. Moscow: Gosudarstvennoe izdatel'stvo politicheskoi literatury.

Markish, Shimon. 1985. *Na evreiskie temy. Vasilii Grossman*. 2 vols. Jerusalem and New York: Biblioteka Aliya, Sifrit-Aliyah.

Popper, Sir Karl. 1973. *The Open Society and Its Enemies*. Vol. 1. 5th Ed. London: Routledge and Kegan Paul.

Prokhorov, A.M. Ed. 1976. "Tatsit." *Bol'shaya Sovetskaya Entsiklopediya*. 3rd Ed. vol. 25. Moscow: Sovetskaya entsiklopediya, 305–06.

Spengler, Oswald. 1980. *Der Untergang des Abendlandes. Umrisse einer Morphologie der Weltgeschichte*. Munich: Verlag C.H. Beck.

Stalin, J. 1945. *Voprosy Leninizma*. 11th Ed. Moscow: Ob"edinenie gosudarstvennykh izdatel'stv.

Struve, Gleb. 1971. *Russian Literature under Lenin and Stalin. 1917–1953*. Norman: Oklahoma University Press.

_____. 1972. Rev. of *Vsyo techyot*, Vasilii Grossman. *Slavic Review*. 31 4: 943–46.

"Synthesis with Slaves." 1973. *Times Literary Supplement* 23 February: 197. Unattributed.

Tacitus, Cornelius. 1989. *The Annals of Imperial Rome*. Trans. Michael Grant. 7th Ed. Harmondsworth: Penguin Books.

Vatai, Frank. 1984. *Intellectuals in Politics in the Greek World, From Early Times to the Hellenistic Age*. London: Croom Helm.

Vodolazov, G. 1989. "Lenin i Stalin, filosofsko-sotsiologicheskii kommentarii k povesti V. Grossmana Vsyo techyot" *Oktyabr'* 6: 3–29.

Vvedensky, B.A., Ed. 1956. "Tatsit." *Bol'shaya Sovetskaya Entsiklopediya*. 2nd Ed. Vol. 42. Moscow: Sovetskaya entsiklopediya, 18.

Walker, B. 1951. *The Annals of Tacitus. A Study in the Writing of History*, Manchester University Press, Manchester. 1946. "Vyshe znamya ideinosti v literature!" *Znamya* 10 (1946): 27–37. Unattributed.

Zamyatin, Evgeny. 1980. *We*. Trans. Bernard Guerney, Harmondsworth: Penguin Books.

CLASSICAL MOTIFS IN THE POETRY OF ALEKSANDR KUSHNER

David N. Wells, La Trobe University, Melbourne

Reference to ancient Greece and Rome in Kushner's poetry forms part of a much broader engagement with the history and culture of the Russian and European past. It is worth treating separately, however, because of the centrality of the classical world to any definition of European culture and because in many ways Kushner's approach to it exemplifies his more general use of allusion to other authors and creative artists. For Kushner, as we shall see, the classical world is an important instrument of self-definition — both for himself as a poet and for Russia as a society. The increase in the number of classical allusions which can be discerned in Kushner's most recent collections is an indication of the increasingly urgent need for self-definition in a time of political and social flux.

Discussing his use of motifs from antiquity in an interview with A. Kuznetsov in 1986, Kushner made clear the extent of his engagement with them in commenting on the present:

> мы не должны «играть в античность». Используя античные реалии, хотелось бы вести речь о самых серьезных, общезначимых вещах. Это должны быть стихи о сегодняшнем дне, обогащенные памятью о прошлом. (Kushner 1991a, 317)[1]

For all Kushner's notorious preoccupation with themes from everyday life, he has always situated the contemporary in a historical and philosophical

143

context which has given it a broader application than was often admitted by Soviet critics. From his poetry it is clear that for Kushner ancient Greece and Rome are part of a continuum which also comprises modern Russia. This is strikingly illustrated in a poem where the author's thoughts on the Trojan War are interrupted by a telephone call which at first appears to be conveying the news of the death of Patroclus (1986, 89–90). Rome and Leningrad are seen as equivalent in, for example, "Esli kameshki na dve kuchki spornykh" ("If the pebbles in two contesting piles"; 1986, 62), and in an early poem on St. Petersburg he concludes a list of the city's rivers with a reference to the Underworld: "Pryazhku, Karpovku, Smolenku, / Stiks, Kotsit i Akheront" ("Pryazhka, Karpovka, Smolenka, Styx, Cocytus and Acheron"; 1986, 230). As John Elsworth notes, this type of juxtaposition allows the modern world to be interpreted symbolically:

> The mere naming of the mythological rivers achieves a striking and economi-cal association of the poet speaking in the present, the history embodied in the city, and the mythic archetype. (1992, 209)

Similar effects are achieved elsewhere: in poems such as "V poluplashche, odna iz aonid" ("In a short cape, one of the Aonides"; 1986, 133–34), where the image of a contemporary beauty is superimposed on that of a classical muse; or more self-consciously in "Razmashisty sovkhoz Temryukskogo raiona" ("The expanse of a *sovkhoz* in the Temryuk region"; 1988, 116), where the unearthing of an image of Apollo during ploughing on a state farm by the sea of Azov provokes a reflection on the closeness of the past; or in "O, ne tak uzh vazhno, ne tak uzh vazhno" ("Oh, it's not so important, it's not so important"; 1988, 97), where the poet proclaims his affinity for ancient Greece in spite of a lack of knowledge of its language: "Drevnegrecheskie obvetshalye bukvy / Kazhutsya znakomymi, rodnymi" ("The decayed an-cient Greek letters seem familiar and natural").

Of course, Kushner's native St. Petersburg is rich in visual pointers to ancient Greece and Rome in the form of its eighteenth-century neoclassical heritage of architecture and civic statuary, and Kushner recognizes the importance of this when he writes of his city's architecture:

> Как клен и рябина растут у порога,
> Росли у порога Растрелли и Росси,
> И мы отличали ампир от барокко,
> Как вы в этом возрасте ели от сосен. (1986, 61)

Just as maples and mountain ashes grow on your doorstep,
Rastrelli and Rossi grew on ours,
And we distinguished empire style from baroque,
As you at that age pine trees from firs.

Moreover, many of his poems about the city and its environs are inspired by aspects of its neoclassical appearance: the façade of the General Staff Building (1986, 197), for example, or the statues at Pavlovsk (1986, 139–40). The park here has both a Russian and a Roman aspect:

И ей на вышколенных берегах Славянки,
Где слиты русские и римские черты,
То снег мерещится и маленькие санки,
То рощи знойные и ратные ряды. (1986, 79)

On the disciplined banks of the Slavyanka,
Where Russian and Roman traits are merged,
[Nature] imagines now snow and little sledges,
Now sultry groves and martial files.

In several places, Kushner elaborates on the link in terms of its effect on poetry in general and on Russian poetry more specifically. In one poem, "Nevy prokhladnoe dykhan′e" ("The cool breath of the Neva"), included in the 1978 collection *Golos* (*Voice*) (1986, 56), Kushner asserts that there has long been no distance at all for the Russian muse between the banks of the Neva and the Greco-Roman civilization of the Black Sea. The qualities of the two traditions are anthropomorphized in terms of classical mythology ("I nimfa nevskaya glyadit na nereidu" ["And the Russian nymph looks at the nereid"]), but in spite of the superficial rivalry between the two nymphs they are shown to merge into each other with a complex interchange of attributes to the great benefit of the Russian poet:

Та снится синею, затем что — зеленой,
Потом меняются, одалживая цвет,
И каплю пресную запив глотком соленой,
То топчешь галечник, то гладишь парапет.

You dream of her as blue, while the other is green,
Then they change, lending each other color,
And washing down a drop of fresh water with a mouthful of salt,
Now you trample the shingle, now you stroke the parapet.

Elsewhere, however, the identity between St. Petersburg and the Russian classical south seems less absolutely secure. In the title poem of the 1984 collection *Tavrichesky sad* (*The Tauride Garden*), the garden is seen as a point of entry from the sensual deprivation of a Russian winter to a brighter, more vital Helladic world (1986, 77). Certainly, Kushner insists that this world can also exist in the present in love, in language and in poetry, but it is clear too that it requires a certain effort to recreate it: "Ne goryui. My eshchyo perepishem sud'bu" ("Do not grieve. We will rewrite fate again"). The position adopted here is in many ways rendered more explicit in the poem "Apollon v snegu" ("Apollo in the snow"; 1988, 133–34), written in 1975, but not published at the time because of political opposition to it (see Kushner 1991a, 5; Elsworth 1992, 200, 214). The impetus for this poem is the sight of the statue of Apollo in the park at Pavlovsk under a covering of snow. As in "Tavrichesky sad," the snow becomes a metaphor for the difficulty of writing poetry so far from the center of classical inspiration and from other Apollos in olive groves and by the shores of sparkling seas. However, here Kushner goes further and gives the poem a much clearer political coloration through his description of the northern Apollo's song: "Zamerzayut, pochti ne slyshny, / Stony liry i gasnut v snegu" ("The groans of the lyre freeze, almost inaudible, and are extinguished in the snow"). Because of the difficulty of being heard in Russian conditions — and metaphors of climate have long been used to refer to the vagaries of censorship and political control over the arts — Apollo's song is sweeter to those who are able to hear it and also represents the embodiment of a particular courage in the face of authority: "Eto — muzhestvo, eto — metel', / Eto — pesnya, odetaya v drozh'" ("It is courage, it is a snowstorm, It is a song dressed in trembling").

In the poem "I v sleduyushchy raz ya zhit' khochu v Rossii" ("Next time too I want to live in Russia"; 1986, 79), Kushner suggests that he is injured as a poet by not being able to visit western Europe: "mne zhal' ego, on mir ne povidal. / Kakie b on stikhi o Rime napisal!" ("I am sorry for him, he did not see the world. What poems he would have written about Rome"). This statement, as Carol Ueland has noted (1988, 376), must be intended ironically, since in fact Kushner wrote many poems on Roman themes well before the advent of *glasnost'* allowed him the possibility of travel. Yet there remains a nostalgia for the inaccessible source of inspiration, discernible also in, for example, "Ty gorish', Kolizei, kak bol'shoi restoranny pirog" ("You shine, Colosseum, like a big restaurant pie"; 1988, 15), which again contrasts the warmth of Italy with the harshness of the Russian climate.

Given the broad approach to the classical world which has been outlined above it is not surprising that Kushner regularly uses ancient sources to elucidate and deepen a wide range of contemporary themes. Often the classical component is incidental, as in "Kogda shumit listva, togda mne gorya malo" ("When the leaves rustle I feel little grief"; 1986, 91), where the poet's knowledge of the late Roman emperor Philip is used to illustrate the generation gap between him and a boy playing in the courtyard outside his window; or in "Pomnyu, v detstve na ulitsakh bylo ne mnogo lyudei" ("I remember in my childhood there were few people in the streets"; 1988, 68–68), where the quietness of the streets in the Leningrad of Kushner's childhood is compared to the supposedly slow pace of life in Mycenaean Crete; or in "Ne privykai ko mne" ("Do not get used to me"; 1992, 36), which uses Lethe to symbolize forgetting. Sometimes the classical reference is even flippant, inspired by a chance resemblance and apparently without any deeper significance, as in "Nochnoi parad" ("Night Parade"; 1986, 263–64), where a tug boat is compared to Orpheus followed by two Eurydices, or in "Po dorozhke sadovoi khodit'" ("Walking along the garden path"; 1986, 171), in which the fate of snails in a garden is compared mock-heroically to that of Iphigenia or Clytemnestra. At least as often, however, the allusion is integrated much more fully into the poem as a whole. One of the commonest ways in which Kushner achieves this is by means of dramatization, by taking a scene from history or mythology and presenting it in an unexpected light in accordance with his own preoccupations. In "Perevaliv cherez Al'py, varvarsky gorodok" ("After crossing the Alps, a barbaric little town"; 1986, 167), for example, Kushner starts from a passage in Plutarch's *Life of Caesar* in which Caesar states that he would rather be the first man in a provincial city than second in Rome (Plutarch 1919, 468–69)[2] and evokes the circumstances in which the statement was made, using the episode as evidence in a discussion on the unchangeability of human nature. In "Pri mne ona v kotel ponurogo barana" ("In my presence she had a decrepit ram placed in a cauldron"; 1988, 32), he offers a reworking of the story of Medea and Pelias (cf. Graves 1960, 2: 251–52). In Kushner's version, the legend is used to make a general comment about maturity and the process of aging. Pelias is indeed persuaded that Medea has the power to restore him to youth by cutting him up and boiling him in her pot just as she has restored an old sheep to lambhood, but he decides that he has no desire to relive the turbulence and insecurity of youth, and rejects her offer:

DAVID N. WELLS

— Не хочешь ли и ты? Пожалуйста. В два счета! —
Но я представил жизнь, с младенческих ногтей
Подвластную тоске, и школьный запах пота,
И месиво забот, и марево страстей.

— Медея, — говорю, — кого-нибудь другого
Найди ... и белый пух младенческих волос
Внушает жалость мне ... жить вечно или снова —
Желанье это я, должно быть, перерос.

— Would you like to do this too? By all means. In a trice! —
But I imagined a life subject to anxiety
from its baby nails, and the smell of sweat at school,
and a mass of cares and a haze of passions.

— Medea, I say, find somebody else ...
and I feel pity for the white down of the baby's hair ...
I must have outgrown the desire to live
for ever or a second time.

One critic has claimed that all Kushner's work takes the form of conversations (Chuprinin 1983, 210), and certainly, even when not literally cast as dialogue, his poems often imply formally the active participation of the reader as interlocutor. This particular technique of dramatization is often used as a device to bring the present into contact with the ancient world. Thus "Pri mne ona v kotel," which concludes with Pelias addressing Medea, begins with him addressing the reader directly. "Mne, Plinii, mne pozvol' zadanie tvoe" ("Allow me, Pliny, to carry out your request"; 1988, 114–15), in which Kushner retells a story about a boy and a dolphin narrated by Pliny in a letter to Caninius Rufus (1915, 250–57),[3] takes the form of a dialogue with the Roman writer. In the final stanza, however, where Kushner relates Pliny's story to the present and uses it as an object-lesson in the universal human capacity for both good and evil, he again speaks directly to the reader:

Не правда ль, все века преступны и темны,
Но мальчик вечно добр и плеск дельфиний гулок.

Is it not true that all ages are criminal and dark, but a boy is
eternally kind and the splash of a dolphin resonant.

The tendency to philosophize that has often been noted in Kushner's verse (Marchenko 1966, 43; Ueland 1988, 372) frequently resolves itself almost as a lecture directed at the reader and marked with rhetorical questions and exclamations. Occasionally Kushner includes reference to ancient Greek thinkers such as Aeschylus (1988, 57), Empedocles (1991, 50) or Plato (1991, 81). Kushner's reference to external texts is often itself dialogic, and there are several examples involving classical writers. Thus "Dvum poetam v komnate odnoi" ("Two poets in one room"; 1986, 177–78) discusses Raphael's painting *The School of Athens*, and its portrayal of Aristotle and Plato, the thoughts of each in tune with the other's. "Est' muzyka v pribrezh-nom trostnike" ("There is music in the reed on the riverbank"; 1986, 134), considers the relationship between nature and poetry and combines a reference to Ausonius in its first line with an allusion to Tyutchev's poem "Pevuchest' est' v morskikh volnakh" ("There is a melodiousness in the sea's waves"), which used the same line from the Roman author as its epigraph: "est in harundineis modulatio ripis" ("Reed-grown banks also have their tuneful harmonies"; Ausonius, 114–15).[4]

The Greek mythological tradition has always been an important source of inspiration for Kushner and there are several mythological patterns which recur with some regularity. One of the most persistent motifs is the Greek underworld, and especially the river Lethe. For a poet as concerned as Kushner with the literary tradition, the process of remembering and forgetting is naturally of particular importance. The link in Kushner's poetry between Hades and St. Petersburg has already been mentioned. In other poems, the process of forgetting and loss is discussed using underworld imagery. In the early poem "Uekhav, ty vybral prostranstvo" ("When you left, you chose space"; 1986, 204) time and space are defined as two equivalent means by which memory may be erased: "Vot vidish': dve raznye Lety, / A pit' vsyo ravno iz kakoi" ("There, you see: two different Lethes, And it is all the same from which you drink"). More recently, Hades has been used as a metaphor for autumn (Kushner 1986, 55), and in "Ya skazhu tebe, gde khorosho ..." ("I will tell you where it is good ..."; 1990, 91) the image of Lethe is invoked in order to suggest that the unpalatable present can be forgotten by recourse to the world of the imagination.

The legend of Orpheus and Eurydice is used several times in Kushner's love poetry as a metaphor for the pain of loss (cf. Graves 1960, 1: 112). In "Zasnyosh' i prosnyosh'sya v slezakh ot pechal'nogo sna" ("You will fall asleep and wake up in tears from a sad dream"; 1986, 27–28) a grieving lover is compared to the figure of Orpheus: "Kogda tot poshyol, kameneya, k Kharonu vtorichno" ("When, turning to stone, he went to Charon the second time"). In "Vospominanie o lyubvi" ("Memory of Love"; 1986, 34) Kushner reverses the traditional legend, claiming that the reason he will not look back is not that he will thereby lose his love (who is already lost), but that to do so will merely recall the pain of separation. Nevertheless, like Orpheus, he finds the burden of restraint impossible to bear. The myth here is used to explain the subconscious process which is at work in the impossibility of self-denial (Elsworth, 1992, 203). In the recent poem "Novy Orfei" ("The New Orpheus"; 1991b, 94–96), the Orpheus legend is used to explain the psychology of reunion with Kushner's Russian friends whom he has not seen since they emigrated to New York. The poet experiences the desire to return to the past, but realizes that relationships have changed and that this is no longer possible. Elsewhere it is Orpheus' talent as a poet and singer which is brought to the reader's attention: in a poem on the origins of poetry Kushner evokes the image of Orpheus charming wild beasts with his music (1986, 173–74).

Another myth which has received repeated attention is the story of Theseus and the Minotaur (cf. Graves 1960, 1: 337–39). The Minoan labyrinth is an obvious metaphor for the human subconscious, and Kushner uses it as such in a number of poems, generally emphasizing the triumphant return of the hero after the Minotaur's death. In the recent "Spit Ariadna, ruki zalomiv" ("Ariadne sleeps, her hands broken off"; 1992, 37) Kushner makes the psychological interpretation of the myth explicit, providing the following definition of the Minotaur: "Ty smotrish': gde / Zver', mnoi zakoloty? V serdechnom tesnote, / V dushevnom sumrake" ("You are looking for the beast which I speared? It is in the narrowness of our hearts, in the half-light of our souls"). Yet in general he avoids this use of the Minotaur image in his poetry, preferring the solution to the threat. Thus in "Issledovav, kak Kritsky labirint" ("After exploring, like the Cretan labyrinth"; 1986, 291–92) Kushner applies the legend to the analysis of an unspecified depression and the subsequent gradual recovery from it. Elsewhere he compares the inspiring pattern of the night sky with the labyrinth at the moment that Theseus has just left it (1986, 68), and describes how a Minotaur-like figure is tamed by the innocence of a small girl (1986, 147–48). Other poems again identify the Minotaur as a political threat, rather than as a psychological one, and here it is a more ambiguous image. Kushner notes (1991b, 26–27) that under present conditions the politics of terror at least is no longer in operation: "Minotavr ne dokhnet tyazhelo, / Ne potrebuet strakha i drozhi v otvet" ("The Minotaur does not breathe heavily, demanding fear and trembling in reply"). Elsewhere, however, he is less sure, asking: "Myortv Minotavr nash / Ili ustal, spit?" ("Is our Minotaur dead, or tired, asleep?"; 1991b, 38).

Particularly in his most recent poetry, where he has been able to develop political themes more openly, Kushner has been drawn to Imperial Rome as a source of parallels and images. The comparison between the Roman empire on the one hand, with its alternation of benign and corrupt rulers, its gradual decay and disintegration, and the Soviet Union on the other, as it divests itself of its imperial legacy, is a compelling one, and it has proved very fruitful for Kushner's poetry.

The repressive measures of the early Roman empire, particularly the reigns of terror under Nero and Domitian, are a natural metaphor for the excesses of Stalinism. Kushner was able to broach these themes indirectly, without making their connection with the Soviet order explicit, in poems of the early 1980s. Thus in "Kakoi, Oktaviya, veter sil'ny" ("What a strong wind there is today, Octavia"; 1986, 91–92) he recalls Tacitus' account of the exile and murder of Nero's wife (1937, 203–13),[5] and in "Na vybor smert' emu predlozhena byla" ("A choice of deaths was offered him"; 1986, 89) he reconstructs the circumstances of a judicial suicide. Both these poems contain mechanisms that have the effect of distancing the episodes they describe from the present. In the Octavia poem, the poet's own problems obtrude as more important; in "Na vybor smert'…" the suicide serves to introduce a lengthy comparison between Greek and Roman attitudes to life. But at the same time, the vividness and specificity with which Kushner conveys the Roman past has the effect of making it appear of great relevance to the contemporary world.

In later poems the parallels between Roman and Soviet history are brought out much more clearly. In "Posledny, kto byl lyut i dik, — Domitsian —" ("The last who was cruel and wild — Domitian"; 1988, 42) Kushner defines Roman and, by implication, Russian history as a series of storms and periods of calm, placing his words in the mouth of an imaginary Roman and concluding: "Tak mog iz rimlyan kto-nibud' / Skazat'…. I my emu kivaem s ponimaniem" ("Thus might a Roman have said…. And we nod to him in understanding"). The point is then reinforced by a concluding stanza which asks how the pattern of history may be repeated in the twenty-first century. In a poem dedicated to Bella Akhmadulina, "Kakoe ravenstvo? Smugla i pyshnokryla" ("What equality? Dark and with downy wings"; 1991b, 70), the example of Nero is evoked to illustrate the point that death does not make all people equal: the tyrant is remembered by everybody, but his victims remain anonymous, forgotten as individuals. In another striking poem, "Prozhivi Katull eshchyo let desyat'" ("Had Catullus lived ten years longer"; 1991b, 67), Kushner catalogues the political degeneration — the murder of Julius Caesar and the ensuing struggle for power — that occurred in the years immediately following Catullus' death. The connection with the political development of Russia is emphasized by the heavily ironic line: "Tsezar' zhiv dlya nego i budet vechno / Zhiv" ("Caesar is alive for him and will live eternally") alluding to the endlessly repeated Soviet slogan about Lenin.

Another group of poems refers to the collapse of the Roman empire and the analogous situation in present-day Russia. "Mne i Rimskoi imperii zhal'" ("I am also sorry for the Roman empire"; 1991b, 17–18), while acknowledging that the fall of Rome was inevitable, bemoans the loss to the cultural heritage of Latin as a living language. Kushner goes on to insist that in the Russian case the collapse of empire will not result in the destruction of the language and culture. The poem immediately following in *Nochnaya muzyka* (*Night Music*) (Kushner 1991b, 18–19) contains a broadly similar message. Although the political order is uncertain, there is hope for the future: "Ya nadeyus' ne znayu na chto, na gryadushchy vek" ("I hope for I know not what, for the coming century"). The poem concludes with a plea to the contemporary Petronius, as he satirizes a period of decadence, not to be too harsh in his judgements: "Oboidyotsya, Petronii. Ne predrekai razvyazki / Mrachnoi, ty ved' ne polovets, ya zhe ne pecheneg" ("Things will turn out all right, Petronius. Do not foretell a gloomy outcome, for you are not a Polovtsian, I am not a Pecheneg"). Elsewhere, in "Teper' ya znayu, kak" ("Now I know how"; 1992, 34), Kushner finds a key to the understanding of contemporary events in the example of the fourth-century poet Ausonius, who himself lived at a time of political dissolution. In Kushner's view, the type of poetry which Ausonius wrote, with its emphasis on domestic, even banal themes, is wholly understandable in a world with no stable values, where "nagleet got / I shtukaturka vniz letit" ("The Goth is becoming insolent and the plaster is flying loose"). He finds that a similar sort of poetry is also appropriate for present-day Russia, where the domestic round provides the only fixed point in a world characterized by breakdown: "Teper' ya znayu, gde / Spasen'e dlya zhivykh" ("Now I know where rescue lies for the living"). In many ways of course Kushner has, until recently at least, avoided grand themes and concentrated on the everyday in precisely the same fashion as Ausonius (see, for example, Urban 1986, 152).

If at present Ausonius seems the classical poet with whom Kushner has the greatest affinity, the figure who appears most consistently in his recent verse is Catullus, another writer whose work generally avoids public themes. One poem from *Nochnaya muzyka* (Kushner 1991b, 68) contains a tribute to Catullus' ability to coax poetic immortality from as superficially prosaic a creature as a sparrow, and insists that poetry is not dependent on the weightiness of its subject matter for its significance: "Kto skazal, chto nuzhny poetu temy, / Chto oni tem nuzhnee, chem vesomei" ("Who said that a poet needs themes, that they are more necessary the weightier they are"). Although Kushner does not refer to Catullus in this poem by name, he incorporates many details from the poet's biography into his text, mentioning Rome,

Verona and the dedication of Catullus' work to Cornelius Nepos. There are also direct textual allusions: compare, for instance, "Luchshy sbornik, ottertyi pemzoi zhestkoi" ("The best collection, rubbed down with hard pumice-stone") and "Cui dono lepidum novum libellum / arida modo pumice expolitum?" ("To whom am I to present my pretty new book, freshly smoothed off with dry pumice-stone?" Trans. F.W. Cornish.) (Catullus 1950, 2–3). Likewise, "O tebe, primostivshemsya na lone / Obnazhyonnoi podrugi ravnodushnoi ..." ("About you, installed in the lap of his naked, nonchalant friend") and "Passer, deliciae meae puellae, / quicum ludere, quem in sinu tenere" ("Sparrow, my lady's pet, with whom she often plays whilst she holds you in her lap." Trans. F.W. Cornish.) (Catullus 1950, 2–3).[6]

In several other poems Kushner makes use of real or imagined episodes from Catullus' life in order to dramatize themes of his own. This device is most strikingly used in "Prozhivi Katull eshchyo let desyat'," which has already been discussed, and in "V real'nosti nel'zya — v romane mozhno" ("In reality you can't, in a novel you can"; 1991b, 66). This poem takes the form of an imaginary conversation between Catullus and Caesar, who consoles the poet for the sorrows of his life and assures him that the lasting values of his poetry will make those sufferings worthwhile. Kushner succinctly affirms the significance of Catullus' verse for the Russian present by insisting that even translations have the power to move the reader: "Prochtyot ikh kto-to: dazhe v perevode / Oni ego vzbodrili i plenili ... " ("Someone will read them: even in translation they have cheered and captivated him ... "). In other poems points are illustrated by incidental reference to Catullus. Kushner reflects on what views Catullus may have seen while in Bithynia (1986, 137), and uses him as an emblem of all that fascinates him about Rome: "tam, gde kipela vrazhda, / Gde Katull prokhodil, bormocha: — Chto za drian', svolota!" ("Where enmity seethed, where Catullus walked past muttering, 'What rubbish, what swine!'"; 1991b, 105). In one poem from *Zhivaya izgorod'* (*Hedgerow*), "Kak pisal Katull, propadaet golos" ("As Catullus wrote, speech disappears"; 1988, 86), Kushner enters directly into a dialogue with the author of what he calls elsewhere his favourite book ("Luchshy sbornik": 1991b, 68), paraphrasing and later quoting in Russian Catullus No 51. Compare:

> Как писал Катулл, пропадает голос,
> Отлетает слух, изменяет зренье
> Рядом с той, чья речь и волшебный образ
> Так и этак тешат нас в отдаленье.

As Catullus wrote, speech disappears, hearing vanishes, vision fails next to her, whose words and magical image please us so much at a distance.

> lingua sed torpet, tenuis sub artus
> flamma demanat, sonitu suopte
> tintinant aures, gemina teguntur
> lumina nocte.

> my tongue falters, a subtle flame steals down through my limbs, my ears ring with inward humming, my eyes are shrouded with twofold night. [Trans. F.W. Cornish] (Catullus 1950, 60–61)[7]

Kushner also adapts the first words of Catullus No. 85: "Odi et amo" ("I hate and I love"): "Nenavidim i lyubim" ("We hate and we love"). He makes a distinction between "vlyublennost'" ("falling in love") and "lyubov'" ("love"), which in his view Catullus ignores. In Kushner's understanding, the state of insecurity which Catullus describes is not love but "vlyublennost'," while the emotion that genuinely deserves the name of love is something calmer and nobler, born only out of maturity.

Kushner, like many other Russian poets of his generation and especially those closely associated with St. Petersburg — for example, Iosif Brodsky, Evgenii Rein and Anatolii Naiman — sees himself in many ways as a continuator and preserver of the Russian modernist tradition. Coming of age during the Khrushchev thaws, Kushner turned naturally to the poetic values of the last pre-revolutionary generation rather than to the compromised aesthetic of socialist realism. He was inspired by the example of Anna Akhmatova, the last surviving major figure of the Russian Silver Age, whom he met several times and who encouraged him in his writing (see Kushner 1991a, 378–91). Kushner's interest in the period is attested by several articles he has written on such writers as Blok, Mandel'shtam and Annensky, and, in his poetry, by numerous direct and indirect quotations from the work of the Silver Age writers. In recent years Kushner's political verse has included poems focussing on events in early twentieth-century history. For example, in "Gadanie" ("Fortune-Telling"), he presents a fortune-teller weighed down by the vision of the future lives of her clients that she is able to read in the cards; in "Vospominaniya" ("Memories") he uses the persona of a survivor of the Terror who is recalling the friends of his youth — most of them now dead — and their respective fates (1988, 22, 18–19). There have also been references to literary-historical themes: in "Vospominaniya" Kushner evokes a young woman reading her poetry to Akhmatova at the height of the latter's early fame; elsewhere he recreates details from the life of Chekhov (1988, 24–25).

However, Kushner's recuperation of the Silver Age has always been closely linked with his use of material from the Greek and Roman traditions. As his poetry has developed, the connection has taken a variety of forms. In his earlier verse it is largely confined to a repetition of motifs from the common currency of St. Petersburg poetic style, a reflection of the city's neoclassical heritage in terms similar to those of the modernist writers. Thus, Kushner is inspired by the same classical statues as his predecessors and like them he refers regularly to the muses. From his earliest work he draws on the vision of St. Petersburg as necropolis, and the association of the Neva with the river Lethe, which is encountered, for example, in Akhmatova and Mandel'shtam (Kushner 1986, 229, 268; Ueland 1988, 371). In one memorable early poem, "Pamyati Anny Akhmatovoi" ("In Memory of Anna Akhmatova"; 1986, 228–29), Kushner pays tribute to the older poet in a way which both acknowledges Akhmatova's own debt to the classical tradition (see Wells 1990) and confirms its importance for Kushner in defining Russian modernism. The poem describes Akhmatova's stately progress across the rivers of Hades and combines an account of the underworld conceived in classical terms — "Pred neyu volny katyat / Kotsit i Akheront" ("Before her Cocytus and Acheron roll their waves") — with a series of allusions to her biography: "Druguyu by dorogu, / V Komp'en ili Parizh…" ("It might have been another road, to Compiègne or to Paris…"), "No dyshit grud' ne chashche, / Chem v Tsarskom gde-nibud'" ("But her breast breathes no faster than it used to anywhere in Tsarskoe Selo"), "Takoi, kak Modil'yani / Eyo narisoval" ("Just as Modigliani portrayed her").

In Kushner's later writing, the biographies of other modernist writers are also linked with classical themes. Thus in "Ne slishkom slozhen byl professorsky vopros" ("The professor's question was not too difficult"; 1988, 131), Kushner imagines the young Mandel'shtam struggling to answer a classroom question about Aeschylus. This scene prefaces a discussion about Mandel'shtam's approach as a poet to the classical tradition. Kushner emphasises that although Mandel'shtam's classical scholarship is often at fault, he nevertheless has an instinctive understanding of the ancient world which he is able to translate effectively into a commentary on the present by virtue of his talent as a poet: "No rifma ubedit, / I v ritme pauzy tak khoroshi i sdvigi" ("But the rhyme convinces, and the pauses and displacements in the rhythm are so good"). The poem ends with an allusion to a passage from Mandel'shtam's own work which stands as an epigraph to Kushner's poem: "Kogda-to zhil uzhe, druzhil vo t'me vekov / S Eskhilom-gruzchikom, Sofoklom-lesorubom" ("Once he lived and was friends in the darkness of the ages with Aeschylus the stevedore and Sophocles the lumberjack").[8] Kushner thus projects Mandel'shtam's approach to the Greek tradition onto his own view of the task of the poet. In this context it is significant that Mandel'shtam's "Gde svyazanny i prigvozhdenny ston" ("Where the bound and nailed groan"; 1967, 240–41), which is primarily concerned with the status and function of the poet under Stalin, and from which the epigraph is taken, contains a further classical allusion to Prometheus, who is seen as an analogue of the poet suffering "for having dared where others would have fallen back" (Baines 1976, 188).

In "Razmashisty sovkhoz Temryukskogo raiona" (1988, 116) Kushner juxtaposes the discovery of the statue of Apollo and a reference to the post-symbolist journal *Apollon*. In the same way as ancient Greece is available to the contemporary world but hidden just below the surface, so is the world of Annensky. A chance encounter with his wife's aunt, who turns out to be the girl in the green sash to whom Annensky devoted his poem "Oduvanchiki" ("Dandelions"), brings this point home (Annensky 1990, 88–89). The poem further evokes the modernist world by referring to two other works by Annensky: compare the lines "My ryadom s 'Apollonom,' / Vblizi sharmanki toi, ot skripki v dvukh shagov" ("We are next to *Apollo*, close to that barrel organ, two paces from the violin") with Annensky's poems "Staraya sharmanka" ("The Old Barrel Organ") and "Smychok i struny" ("Bow and Strings"), which deal with the power of barrel-organ and violin music respectively (1990, 90–91, 87). The poet himself is thus included within the ambit of the literary-historical periods — classicism and modernism — with which he most closely identifies and on which he most commonly draws.

In the poem "O da, ona mogla b vnushit' Orfeyu" ("Oh yes, she could have inspired Orpheus"; 1991b, 28) Kushner discusses the Orpheus legend, and attempts to explain Orpheus' turning back in terms of the "feminine" aspect of his soul, in the context of an examination of Tsvetaeva's poetry. Tsvetaeva is at no point mentioned by name, but is adequately identified through references to certain localities associated with her biography: her native Moscow, Germany, where she lived in the first years after emigrating from Russia, and the Vendée, which "she regarded as the homeland of her soul" (Karlinsky 1985, 161): "S nei / Germaniyu lyubivshei i Vandeyu…" ("With her, who loved Germany and the Vendee"); "Pisavshaya v Moskvu ob etoi sile / Svoei…" ("Writing to Moscow about this strength of hers"). There is also mention of salient aspects of her poetic style. Kushner notes that the early enthusiasm of himself and his friends towards her work was followed by a degree of disillusionment with Tsvetaeva's verbal and emotional acrobatics: "ottalkivan'ya ot takikh strastei / Izbytochnykh" ("rejection of these excessive passions"). The Orpheus legend of course is also one to which Tsvetaeva was especially attracted, associating it particularly with Voloshin (see Tsvetaeva 1979, 58).

Other poems link the classical world and Russian modernism by the use of rather less direct textual allusion. For example, in "Vremena ne vybirayut" ("People do not choose their times"; 1986, 22–23) Kushner insists that a Hesiodic Golden Age has never existed and that suffering and courage are necessary in all epochs: "Chto ni vek, to vek zhelezny" ("Whatever the age it is an iron age"). At the same time, he provides numerous examples of eras that were worse than the present (the poem was written in the late 1970s). He names specifically the reign of Ivan the Terrible and the Florentine plague, but refers to the Stalinist Terror only indirectly through the expression "Vek moi, rok moi" ("My age, my fate"), echoing Mandel'shtam's phrase "Vek moi, zver' moi" ("My age, my beast") from his poem "Vek" ("The Age"), written in 1923, but foreseeing future events (Mandel'shtam 1967, 102–03). Mandel'shtam himself refers in this poem to the Golden Age, admitting that it cannot be recreated. Kushner's poem also alludes to work by Gumilyov and Blok (Ueland 1988, 374; Elsworth 1992, 212), both of whom died in 1921, like Mandel'shtam, victims in one way or another of the revolution. These references transform what is on the surface a fairly unexceptionable, abstract poem about time and fate into something with a much more concrete message about the duty of the poet to bear witness to the era in which he or she lives. The same Mandel'shtamian subtext is referred to in "Posledny, kto byl lyut i dik — Domitsian" (Kushner 1988, 42), which, as we have seen, addresses the theme of the Terror much more directly. Here, in the spirit of ancient Rome, the age is seen as a wolf: "Nam vypal volk — ne vek" ("We received a wolf, not an age"). This wolf may perhaps be tamed, but its behavior into the twenty-first century is not altogether predictable.

Kushner's use of material from the Greek and Roman tradition is complex and wide-ranging. It is clear, however, that classical motifs in his poetry are clustered around a small number of fundamental themes. They are used in the exploration of universal psychological processes and they are especially important in Kushner's self-definition as a poet, not only because of his direct response to classical writers, but because he connects the classical tradition very closely with the Russian modernists. Increasingly in his recent poetry, Kushner has been concerned with the question of the poet's role in society and has sought inspiration in the example of figures such as Catullus or Ausonius. Most strikingly, he has used the history of the Roman empire to illuminate both the Stalinist Terror and the apparent collapse of Soviet/Russian society. How Kushner's use of classical material will develop in the future cannot yet be known, but it seems certain that it will continue to play a central and productive part in his poetry.

NOTES

1. "We should not 'play at antiquity.' In using the ancient world I would wish to talk about the most serious, the most broadly significant things. These should be poems about today, enriched by the memory of the past." (All translations are mine unless otherwise indicated.)
2. *Caesar*, 11.3-4.
3. *Letters*, 9.33.
4. *Epistles*, 29.
5. *Annals*, 14.60-4.
6. Catullus, 1-2.
7. Catullus himself is, of course, paraphrasing Sappho here, but Kushner is concerned only with the Roman author.
8. Kushner's epigraph reads: "No eti guby vvodyat pryamo v sut' / Eskhila-gruzchika, Sofokla-lesorubtsa…" ("But these lips lead straight to the essence of Aeschylus the stevedore, Sophocles the lumberjack…") The aposiopsis is not present in Mandel'shtam and serves to draw the reader's attention to the remainder of the poem from which the epigraph is taken.

WORKS CITED

Annensky, I.F. 1990. *Stikhotvoreniya i tragedii*. Leningrad: Sovetsky pisatel'.

Ausonius. 1921. *Ausonius*. Ed. Hugh G. Evelyn White. Vol. 2. London: Heinemann.

Baines, Jennifer. 1976. *Mandelstam: The Later Poetry*. Cambridge: Cambridge University Press.

Catullus. 1950. *Catullus, Tibullus and Pervigilium Veneris*. Ed. F.W. Cornish, J.P. Postgate and J.W. Mackail. Rev. edn. London: Heinemann.

Chuprinin, Sergei. 1983. *Krupnym planom. Poeziya nashikh dnei: problemy i kharakteristiki*. Moscow: Sovetsky pisatel'.

Elsworth, John. 1992. "The Poetic Vision of Aleksandr Kushner." *Symbolism and After: Essays on Russian Poetry in Honour of Georgette Donchin*. Ed. Arnold McMillin. London: Bristol Classical Press.

Graves, Robert. 1960. *The Greek Myths*. Rev. edn. 2 vols. Harmondsworth: Penguin.

Karlinsky, Simon. 1985. *Marina Tsvetaeva: The Woman, Her World and Her Poetry.* Cambridge: Cambridge University Press.

Kushner, A.S. 1986. *Stikhotvoreniya.* Leningrad: Khudozhestvennaya literatura.

_____. 1988. *Zhivaya izgorod': kniga stikhov.* Leningrad: Sovetsky pisatel'.

_____. 1990. "Iz lirika." *Druzhba narodov* 7: 89–92.

_____. 1991a. *Apollon v snegu: zametki na poliakh.* Leningrad: Sovetsky pisatel'.

_____. 1991b. *Nochnaya muzyka: kniga stikhov.* Leningrad: Lenizdat.

_____. 1992. "Devyat' stikhotvorenii." *Znamya* 2: 34–37.

Mandel'shtam, O.E. 1967. *Sobranie sochinenii v tryokh tomakh.* Ed. G.P. Struve and B.A. Filippov. Vol. 1, 2nd edn. Washington: Inter-Language Literary Associates.

Marchenko, A. 1966. "Chto takoe ser'yoznaya poeziya?" *Voprosy literatury* 11: 35–55.

Pliny. 1915. *Pliny: Letters.* Ed. William Melmoth. Revised by W.M.L. Hutchinson. Vol. 2. London: Heinemann.

Plutarch. 1919. *Plutarch's Lives.* Ed. Bernadotte Perrin. Vol. 7. London: Heinemann.

Tacitus. 1937. *Tacitus: The Histories and the Annals.* Ed. Clifford H. Moore and John Jackson. Vol. 4. London: Heinemann.

Tsvetaeva, M.I. 1979. *Izbrannaya proza v dvukh tomakh 1917–1937.* Vol. 2. New York: Russica.

Ueland, Carol. 1988. "Aleksandr Kushner and the Re-Emergence of the Leningrad School." *Studies in Comparative Communism* 21, 3/4: 369–78.

Urban, Adol'f. 1986. "Pyataya stikhiya." *Neva* 9: 51–58.

Wells, David N. 1990. "Three Functions of the Classical in Akhmatova's Poetry." *The Speech of Unknown Eyes: Akhmatova's Readers on Her Poetry.* Ed. W.A. Rosslyn. 2 vols. Nottingham: Astra Press. Vol. 2: 183–99.

THE WANDERING GREEK: IMAGES OF ANTIQUITY IN JOSEPH BRODSKY[1]

Dan Ungurianu, University of Wisconsin

Classical motifs are plentiful in the work of Joseph Brodsky. They range from separate details and names sparkling here and there to whole poems and poetic cycles and include references to classical mythology, history and art. In the frequency of his allusions to antiquity Brodsky far surpasses any contemporary Russian poet (with the exception perhaps of Kushner). This fact alone suggests the significance of classical motifs in Brodsky, to say nothing of Brodsky's own declarations about his "classicism." "Ya zarazhyon normal'nym klassitsizmom,"[2] writes Brodsky in 1965, very early in his literary career (1970, 142). Twenty years later, in 1985, he confirms this, speaking about "the inoculation of the 'classical rose,'" to which he subjected himself for the greater part of his life (1986, 395–96).

The words "classical rose" evoke Khodasevich and point to a link between Brodsky's "classicism" and the "classical" tradition in Russian poetry. In fact, virtually all of Brodsky's art demonstrates a similar interplay of foreign and native sources, an interplay which David M. Bethea adeptly terms "triangular vision":

> Brodsky ... constantly looks *both ways*, both to the West and to Russia, as he continues Mandelstam's dialogue with Hellenicism. This vision can be called triangular in that a Russian source ... is subtly implanted within a Western source ... so that each source comments on the other, but as they do so they

also implicate a third source — Brodsky himself.... This ingenious triangu-
larity happens often enough to be, for the mature Brodsky, a kind of signa-
ture. (1994, 49)

When Brodsky alludes to contemporary Anglo-American poetry or even the
English Metaphysics and Dante, his sources are usually specific and trace-
able. However, antiquity is present in his work not in the form of allusions
to a particular author or piece, but primarily as a pool of images with certain
symbolic meanings and as a framework for cultural, philosophical and
historical concepts.[3] For this reason, I will concentrate not on the origin of
classical motifs, but rather on their usage by Brodsky. As to Russian influences, I will single out that of Mandel'shtam, whose notion of Hellenicism[4]
shaped Brodsky's vision of antiquity to such a degree that when looking for
the roots of Brodsky's attraction to classical imagery, one inevitably comes
across the Mandel'shtam connection. In the essay entitled "The Child of
Civilization," "the second Osya" elaborates on the famous phrase coined by
his great predecessor, "nostalgia for world culture":

> The notion of a world culture is distinctly Russian. Because of its location
> (neither East nor West) and its imperfect history, Russia has always suffered
> from a sense of cultural inferiority, at least toward the West. Out of inferiority
> grew the ideal of a certain cultural unity 'out there' and a subsequent intellec-
> tual voracity to anything coming from that direction. This is, in a way, a
> Russian version of Hellenicism. (Brodsky 1986, 130)

These words are self-referential for Brodsky, as are most of his writings on
Mandel'shtam. At least in his early period, Brodsky was driven by this same
intellectual voracity for Western culture, especially under the circumstances
of the Soviet political situation, when longing was reinforced by the need for
defense. As Brodsky recalls in an interview: "There was that sentiment in all
of us.... It was defending culture, but in the broad sense, it wasn't Russian
culture or Jewish culture, it was simply defending civilization against the
barbarians" (1991, 36). Classical culture was, indeed, one of the cornerstones
of that civilization.

Classical motifs appear very early in Brodsky's work, reflecting the poet's
enchantment with antiquity and signaling his Russian "Hellenic" orientation
as well. This is seen already in one of his first "classical" poems — "Veliky
Gektor strelami ubit" ("The great Hector has been killed by arrows") of 1961
— a beautiful vignette, an animated picture from a Greek vase, reminiscent,
incidentally, of Pushkin's "antique" stylizations, especially "Tsarskosel'-
skaya statuya" ("The Statue of Tsarskoe Selo"). Another similar poem is

"Enei i Didona" ("Aeneas and Dido") (1969), in which Brodsky revives in perfect classical settings a famous story from Virgil, and also alludes to a piece by Akhmatova (see Zelinsky 1987). This poem vividly demonstrates the two-pronged nature of Brodsky's classical motifs, with their sources in both antiquity and twentieth-century Russia.

Such a double connection can be traced in Brodsky's use of geographical names as well. He repeatedly refers to the Crimea as *Tavrida*, to the Black Sea as *Pont*, and to the Don as *Tanais*; even the school friend who got stranded in Sochi calls himself "Yazon, zastryavshy na zimu v Kolkhide" (1970, 127).[5] Brodsky follows here the old Russian poetical tradition (of which Mandel'shtam and his Crimean poems are a prominent example), that stems from "Russian poetry's traditional regard for the Crimea and the Black Sea as the only available approximation of the Greek world, of which these places ... used to be the outskirts" (Brodsky, 1986, 126). In addition, however, it seems that Brodsky is simply too enchanted by antiquity to miss the opportunity to say out loud the Greek toponyms.

In accordance with this longing, Brodsky on several occasions identifies his persona with ancient heroes. An extended autobiographical use of classical motifs is found in "K Likomedu na Skiros" (1967) ("To Lycomedes on Scyros"). There, behind the Brodskian version[6] of the Theseus myth, one can easily discover the facts of the poet's own life. Theseus won a victory over the Minotaur, but instead of enjoying his glory, he is frustrated because Ariadne is left in the embrace of Bacchus. Equally frustrated was the young Brodsky when, having won his battle with the Soviet monster, he discovered M.B., the dark lady of his songs, in the embrace of another man. In "Anno Domini" (1968),[7] betrayal by the beloved woman is joined with separation from the son. The latter theme becomes central in a poem written after Brodsky's forced emigration — "Odissei Telemaku" ("Odysseus to Telemachus") (1972), in which Odysseus' situation is clearly similar to that of the poet: a sea divides both of them from their sons. Odysseus' words about his "victory" in the war recall Theseus in "K Likomedu" and must reflect the bittersweet outcome of Brodsky's own "Trojan war":

Троянская война
окончена. Кто победил — не помню.
Должно быть, греки: столько мертвецов
вне дома бросить могут только греки.

The Trojan War
is over. I don't remember who won.
Presumably, the Greeks: so many corpses
could be cast outside the homeland only by the Greeks. (1977a, 23)

And in contrast to the happy ending of Odysseus' travels, the persona of the poem is not at all sure whether he will come back.[8]

Political hints are present in "Odissei Telemaku" as well: the mention of high casualties among the Greeks in "The Trojan War" evokes traditional Russian ways of waging wars (Kreps 1984,155). However, such allusions can hardly be called political in the proper sense of the word, because they represent not an effort to encode some political realia, but rather an attempt to "depoliticize" those realia by sublimating them to the mythological level. And in general, Greek poems in Brodsky involve mostly mythical and epic images and are practically devoid of political "lining."

Direct political implications appear frequently only in Brodsky's Roman poems, which towards the beginning of the seventies supplant the Greek ones.[9] This progression follows Mandel'shtam's trajectory, as described by Brodsky himself: "Toward the twenties, the Roman themes gradually overtake the Greek and biblical references largely because of the poet's growing identification with the archetypal predicament of 'a poet versus an empire'" (1986, 128).

Brodsky's picture of the Roman Empire bears a clear resemblance to the Soviet Union, the heir of the "Third Rome" (a term the poet uses on numerous occasions). It is a huge state ruled by an all-mighty Caesar in the center and his proconsuls in ethnically diverse provinces ["Anno Domini," "Post Aetatem," "Pis'ma rimskomu drugu" ("Letters to a Roman Friend")]. Its borders are tightly guarded ("Post Aetatem"). It wages constant wars in remote locations: "Kak tam v Livii, moi Postum, — ili gde tam? / Neuzheli do sikh por eshchyo voyuem?" (1977a, 13).[10] The center is corrupted: "Kak tam Tsezar'? Chem on zanyat? Vsyo intrigi? / Vsyo intrigi, veroyatno, da obzhorstvo (1977a, 11)."[11] So are the provinces: "Vse namestniki — voryugi" (1977a, 12).[12] The empire is in stagnation[13] and its bulky ship[14] moves slowly in a narrow channel:

Все вообще теперь идет со скрипом.
Империя похожа на трирему
в канале для триремы слишком узком.
Гребцы колотят веслами по суше,
и камни сильно обдирают борт.
Нет, не сказать, чтоб мы совсем застряли!
Движенье есть, движенье происходит.
Мы все-таки плывем. И нас никто
Не обгоняет. Но, увы, как мало
похоже это на былую скорость! (1977b, 94)

Everything now is dragging along.
The empire looks like a trireme
in a canal which is too narrow for a trireme.
The rowers beat their oars upon the land
and rocks scratch deeply at the sides.
No, that is not to say that we're entirely stuck!
There is movement, movement still takes place.
We are still sailing and no one
passes us. But alas, how little
this resembles our former speed!

Some other details are strikingly Soviet as well:

Движенье перекрыто по причине
приезда Императора. Толпа
теснит легионеров — песни, крики;
но паланкин закрыт (1977b, 87)

Traffic is blocked because of
the Emperor's visit. The crowd
pushes the legionaries — songs, cries,
but the palanquin is closed.

It is possible to find even direct quotations from contemporary political life; for example:

Известный,
известный местный кифаред, кипя
негодованьем, смело выступает
с призывом Императора убрать
(на следующей строчке) с медных денег. (1977b, 89–90)

A famous,
famous local bard, boiling
with indignation, boldly appeals
to remove the Emperor
(and the next line reads) from copper coins.

This bard is, of course, Voznesensky with his notorious appeal to remove Lenin's portrait from banknotes (Kreps 1984, 238–39). There are allusions to Brodsky's own political circumstances as well. In a fragment written during his exile, Brodsky compares himself to Ovid:

Назо, Рима не тревожь.
Уж не помнишь сам
тех, кому ты письма шлешь.
Может, мертвецам. (1992, 396)

Naso, do not disturb Rome.
You do not remember any longer
those to whom you send your letters.
Perhaps — to dead men.

This poem should be viewed in the light of the Russian Ovidian tradition and especially in the context of the famous Mandel'shtamian "Ya vernulsya v moi gorod" ("I came back to my city"): "U menya eshchyo est' adresa, / po kotorym naidu mertvetsov golosa."[15] The same is true for another piece dating back to this period, "Nazo k smerti ne gotov" ("Naso is not ready for death"), which resonates with Mandel'shtam's line: "Ya eshchyo ne khochu umirat'"[16]). In "Post Aetatem" the authorities adopt new tougher laws against paupers, prompting the wandering Greek ("brodyaga-grek") to flee the country. At his famous trial Brodsky himself was accused of *tuneyadstvo*, social parasitism, and indeed became a "wandering Greek," a fragment of Hellenic civilization in the Post-Hellenic, "Roman" world.

The list of Soviet allusions in the Roman poems could be continued, but it is important to bear in mind that Brodsky is by no means a political poet, one of those "local bards" trying to bite the authorities. His position is not that of defiance but — to use Venclova's paraphrase from Akhmatova — that of "the stoic's splendid contempt" (Venclova 1990, 138):

Если выпало в империи родиться,
лучше жить в глухой провинции у моря.
И от Цезаря далеко и от вьюги.
Лебезить не нужно, трусить, торопиться. (1977a, 12)

If it befell you to be born in an empire
it is better to live in a remote province by the sea.
Far from the Caesar and the blizzard.
One does not need to fawn, to fear, to hurry.

Attempts to change anything in the Empire or to flee from it are seen as futile (Tullius in *Marbles* voluntarily returns to prison), because Brodsky's concept of Empire is not purely political, but rather philosophical; it is an existential category based on his view of time, space and death.

Time is one of the central themes of Brodsky's writing, and, in his view, the preoccupation of every poet: "A poet always deals with time, one way or another. Whether he is young or decrepit.... Because what is a song anyway but restructured time?" (1989, 71). Time in Brodsky is in direct opposition to space.[17] Space consists of objects,[18] on which time wages war, making them rot and turn into dust. Space in turn "retaliates," supplanting time with the monotonous infinity of the spatial continuum. The human spirit (especially a poetic one) belongs to the temporal realm, while human flesh is a part of the material spatial world. Therefore human beings are inevitably caught in a kind of double trap. Space is hostile to the human spirit and strives to take it over. Time, paradoxically enough, proves to be an accomplice in this: destroying the carnal vessel of spirit, it halts the attempts of the latter to master Chronos, and in so doing pushes men into the wasteland of space. Death brings total objectification, turning humans into a mere thing.[19] Although people are thereby relieved of suffering and emotional chaos, they are also deprived of the temporal dimension, which to Brodsky as a human being and as a poet is of a higher order and dearer: "Space to me is, indeed, both lesser and less dear than time. Not because it is lesser but because it is a thing, while time is an idea about a thing. And choosing between a thing and an idea, the latter is always to be preferred, say I" (1986, 435). One of the pivotal concepts in Brodsky's philosophy is the time–space dichotomy, with people being squeezed between the two and facing imminent destruction unless they manage to leap into time. Hence Brodsky's main existential preoccupation: how to make this leap, or to put it more simply, how to overcome death. For Brodsky, whose worship of language borders on religion, this appears to be possible through the restructuring of time by poetry, as he describes it in connection with Mandel'shtam:

> Mandelstam's verse ... expresses the slowing-down, viscous sensation of time's passage.... The words, even their letters — vowels especially — are almost palpable vessels of time; they allow the moment to continue, to "linger beyond its own natural limit." (1986, 125)

Antiquity provides Brodsky with rich imagery for these topics, and classical motifs play a vital role when the poet addresses the time–space–death relationship. It is in connection with antiquity that Brodsky first gives a completed picture of a living creature transformed into a thing when, in the poem "Podsvechnik" ("A Candlestick"), a dying satyr turns into a statue: "Shagnuv za Rubikon, on zatverdel ot peis do genitalii" (1970, 118).[20] This metamorphosis is replayed in "Tors" ("Torso"):

Встань в свободную нишу и, закатив глаза,
смотри, как проходят века, исчезая за
углом, и как в паху прорастает мох
и на плечи ложится пыль — этот загар эпох. (1977a, 39)

Stand in a free niche and, rolling up your eyes,
watch the centuries pass, disappearing around
the corner, and the moss grow in your groin
and your shoulders get covered with dust, this tan of ages.

The same motif is repeated over and over again in Brodsky's work and in
almost every instance it involves reminiscences of antiquity (seen through
the eyes of Medusa, one might add). In "Post Aetatem," the servants of the
proconsul freeze like statues: "Slugi bezuchastno glyadyat pered soboi, kak
izvayan'ya" (1977b, 88).[21] So does the wandering Greek:

Невероятно жарко;
и грек сползает с камня, закатив
глаза, как две серебряные драхмы. (1977b, 90)

It's incredibly hot.
And the Greek slides from the rock, rolling up
his eyes like two silver drachmas.

"Zakativ glaza" is a symptom of petrification familiar from "Tors." Another
detail in this poem, the hot climate, is "loaded" as well. Such weather is quite
appropriate for becoming immobilized. It also suggests a link with Mandel'shtam, since, as Brodsky remarks, his classical poems are usually set in
late summer (1986, 126). The same is often true of Brodsky. "Post Aetatem,"
with its alternation of extremely hot and cooler weather, is probably set in
that season, as are "Pis'ma rimskomu drugu": "Skoro osen', vsyo izmenitsya
v okruge" (1977a, 11).[22] Autumn implies impending decay and death, and,
in fact, "Pis'ma" deal with that theme and most likely result in the death of
their persona. August is also the time of "Rimskie elegii" ("Roman Elegies"),
in which statues abound and the persona constantly feels the imminent
possibility of becoming petrified: "Privalis' luchshe k portiku, skin' bakhily,
/ skvoz' rubashku stena kholodit predplech'e" (1987, 113).[23]

These lines evoke the model defined in "Tors": "Vstan' v svobodnuyu
nishu." A similar pattern is found in "Natyurmort" ("Still Life") where the
persona, presumably on the verge of suicide, feels that he is turning into a
marble statue:

Я неподвижен. Два
бедра холодны, как лед.
Венозная синева
Мрамором отдает. (1977b, 110–11)

I am immobile, my two
hips are cold as ice.
My bluish veins
smack of marble.

Moreover, marble sculptures — busts of classical writers — are more than plentiful in *Marbles*.

Death is described as petrification, the turning of a living being into a "statue,"[24] but transformations do not stop at this point: statues follow the usual destiny of things, dilapidating and eventually crumbling to dust. The process of continued degradation is depicted in "Tors":

Кто-то отколет руку, и голова с плеча
скатится вниз, стуча.
И останется торс, безымянная сумма мышц. (1977a, 39)

Someone will chip off a hand and the head
will roll down the shoulder, knocking.
And the torso will remain, the anonymous sum of muscles.

The poet's own body turns into ruins: "Vo rtu razvaliny pochishche Parfenona" or "V polosti rta ne ustupit karies / Gretsii drevnei po men'shei mere" (1977a, 24).[25] His whole life is a ruin:

Вот и прожили мы больше половины.
Как сказал мне старый раб перед таверной:
"Мы, оглядываясь, видим лишь руины."
Взгляд, конечно, очень варварский, но верный. (1977a, 12)

Well, we've lived more than half.
As an old slave told me in front of a tavern:
'Looking back, we see only ruins.'
It is of course a barbaric view, but a correct one.

This personal "ruination" corresponds to a broader picture:

Для бездомного торса и праздных граблей
ничего нет ближе, чем вид развалин.
Да и они не ломаном "р" еврея

узнают себя тоже; только слюнным раствором
и скрепляешь осколки, покамест Время
варварским взглядом обводит форум. (1987, 111–12)

For the homeless torso and idle hands
there is nothing dearer than the sight of ruins.
And they too, in the broken 'r' of a Jew,
recognize themselves; only with saliva
can you glue together the fragments whilst Time
looks around the forum with a barbaric glance.

Of course, all Brodsky's poetry can be viewed as an attempt to overcome the gravity of space, escaping into a higher dimension, into time, but many of his classical poems demonstrate this urge very vividly. Here again Brodsky emulates Mandel'shtam:

> In almost every case when Mandelstam happens to deal with this theme of time, he resorts to a rather heavily caesuraed verse which echoes the hexameter either in its beat or in its content.... As a rule, this kind of a poem ... directly or indirectly evokes the ancient Greek background. (1986, 126)

And indeed in Brodsky's very first classical poem ("Veliky Gektor"), the topic itself is a lingering moment, which is reinforced by the poet's extensive use of *ziyanie* (hiatus),[26] a device normally not typical of him. Similarly, in "Enei i Didona" ("Aeneas and Dido") a static scene is animated meticulously and then linked to the remote future. The sensation of retarded time runs through virtually all of Brodsky's classical poems and culminates in open declarations in *Marbles* that time is the main subject of a poet's preoccupation. This obsession with time, Brodsky emphasizes, is a prerogative of poets and only of poets: "Main thing, don't mix them up with emperors. Nor with the orators. Nor with playwrights. Only poets" (1989, 53).[27]

Hence we return to the topic of Empire in Brodsky, but now in a broader philosophical context and in connection with the poet's view of history, which is outlined in his essay "Flight from Byzantium." Brodsky sees two main principles in world history — Greek and Roman. The Western tradition is Greek in origin: "one of order (the Cosmos), of proportion, of harmony, of the tautology of cause and effect (the Oedipus cycle) — a tradition of symmetry and the closed circle, *of return to the origin*" (1986, 401–02). Rome broke away from the Greek tradition and became preoccupied with the spatial realm: "As its Empire grew, Rome ... fled from that culture. The flight began, in fact, with the Caesars and with the idea of absolute power" (1986, 410). Every empire, be it Rome, Byzantium, Russia, or the USSR, represents the triumph of space and endless linear movement. Rome in this respect is the opposite of Greece and is more akin to the East. In Brodsky's view, the first proponent of linearity in literature was a Roman writer, Virgil: "Virgil … was the first — in literature, at least — to apply the linear principle.… It was dictated by the expansion of the Empire, which had reached a scale in which human displacement had indeed become irreversible" (1986, 402). The linear attitude was transferred even to time itself, which grew to be perceived as something spatial: a plane, or rather a road, leading to a certain point in the future. Such a concept resulted, according to Brodsky, in social utopias, including Christianity (1986, 402).[28] Christianity was also closer to the imperial tradition by virtue of its monotheism: "Polytheism was synonymous with democracy. Absolute power — autocracy — was synonymous, alas, with monotheism" (1986, 410). Brodsky's sympathies clearly lie with Greek principles:

> Bearing in mind the culture we call ancient or classical … I can only say that the longer I live the more this idol worship appeals to me, and the more dangerous seems to me monotheism in its pure form. There is little point, I suppose, in laboring the matter, in calling the spade the spade, but the democratic state is in fact the historical triumph of idolatry over Christianity. (1986, 410–11)[29]

But for Brodsky these Greek principles are fragile and might prove not to be very lasting, as can be seen in his futuristic totalitarian utopia, where the ultimate Empire brings an end to "our era." This motif sounds for the first time very early, in 1966, when the poet muses in "Ostanovka v pustyne" ("A Stop in the Desert") about the coming of another era:[30]

> Сегодня ночью я смотрю в окно
> и думаю о том, куда зашли мы?
> И от чего мы больше далеки:
> От православья или эллинизма?
> К чему близки мы? Что там, впереди?
> Не ждет ли нас теперь другая эра? (1970, 168)

> Tonight I look out the window
> and think, where have we gone?
> And what are we further from:
> Orthodoxy or Hellenicism?
> What are we close to? What is ahead?
> Is a different era awaiting us?

Four years later Brodsky addresses this topic in the cycle "Post Aetatem Nostram." There he introduces into an otherwise "purely" Roman setting a futurological element, describing in poem VII a huge steel tower, one of whose functions is to be a prison for a certain fixed number of inmates arrested arbitrarily not for crimes but on a percentage basis. In 1984 Brodsky unfolds this idea in an entire play, *Mramor* (translated into English in 1989 as *Marbles*), the action of which takes place in a cell of the steel tower during the second century *post aetatem nostram*, when the new Roman Empire will rule the Earth: "Because Rome's destiny is to rule the world. As the poet has it" (1989, 31). As Vail and Genis have noted, Brodsky reiterates "with a masochistic delight" "a reflection–prediction in the magic mirror of the eternal city — the prophetic symmetry *MIR — RIM* (world — Rome)" (1990, 206). In order to create the image of the ultimate Empire Brodsky refers to the legacy of Rome, the archetype of Empire.

The ultimate Empire also means the ultimate triumph of space, which is irreconcilable with time and poetry. Speaking of Mandel'shtam's destiny, Brodsky described this conflict strikingly, as follows:

> It was a case of pure polarization. Song is, after all, restructured time, toward which the mute space is inherently hostile. The first has been represented by Mandelstam; the second chose the state as its weapon. There is a certain terrifying logic in the location of that concentration camp where Osip Mandelstam died in 1938: near Vladivostok, in the very bowels of the state-owned space. (1986, 137)

This statement sheds light on Brodsky's stance of splendid contempt in his relation to the Empire: since the latter represents space, which in turn is a synonym of death, it is senseless to resist the Empire on its own plane. The only possible escape is in the restructuring of time, in poetry.

However, Brodsky plots yet another escape route, which seems paradoxical and self-contradictory: on several occasions he states that the way out of spatiality and death is in the Empire itself, in the world of petrified bliss, as it is described in "Tors":

> Если вдруг забредаешь в каменную траву,
> выглядящую в мраморе лучше, чем наяву,
> или заметишь фавна, предавшегося возне
> с нимфой, и оба в бронзе счастливее, чем во сне,
> можешь выпустить посох из натруженных рук:
> ты в Империи, друг.

If you suddenly find yourself in stone grass,
which looks better in marble than in reality,
or you notice a faun given over to play
with a nymph, and both are happier in bronze than in dreams,
you can drop the staff from your calloused hands:
you're in the Empire, friend.

Brodsky continues:

Это — конец вещей, это — в конце пути
зеркало, чтоб войти. (1977a, 39)

This is the end of things, this is a mirror to enter
At the end of the path.

This idea is expressed unequivocally in *Marbles*: "Rome's task is to merge
with time" (1989, 13).

In explaining this paradox, one might assume that here Brodsky got
carried away by a certain mathematical logic inherent in his time–space
dichotomy: if space and time are in direct opposition, then the reduction of
space to zero will result in an automatic going into time: "Skhodya na konus,
/ veshch' obretaet ne nol', a Khronos" (1977b, 106).[31] Brodsky is appalled by
death, which will leave him in the embrace of "mute space," but is simultaneously attracted to it, tempted by the idea that dying can break the chain of
spatiality, thus enabling him to overcome death itself, "having trampled
death by death," so to speak:

"Не умер" повторяли зеркала ...
Нас ждет не смерть, а новая среда. (1970, 117–18)

"He didn't die" the mirrors repeated ...
We are awaited not by death, but by a new environment.

The same logic is present in the words of Tullius in Marbles, who asserts that
the less space one has, the closer one is to time:

[Prison] virtually pushes you out physically. Into time ... into Chronos. For
the absence of space is the presence of time.... Solitary, though, might be
better.... Beyond that, of course, there is only a coffin. Where space comes to
an end, and you become time yourself. Cremation, though, would be even
better. (1989, 49)

Of course, the Empire represents not a spatial zero but, on the contrary, infinity. However, it is at this point that opposites come together: "The meaning of the Empire ... is in rendering space meaningless. When so much is conquered, it's all the same" (1989, 46). Maximum space amounts to no space, presumably opening the door into time. But, as Tullius admits in *Marbles*: "Suicide ... is not a way out. It's no exit, it's just the word 'Exit' painted on a wall" (1989, 44).

One can also suppose that the Empire casts a spell for Brodsky because it creates for a poet like him "optimal" conditions for writing. Hence Brodsky's masochistic attraction to the Empire; he sees his arrival in the United States from the totalitarian Soviet Union only as a change of empires:

> Как бессчетным женам гарема всесильный Шах
> изменить может только с другим гаремом,
> я сменил империю. (1977a, 100)

> As the all-powerful shah can betray his countless wives
> only with another harem,
> I changed empires.

But even an experimenting "layman" like Tullius recognizes that true mastery of time comes only from poetry. And Brodsky himself, although he utilizes the conditions in the Empire to "restructure time," does so exclusively by means of poetry, following in the footsteps of his great predecessor, the "first" Osya, who also used the somewhat forced "help" of the Empire to reach the last limits of its vast space. "And he ran," writes Brodsky, "till there was space. When space ended, he hit time" (1986, 139). He hit time not because of his death in a concentration camp (a less refined version of the Tower), but because of his poetry. Thus the spell of the Empire is the spell of death. Just as dying by itself cannot trample death, nor can the Empire release one from the grip of space; this is achieved by poetry.

There is yet another consideration: articulating his views about the idea of the Empire in "Flight from Byzantium," Brodsky projects his shocking impressions of Istanbul onto Rome (and for that matter Russia), and takes the idea of Rome's opposition to Greece and the Hellenistic principle to its extreme. In his poetry we find a less gloomy portrayal:

> Я счастлив в этой колыбели
> Муз, Права, Граций,
> где Назо и Виргилий пели,
> вещал Гораций. (1987, 93)

> I am happy in this cradle
> of Muses, Law, Graces,
> where Naso and Virgil sang,
> Horace spoke.

But as Brodsky admits in "The Child of Civilization," Petersburg, his home in the Third Roman Empire, is a Hellenistic city (1986, 130). The notion of the Empire proves to be more complex. One of the main features of the Empire is an abundance of statues: in this respect Rome and Petersburg are similar. "I ya kogda-to zhil v gorode, gde na domakh rosli / statui," writes Brodsky in a poem dedicated to his Italian friends (1987, 181).[32] But the statue is indeed an ambivalent symbol.[33] On the one hand, it is a *veshch'* — a de-animated and reified body — on the other, it is a work of art, representing if not restructured time, then restructured space: "Na kachestvo prostranstva / nikak ne reagiruyushchy byust" (1987, 137).[34] A statue offers some kind of "impersonal immortality," even when it is dilapidated (Nivat 1990, 95): "Plot', prinyavshaya vechnost' kak anonimnost' torsa" (1987, 116).[35] Or at least, by translating flesh into marble, a statue increases the body's "life span." However, this is not an ideal solution, as Brodsky says in his "Exegi monumentum" variation:

> Я не воздвиг уходящей к тучам
> каменной вещи для их острастки.
> О своем — и о любом грядущем
> я узнал у буквы, у черной краски. (1987, 113)

> I did not erect a stone thing,
> going toward clouds for their intimidation.
> About my own and any other future
> I learned from the letters and the black paint.

Brodsky states once again that the only way to flee from the inevitable annihilation in the world of things and to master time lies in restructuring it with language, with poetry, with the pulse of prosody.

* * *

The major meanings of the classical motifs in Brodsky's poetry are not isolated from each other, but are present simultaneously, making images of antiquity polysemantic and multifaceted. This is true of the first antique poem by Brodsky, "Veliky Gektor," which is not simply a Greek "study" by a young self-proclaimed classicist, but also an "exercise" in making the moment linger in the spirit of Mandel'shtam's Greek poems. The multidimensionalism of Brodsky's classical poems grows as he progresses as a poet and shapes more clearly his notion of antiquity. Two good examples of this are his poems from *Uraniya*: "Byust Tiberiya" ("The Bust of Tiberius") and "Rimskie elegii."

The situation in "Byust Tiberiya" (1987, 135–37) evokes the old cliche: a poet addressing the statue of a great man. Brodsky starts with an appropriate greeting: "Privetstvuyu tebya dve tyshchi let spustya." The first two words fit quite nicely into the solemn "Ave, Caesar," but the subsequent colloquial "tyshcha" introduces another tonality, which fully manifests itself in the next two lines: "Ya tozhe byl zhenat na blyadi. / U nas nemalo obshchego."[36] Moreover, this is an address to one of the major symbols of terror and cruelty in human history, to one of those figures about whom historians normally write in a very different key, as in Karamzin's exclamation: "Monsters outside the law, outside the rules and probabilities of the mind: these horrible meteors, these wandering flames of unbridled passions light for us through the ages the abyss of possible human depravity, so seeing this we shudder" (1892, 274). The poet openly departs from this solemn rhetorical tradition.

К тому ж
вокруг-твой город. Гвалт, автомобили,
шпана со шприцами в сырых подъездах,
развалины. (1987, 135)

Besides
around is your city, noise, automobiles,
punks with syringes in damp doorways,
ruins,

Brodsky proceeds, introducing a scene of modern Rome. The last element in this picture is ruins, an extremely "charged" motif in Brodsky, as we have seen. Here they represent the realia of the city and also hint at the future destiny of today's busy world.

The poet returns his glance to the bust and, sighing elegiacally "Akh, Tibery" ("Oh, Tiberius"), he begins to "revive" the emperor. This sigh is repeated three times in the poem: whenever he wants to animate the bust, Brodsky resorts to it like a sort of artificial resuscitation. But the value of the elegiac mode has already been deflated. Brodsky's "poetic eye" reconstructs Tiberius' missing body, which proves to be Rome itself:

Все то, что ниже подбородка,-Рим:
провинции, откупщики, когорты,
плюс сонмы чмокающих твой шершавый
младенцев. (1987, 135)

Everything that is beneath your chin is Rome:
provinces, tax-farmers, cohorts,
plus swarms of babes sucking on your rough one.

The ruins are restored to their original boisterous being. It might seem for a moment that the bust itself acquires the gift of speech:

Те самые уста!
глаголющие сладко и бессвязно
в подкладке тоги. (1987, 135)

Those very lips!
mumbling sweetly and incoherently
under your toga.[37]

The toga is another recurrent classical detail in Brodsky. Here it is connected with sex, and later in *Marbles* almost every mention of a toga will be accompanied by sexual remarks, thus emphasizing the contrast between the outburst of the body's biological energy and its imminent petrification.

The framework of the poem expands even further: from the geographical ancient Rome to history, which Brodsky seems to regard with totally alienated, dispassionate eyes as he justifies Tiberius and his cruelty. He also takes on moralizing historians:

Какая разница, что там бубнят
Светоний и Тацит, ища причины
Твоей жестокости! (1987, 135)

What difference does it make what
Suetonius and Tacitus grumble, looking for reasons
for your cruelty!

Human beings appear to be mere leaves:

И защищать тебя
от вымысла — как защищать деревья
от листьев с ихним комплексом бессвязно,
но внятно ропщущего большинства. (1987, 136)

> And to protect you
> from fiction is like protecting trees
> from leaves with their complex
> of a majority complaining incoherently but loudly.

Such a stance seems to be rather strange for a Russian poet in general, and for Brodsky in particular. Let us recall his own words condemning the imperial disregard for human life: "The common denominator of all these deeds is the anti-individualistic notion that human life is essentially nothing — i.e., the absence of the idea that human life is sacred, if only because each life is unique" (1986, 422). In "Byust" he evokes this same topic, punning on the word *sledstvie*, which means "consequence" and "investigation":

> Причин на свете нет,
> есть только следствия. И люди жертвы следствий.
> Особенно, в тех подземельях, где
> все признаются-даром, что признанья
> под пыткой, как и исповеди в детстве,
> однообразны. (1987, 135–36)

> There are no causes in the world
> but only consequences, and people are victims of
> consequences/investigations
> especially in those cells where
> everybody confesses, though confessions under torture
> are monotonous, like confessions in childhood.

So, the complaints of people are monotonous and meaningless, as are their confessions under torture.

Such an attitude toward history becomes more understandable if we return to the tree-leaf metaphor. Here, Tiberius is the tree and other people are leaves; they are just outgrowths of Tiberius' body, which is space, the essence of the empire. So people, at least in Tiberius' plane of operation, are only objects, *veshchi*. Also, Tiberius acts with perfect logic for his spatial dimension where destruction is the only possible outcome:

> Вообще — не есть ли
> жестокость только ускоренье общей
> судьбы вещей? (1987, 136)

> In general, is not
> cruelty just the acceleration of
> the destiny of things?

"*Uskoren'e*" (acceleration) might be a reference to Virgil's Fourth Eclogue:

'Speed on those centuries', said the Parcae to their spindlers,
Concordant with the steadfast nod of Destiny. (1984, 59)

Some four years before "Byust," in 1977, Brodsky had composed his variation on the Fourth Eclogue, and now, as he writes about Tiberius, presumably he still has Virgil's original in mind. There is an obvious coincidence in the wording: "Speed on those centuries" — "acceleration of destiny." But the content is very different. According to the traditional interpretation of the Church (and that is definitely the one the poet is interested in), Virgil predicts the coming of Christ (who was crucified during Tiberius' reign) and the speeding of time towards eternal life. But in "Byust" Brodsky talks about acceleration of space towards eternal non-being.

Having made this gloomy assertion, the poet returns for a moment to the present, reiterating the idea that the Rome of Tiberius is gone:

Фонтаны, бьющие туда, откуда
никто не смотрит — ни сквозь пальцы, ни
прищурившись. Другое время!
И за уши не удержать уже
выбесившегося волка. (1987, 136)

Fountains spurting upwards whence
no one watches, not through one's fingers nor
squinting one's eyes — a different time!
and the mad wolf can no longer be held by his ears.

That is to say, the gods of antiquity who used to inhabit the sky of Rome are gone, and so is Tiberius' power to control his subjects.[38] But despite all this, the principle embodied in Tiberius remains, and Tiberius is even "preferable" to his followers because he represents pure destruction:

Ты был чудовищем, но равнодушным
чудовищем ...
... Гораздо
отраднее — уж если выбирать —
быть уничтоженным исчадьем ада,
чем неврастеником ...
Ты выглядишь естественной машиной
уничтоженья, а вовсе не

рабом страстей, проводником идеи
и прочая. (1987, 136)

You were a monster, but an impassionate
monster ...
... it is much
preferable, if one has to choose,
to be destroyed by the progeny of hell
than by a neurasthenic ...
You look like a natural machine
of destruction, and not at all like
a slave of passions, the bearer of an idea
and so on.

"*Nevrastenik*" and "*provodnik idei*" are, at least in part, Soviet allusions. Such types are a deviation from "natural destruction," but the overall principle is the same.

The poet develops this thought, returning to his own persona described in terms of the familiar ruinary imagery:

Я тоже ...
... превратился в остров
с развалинами, с цаплями. (1987, 138)

I too ...
... turned into an island
with ruins, herons.[39]

This is probably the main point of similarity between him and the emperor, and not the dubious kinship of being married to whores, as it may have appeared in the beginning. Brodsky continues the comparison: Tiberius' head was "cut off" during his lifetime by the sculptor who made the bust: "Golova, otrublennaya skul'ptorom pri zhizni."[40] Something like this has been happening to the poet: "I ya / chekanil profil' svoi posredstvom nastol'noi lampy. / Vruchnuyu."[41] Attempts to change one's life are futile because ahead there is only destruction, both personal and universal:

Раскаяться? Переверстать судьбу?
Зайти с другой, как говориться, карты?
Но стоит ли? Радиоактивный дождь
польет не хуже нас, чем твой историк.
Кто явится нас проклинать?
Звезда? Луна? Осатаневший от бессчетных

мутаций, с рыхлым туловищем, вечный
термит? (1987, 137)

To repent? To redo destiny?
To play another card?
But is it worth it? Radioactive rain
will pour on us like your historian.
Who will come to curse us? A star?
The moon? An eternal termite, fed up with countless
mutations, with a soft body?

Even the words of the poet, in contrast to Brodsky's usual "religion of language," are powerless to change anything:

Что до сказанного мной,
мной сказанное никому не нужно —
и не впоследствии, но уже сейчас. (1987, 137)

As to my words,
nobody needs my words —
and not in the future but even now.

Everything in this world is doomed, apparently proclaims the poet who stoically faces the inevitable. It might appear that such an idea is expressed by the very flow of the poem which starts from one ruin, the bust of Tiberius, encompasses Rome and all of history and, engulfing the poet who happens to be in its way, ends in total destruction.

However, the movement of the poem does not fit into that "stream of lava" pattern, nor does the poem's meaning limit itself to a mere declaration of impending death and corruption. The poem keeps progressing in circles, or to be more precise, in concentric circles. The first circle starts when the poet animates the bust, which swells to the size of the Roman Empire and then shrinks, returning to the sculpture: "V rezul'tate — byust."[42] Immediately with the first line of the second stanza another circle begins, and its radius is already much bigger: it again revives the bust and ancient Rome and also encompasses world history. Then it too returns to the statue: "Na kachestvo prostranstva nikak ne reagiruyushchy byust."[43] After that the bust is instantly animated again ("Ne mozhet byt', chto ty menya ne slyshish'!"[44]), and the third circle starts, which is even greater and includes the poet and the future of mankind. And again everything returns to its circuits: in the dust of annihilated Earth, the future termite discovers the bust, which is now a "collective" bust of Tiberius and the poet, who have been merged together by a common destiny: "Natknuvshis' v nas / na nechto tvyordoe."[45]

But there is yet another circle, the last ring that encompasses everything in the poem. The poem starts when, in an abandoned gallery, the poet comes across the bust and inspires life into it through his "Akh, Tiberii." The poem ends in exactly the same way: amid the dust of the abandoned Earth a termite encounters the bust, and the termite behaves in a way strikingly similar to the poet's actions in the first lines:

«Бюст, — скажет он на языке развалин
и сокращающихся мышц, — бюст, бюст.» (1987, 137)

"A bust," he will say in the language of ruins
and contracting muscles, "a bust, a bust."

What ultimately prevails is not destruction, but language, drawing a new circle, the radius of which is infinity, because language deals with time and transcends the limits of the spatial world. As Brodsky puts it in his "Fourth Eclogue":

Кириллица, грешным делом,
разбредясь по прописи вкривь ли, вкось ли,
знает больше, чем та сивилла,
о грядущем. О том, как чернеть на белом,
покуда белое есть, и после. (1987, 123)

The Cyrillic letters,
wandering astray on the page,
know more than that Sibyl
about the future.
About how to show black on white
as long as white exists and after.

Language will exist as long as things exist and afterwards, so the poet's lamentation in "Byust" — with all its obvious seriousness — proves to be somewhat of a ploy. He turns the whole poem into an "Exegi monumentum," and this monument is not "a stone thing," but poetry. Then "we" in "Natknu-vshis' v nas / na nechto tvyordoe" refers not to Tiberius and Brodsky, but to Brodsky and poets in general, and through this line shines the old "Non omnis moriar." Having buried the world and himself under the ruins of spatiality, the poet emerges from its dust and, sticking out his tongue (yazyk), cries: "Byust! Byust! Byust!" Such amazing about-faces are typical of Brodsky, showing that beneath his established mask of a grim Stoic there hides a buffoon who can pretend to be dying, but then suddenly open his eyes, disentangle himself from the folds of the petrifying toga, and erect another monument of sorts, making one of those eloquent gestures:

> Скрестим же с левой, вобравшей когти,
> правую лапу, согнувши в локте. (1977a, 42)

> So let us cross with our left clenched fist ...
> our right arm, bent at the elbow.

Brodsky's views of poetic language, time and space are manifested vividly in another Roman poem: "Rimskie elegii." Here he gives a striking picture of how poets pass into time, described in stanza X:

> Рим, человек, бумага;
> хвост дописанной буквы — точно мелькнула крыса.
> Так уменьшаются вещи в их перспективе, благо
> тут она безупречна. Так на льду Танаиса,
> пропадая из виду, дрожа всем телом,
> высохшим лавром прикрывши темя,
> бредут в лежащее за пределом
> всякой великой державы время. (1987, 115–16)

> Rome, a human being, paper;
> the tail of a drawn letter — as if a rat had scurried by.
> Thus things dwindle in their perspective,
> which is impeccable here. Thus on the ice of Tanais,
> vanishing from sight, quivering all over,
> having covered top of their heads with dried-up laurels,
> they wander into time, lying beyond the limit of any great power.

These lines might also imply Mandel'shtam — both his poetry and his horrible end. Perhaps Brodsky found himself on the dead poet's territory when, at the beginning of the previous stanza (IX), he undertook a description of Rome's architecture which turned out to be very Mandel'shtamian in its "anatomical" imagery (including "vertebra" — a word heavily charged in Mandel'shtam): "Skorlupa kupolov, pozvonochniki kolokolen. / Kolonnady, raskinuvshei chleny, pokoi i nega" (1987, 115).[46] These words certainly produce some kind of Russian reference because Brodsky suddenly abandons Rome to "travel" to the North:

> В этих широтах все окна глядят на Север,
> где пьешь тем больше, чем меньше значишь.
> Север! в огромный айсберг вмерзшее пианино,

мелкая оспа кварца в гранитной вазе,
не способная взгляда остановить равнина,
десять бегущих пальцев милого Ашкенази. (1987, 115)

In these latitudes all windows face North,
where the less you mean, the more you drink.
North! A piano frozen into a huge iceberg,
Pockmarks of quartz in a granite vase,
a plain unable to stop a glance,
ten fingers of the dear Ashkenazi.[47]

Brodsky returns to Italy, but at the beginning of the next stanza he has a line which reverberates with Mandel'shtam's notion of speech and speaking, the movement of lips: "Vyp'em chayu, litso, chtoby razdvinut' guby" (1987, 115).[48] Then follows a rather strange transition: from the tail of a letter (compared to a rat) to the passage into time across the ice of the frozen Tanais. To explore this, let us recall Mandel'shtam's poem "Polnoch' v Moskve" ("Midnight in Moscow"), which is also an urban elegy of sorts, set in the summer. There Mandel'shtam describes the winding of a clock with weights as catching time by its tail: "Uzh do chego sherokhovato vremya, / A vsyo-taki lyublyu za khvost ego lovit'" (1991, 1: 183).[49] In Brodsky we see a letter's tail leading to time. But why the frozen Tanais? Tanais is the modern Don, and Voronezh, the place of Mandel'shtam's exile, lies in close proximity to the Don. Furthermore, Tanais was considered by the ancient Greeks to be the Eastern border of Europe. Mandel'shtam died near Vladivostok — the very brink of Russia (the Greek words *Tanais* and *thanatos* [death] are consonant, especially in the Russian pronunciation). According to Struve, Mandel'shtam perished in December of 1938, during a winter so cold that even navigation from the transit camp had to be interrupted prematurely. Hence, perhaps, "lyod Tanaisa" ("the ice of Tanais"). In a letter from the camp quoted by Struve, Mandel'shtam complains that he is very cold without warm clothes ("Ochen' myorznu bez veshchei" [1991, 1: LI]).[50] In Brodsky we read: "Drozha vsem telom" ("quivering all over"). The laurels find parallels in Mandel'shtam as well. In one of the most piercing of the Voronezh poems written not long before his final arrest, "Zabludilsya ya v nebe ..." ("I got lost in the sky ..."), Mandel'shtam says: "Ne kladite zhe mne, ne kladite / Ostrolaskovy lavr na viski" (1991, 1: 257).[51] Brodsky crowns his migrant into time with "vysokhshy lavr" ("dried-up laurels"), mounting it onto the "temya" ("top of one's head"), which is rhymed with "vremya" ("time") — a rhyme found twice in Mandel'shtam. "Temya" for Mandel'shtam, like "viski" ("temples"), is a word associated with sacrifice and violent death under the epoch's blows.[52] In addition, "Zabludilsya ya v nebe" deals with the same themes as "Rimskie elegii": Italy, poetry, death, immortality. Of course, one cannot help but notice the affinity of the lines in "Rimskie elegii" ("they wander into time, lying beyond the limit of any great power") with Brodsky's own words about Mandel'shtam written some four years earlier: "He ran till there was space. When space ended, he hit time" (1986, 139). Thus Voronezh and Vladivostok show through the Roman ruins, and the Russian frost invades the heat of an Italian August.[53]

Having started with Mandel'shtamian overtones in an architectural description, Brodsky generates a rich web of allusions to the poetry and biography of his predecessor, "the first Osya," whose influence on Brodsky is profound in many areas, including the preoccupation with antiquity and the notion of "Hellenicism." Mandel'shtam is also extremely important for Brodsky's concept of poetic language and the poet. Evoking Mandel'shtam in the Roman settings of "Rimskie elegii," Brodsky pays homage to the great poet and focuses the poem on themes associated with his name. By so doing, Brodsky once again introduces a Russian source into a classical context and, using their mutual reflections, creates images of antiquity which are unmistakably Brodskian, based on the poet's distinctive view of language, time, space and history.

NOTES

1. I would like to express my gratitude to David M. Bethea, Alexander Dolinin, and Angela Brintlinger of the University of Wisconsin–Madison for their generous advice in developing the ideas and arguments in this article.

2. "I am infected with normal classicism." (This and other translations, unless otherwise indicated, are mine. Brodsky has translated some of his poetry himself. However, I have chosen to use my own literal prose translations for one obvious reason: as is often the case with bilingual writers, Brodsky's translations present different versions of the original and are poems in their own right.)

3. There are certain exceptions. For example, in "Byust Tiberia" ("The Bust of Tiberius") there are allusions to Suetonius and Tacitus, as well as to Virgil's Fourth Eclogue (see below). But as a rule, Brodsky's references to antiquity are very general and not based on particular sources. Brodsky differs in this respect from such accomplished antiquarians as, for example, Annensky, Vyacheslav Ivanov and Bryusov, and indeed from many poets of the Russian "Silver Aage" who underwent — to various degrees — classical schooling. This includes

Mandel'shtam, who knew some Latin and Greek (though he supposedly failed his Greek literature exam at St. Petersburg University [Struve 1991, xi]).

4. As Victor Terras rightly remarks: "Mandelstam's ideas in the field of philosophy of language, aesthetics, and poetic theory, which he considers 'hellenistic,' have only a vague and indirect connection with the world of classics" (1966, 252). The same is undoubtedly true of Brodsky; however, as mentioned above, I am interested not in the "archaeological" aspect of his classical allusions, but in the way they are used.

5. "Jason, stranded for the winter in Colchis."

6. One of the possible reasons why Brodsky turned to the story of Theseus was the first publication in the Soviet Union of Tsvetaeva's tragedy "Ariadna" at the end of 1965.

7. This title is obviously connected with the title of Akhmatova's collection.

8. Brodsky's poem, "Odissei Telemaku," contrasts with the ending of "Zolotistogo meda struya" ("The stream of golden honey") by Mandel'shtam: "Odissei vozvratilsya, prostranstvom i vremenem polnyi" ("Odysseus returned, full of space and time") (1991, 1: 64). Not only does Brodsky's Odysseus doubt that he will ever come home, but he also gets caught in the conflict of space and time: "Kak budto Poseidon, poka my tam teryali vremya, rastyanul prostranstvo" ("As if Poseidon, while we were losing time there, / stretched space") (1977a, 23).

9. The following demonstrates the chronology of this shift in major works by Brodsky containing classical motifs:

1961	"Veliky Gektor ..." ("The Great Hector")	Greek.
1962	"Gladiatory" ("Gladiators")	Roman.
1964	"Orfei i Artemida" ("Orpheus and Artemis")	Greek.
1964–65	"Nazo k smerti ne gotov" ("Naso is not ready for death")	Roman.
1965	"Ex Ponto" (Poslednee pis'mo Ovidiya v Rim)	
	(Ovid's Last Letter to Rome)	Roman.
1967	"K Likomedu na Skiros" ("To Lycomedes on Scyros")	Greek.
1968	"Podsvechnik" ("The Candlestick")	Antiquity in general.
	"Anno Domini"	Roman.
1969	"Enei i Didona" ("Aeneas and Dido")	Greek and Roman.
1970	"Post Aetatem Nostram"	Roman.
1972	"Odissei Telemaku" ("Odysseus to Telemachus")	Greek.
	"Tors" ("Torso")	Roman.
	"Pis'ma rimskomu drugu" ("Letters to a Roman Friend")	Roman.
1977	"Ekloga 4-ya (zimnyaya)" ("The Fourth [Winter] Eclogue")	Roman.
1981	"Rimskie Elegii" ("Roman Elegies")	Roman.
1981	"Byust Tiberiya" ("The Bust of Tiberius")	Roman.
1984	*Mramor (Marbles)*	Roman.

Initially, Greek and Roman references are mixed more or less evenly, but from ⬩ late sixties Roman themes prevail. (Years for poems from *Urania* are given ⬩ding to the English-language edition [Brodsky 1988], since in the Russian ⬩ot all the poems are dated.)

10. "How are things over there in Libya, my Postumus, or wherever? / Are we really fighting even now?"

11. "How is the Caesar? What is he up to? Still intrigues? / Still intrigues, presumably, and gluttony."

12. "All governors are thieves."

13. As Lev Loseff writes on this subject: "It would be naive to credit Brodsky with 'inventing' the rhetoric of anti-*zastoi* (stagnation) which gained currency in Soviet society twenty years later, but we have seen that this was exactly what Brodsky came up with at the very beginning of the Brezhnev era when he was trying to pinpoint the essence of the new *Zeitgeist*" (1990, 51).

14. The ship of state is a very common metaphor, but one particularly important instance of it might be in Mandel'shtam's poem, "Sumerki svobody" ("The Twilight of Freedom").

15. "I still have addresses at which I will find the voices of the dead."

16. "I don't want to die yet."

17. The more space there is — the less time, and vice versa: "The absence of space is the presence of time" (1989, 49).

18. "Veshch' est' prostranstvo, vne / koego veshchi net" (1977b, 111). ("A thing is space beyond / which there is no thing.")

19. "Vot ono — to, o chem ya glagolayu: / o prevrashchenii tela v goluyu / veshch'!... / Eto i k luchshemu. Chuvstvo uzhasa / veshchi ne svoistvenno." ("There it is — what I'm talking about: / about transformation of the body into a bare / thing! ... / It's for the best, though. A feeling of horror / is not characteristic of things") (1977a, 27). For an interesting discussion of de-animation and reification in Brodsky, see Polukhina 1989, 146–59.

20. "Having strode across the Rubicon, he hardened from whiskers to genitals."

21. "Servants look straight ahead impassionately like statues."

22. "Soon it will be autumn and everything around will change."

23. "You'd better lean against the portico and toss off your slippers / through your shirt the wall is cold on your shoulders."

24. Another version of this is the anonymity of the Roman toga with its folds. See Georges Nivat's discussion of this image in Brodsky: "The journey into 'antiquity' plays a cardinal role, not just in the poetics, but also in the imagination of Joseph Brodsky. The decapitated, antique statue with the sumptuous folds of its tunic or peplum which at one and the same time reveal and conceal the body, seems to me to be the fundamental image, that can, perhaps, provide the key to the 'Ars Poetica' of the poet of the 'Roman Elegies', of the 'Bust of Tiberius', or the play 'Marble'" (1990, 89). Also noteworthy is the downplayed manner in which Brodsky introduces this important motif in the play: "TULLIUS: Whose member is that? You've an erection. (Climbs out of the bath) Where's my toga?" (1989, 13).

25. "The mouth is in ruins, worse than the Parthenon." "The decay of the mouth cavity will not concede, / at least to Ancient Greece."

26. There are seven of them in the fourteen-line poem: strelami ubit, kusty i, po koleno a, voda uzhe, volny i, voda opyat′, i uvlekaet (1970, 45).

27. As P. Vail′ and A. Genis comment on this phrase: "The poet deals with pure time. All others are forced to use spatial categories: for the emperor it is the country, for the orator — the square, for the playwright — the stage" (1990, 204).

28. In "Flight from Byzantium," Brodsky clearly links Rome and Christianity to the spatial/imperial principle of the East. This idea openly contradicts what Brodsky himself has to say further in the essay, where he remarks sarcastically : "On its way to Rus, Christianity dropped behind it not only togas and statues but also Justinian's Civil Code. No doubt in order to facilitate the journey" (1986, 416). The implications are that Rome and Western Christianity are the opposite of the East. This contradiction can be explained if we assume that Brodsky, who does not elaborate on the matter, sees within Rome and Christianity two conflicting beginnings, Hellenic and Eastern. The former resulted in Roman law and Western Christianity, the latter in the Roman Empire and Eastern Orthodoxy.

29. Thus Brodsky's concept in one way is similar to Mandel′shtam's: they both consider Greek and Roman civilizations to be direct opposites, and the sympathies of both poets are on the side of the Greeks. (See e.g., Mandel′shtam's "Everything Roman is sterile, because the soil of Rome is stony, because Rome is Hellas deprived of grace" (1990, 2: 318).) But their applications of this principle to subsequent history are very different. Mandel′shtam considered Christianity to be a continuation of Hellenicism and included Russia in its sphere. Brodsky saw in Christianity and in Russia descendants of imperial linearity.

30. In "Ostanovka v pustyne" there is also a striking image of the linear "Roman" principle triumphing over the cyclical Hellenic one. Describing the demolition of the Greek church in Leningrad and its subsequent replacement by a concert hall, Brodsky says: "Zhal′ tol′ko, chto teper′ izdaleka / my budem videt′ ne normal′ny kupol, / a bezobrazno ploskuyu chertu" ("It's a pity that now / we'll be seeing from afar not the normal dome, / but an ugly flat line.") The poet concludes: "Tak malo nynche v Leningrade grekov, / da i voobshche — vne Gretsii — ikh malo" ("Nowadays there are so few Greeks in Leningrad, / and in general — outside Greece — there are few") (1970, 166–68).

31. "Being reduced to a point / a thing gains not zero but Chronos."

?. "Some time ago, I too lived in a city, where statues grew on buildings."

The sculptural myth in Russian poetic tradition is discussed by Jakobson (1975, 33), who defines two main "directions" of sculptural imagery: a living being [illegible] into a statue and a statue revived.

[illegible]ot reacting in any way to the quality of space."

[illegible]ccepted eternity as the anonymity of a torso."

36. "I greet you two thousand years later. / I was also married to a whore; we've got a lot in common." Tiberius' second wife, Julia, is implied (see e.g. Suetonius, *Tib.* 25, and Tacitus 62.)

37. This is a direct reference to Suetonius' account of the emperor's depravity: "[He let] babies not yet weaned from their mother's breast to suck at his breast or groin — such a filthy old man he had become!" (*Tib.* 44).

38. This is a direct quotation from Suetonius as well: "His hesitation was caused by fear of dangers that threatened him from many quarters, and often led him to declare that he was holding a wolf by the ears" (*Tib.* 25).

39. This colorful metaphor implies most likely the island of Capri — Tiberius' residence and refuge. Although, as Polukhina points out, it can also refer to Donne's "every man is an island" (1989, 204).

40. "Your head, chopped off by the sculptor while you were still alive."

41. "I too / impressed my profile by means of a table lamp. / By hand."

42. "The result — a bust."

43. "A bust, not reacting in any way to the quality of space."

44. "It cannot be that you do not hear me!"

45. "Having run into us, / into something hard."

46. "The eggshells of cupolas, the vertebrae of bell towers. / The languid leisure of a colonnade which has sprawled out its limbs."

47. One might also point to a certain echo of the poet's name (*ospa/Osip*) and to the theme of music which is so prominent in Mandel'shtam. See Kats 1991, 7–11.

48. "Let's have some tea, face, to push apart the lips."

49. "However rough time might be, / I like catching it by its tail." We may also note that the disappearance into time in Brodsky's Stanza X begins with birds flying away: "Soiki, vsporkhnuv, pokidayut kupy / pinii — ot broshennogo nenarokom / vzglyada v okno" (1987, 115) ("Jays, having taken wing, abandon the clumps / of Italian pines — because of an accidental glance through a window"). These birds bring to mind Mandel'shtam's famous goldfinch, who flies away under the poet's glance and whose tail is described in the poem (1991, 1: 224–25).

50. "I am freezing without warm clothes." "Veshch'" here referring to items of clothing, is used differently than in Brodsky, for whom the neutral meaning "inanimate object" is an important recurrent symbol. However, the presence of this word both in Mandel'shtam's letter and Brodsky's "Rimskie elegii" is fascinating.

51. "Do not put then, do not put the sharply tender laurels on my temples." Laurels are also found in "Polnoch' v Moskve."

52. Cf. Mandel'shtam's "I v visok udaryaet mne vyrvanny s myasom zvonok" (1991, 1: 159) ("And the uprooted doorbell, wires dangling, hits my temple"; "Kholodok shchekochet temya ... / I menya srezaet vremya" (1991: 1: 98) ("The cold tickles the crown of my head ... / And I am cut off by time"); "Snova v

zhertvu, kak yagnyonka, / Temya zhizni prinesli" (1991, 1: 102) ("Again to sacrifice, like a lamb, / They have brought the crown of life"); "Kto vremya tseloval v izmuchennoe temya" (1991, 1: 111) ("Who has kissed time on its tired out crown").

53. Bitter frost is another condition for becoming immobilized in Brodsky. See, for example, "Vremya goda zima" ("The time of year is winter"), which gives the Russian setting for petrification, and "Ekloga 4-ya (Zimnyaya)" ("The Fourth [Winter] Eclogue"). The word "lyod" ("ice") is also present in the variant of Mandel'shtam's "Zabludilsya ya v nebe."

WORKS CITED

Bethea, David M. 1994. *Joseph Brodsky and the Creation of Exile*. Princeton: Princeton University Press.

Brodsky, Iosif. 1965. *Stikhotvoreniya i poemy*. New York, Washington: Inter-Language Literary Associates.

_____. 1970. *Ostanovka v pustyne*. Ed. Max Hayward and George L. Kline. New York: Chekhov.

_____. 1977a. *Chast' rechi: Stikhotvoreniya 1972–1976*. Ann Arbor: Ardis.

_____. 1977b. *Konets prekrasnoi epokhi: Stikhotvoreniya 1964–1971*. Ann Arbor: Ardis.

_____. 1984. *Mramor*. Ann Arbor: Ardis.

_____. 1987. *Uraniya*. Ann Arbor: Ardis.

_____. 1991. Interview. With David M. Bethea. Unpublished.

_____. 1992. *Sochineniya*. Vol. I. St. Petersburg: Pushkinsky fond.

Brodsky, Joseph. 1986. *Less than One: Selected Essays*. New York: Farrar, Straus, Giroux.

_____. 1988. *To Urania*. New York: Farrar, Straus, Giroux.

_____. 1989. *Marbles : A Play in Three Acts*. Translated by Alan Myers, with the author. New York: Farrar, Straus, Giroux.

Jakobson, Roman. 1975. *Puskin and His Sculptural Myth*. Trans. and Ed. by John Burbank. The Hague, Paris: Mouton.

Karamzin, N.M. 1892. *Istoriya gosudarstva rossiiskogo*. Vol. IX. St. Petersburg: Izdanie Evg. Evdokimova.

B.A. 1991. "Zashchitnik i podzashchitny muzyki." In Mandel'shtam, Osip. "*\n muzyki, muzy i muki …*" *Stikhi i proza*. Ed. and commentary by B.A. Kats. \nd: Sovetsky kompozitor. 7–54.

\l. 1984. *O poezii Iosifa Brodskogo*. Ann Arbor: Ardis.

Loseff, Lev. 1990. "Politics/Poetics." In *Brodsky's Poetics and Aesthetics*. Ed. by L. Loseff and V. Polukhina. London: Macmillan. 34–55.

Mandel'shtam, Osip. 1991. Sobranie sochinenii v chetyryokh tomakh. 4 vols. Ed. by G.P. Struve and B.A. Filippov. Moscow: Terra.

Nivat, Georges. 1990. "The Ironic Journey into Antiquity." In *Brodsky's Poetics and Aesthetics*. Ed. by L. Loseff and V. Polukhina. London: Macmillan. 88–97.

Polukhina, Valentina. 1989. *Joseph Brodsky: A Poet for Our Time*. Cambridge: Cambridge University Press.

Struve, Gleb. 1991. "O.E. Mandel'shtam. Opyt biografii i kriticheskogo kommentariya." In Mandel'shtam, Osip. *Sobranie sochinenii v chetyryokh tomakh*. Ed. by G.P. Struve and B.A. Filippov. Vol. 1. Moscow: Terra. v–lx.

Suetonius. 1979. *The Twelve Caesars*. Trans. by R. Graves. Revised Edition. London, New York: Penguin Books.

Tacitus, Cornelius. 1987. *The Annals of Imperial Rome*. Trans. by M. Grant. Revised Edition. London, New York: Penguin Books.

Terras, Victor. 1966. "Classical Motives in the Poetry of Osip Mandel'stam." *Slavic and East European Journal* 4: 249–67.

Vail', P., and A. Genis. 1990. "Ot mira — k Rimu." In *Poetika Brodskogo*. Ed. L.V. Losev. Tenafly, New Jersey: Ermitazh. 198–206.

Venclova, Thomas. 1990. "A Journey from Petersburg to Istanbul." In *Brodsky's Poetics and Aesthetics*. Ed. by L. Loseff and V. Polukhina. London: Macmillan. 135–51.

Virgil. 1984. *The Eclogues*. Trans. by Guy Lee. London, New York: Penguin Books.

Zelinsky, Bodo. 1987. "'Dido und Aeneas' bei Anna Achmatova und Iosif Brodskij." In *Jubilaumsschrift zum 25-jahrigen Bestehen der Instituts fur Slavistik der Universitas Giessem*. Ed. by Gerhard Gieseman. New York: Peter Lang. 265–78.